World Food

INDONESIA

Patrick Witton

WORLD FOOD Indonesia
1st edition – February 2002

Published by Lonely Planet Publications Pty Ltd ABN 36 005 607 983

Lonely Planet Offices
Australia Locked Bag 1, Footscray, Victoria 3011
USA 150 Linden Street, Oakland CA 94607
UK 10a Spring Place, London NW5 3BH
France 1 rue du Dahomey, 75011 Paris

Publishing manager Peter D'Onghia
Series editor Lyndal Hall
Series design & layout Brendan Dempsey
Editor Carolyn Papworth
Mapping Natasha Velleley
Photography Jerry Alexander

Photography
Many images in this guide are available for licensing from
Lonely Planet Images. email: lpi@lonelyplanet.com.au

Front cover – Durian for sale in Yogyakarta, Java
Back cover – Fishing in Jimbaran, Bali

ISBN 1 74059 009 0

text & maps © Lonely Planet Publications Pty Ltd, 2002
photos © photographers as indicated 2002

Printed by
The Bookmaker International Ltd
Printed in China

MAP KEY

○ Place to Eat & Drink	——— Tertiary Road	🕍 Buddhist Temple
Market	——— Lane	☪ Mosque
Building	—•— Railway, Station	✝ Church
Park, Garden	✪ National Capital	⚑ Balinese Temple
—··— International Border	◉ Provincial Capital	▥ Fort
——— Freeway	○ Town	⚲ Monument
——— Secondary Road	🏛 Museum	⏛ Stately Home
	🐾 Zoo	▲ Mountain

About the Author

Patrick's interest in Indonesia was born out of necessity, when he found himself lost in a market on Java at the age of 12. He has since studied Indonesian both in Melbourne and Bandung, and wrote Lonely Planet's *Indonesian Phrasebook*. These days Patrick works as an editor on Lonely Planet's *World Food* series and plays banjo both badly and enthusiastically.

Patrick wishes to thank: Wayan and family in Bali; Made Ria and family in Munduk; Yoyo in Solo; Mahdi, Shot, Lestari, Sum and Parin in Yogya; Ni Linda, Ni Pen, Si Ir and Family in Bukittinggi; Mukami and Robert Jacoby (hold the egg) in Banjarmasin; Ibu Bambang Utoyo and Kris Biantoro in Jakarta, Rachman, Lily and Titin in Setiabudi. Huge trims to the Bandung crew – Asti, Didit, Nolly and Naoko – for fine food, dangdut and for keeping me company at Warteg. Hefty thanks to both Dewi Imam and Chendra for friendship and feasting in Central Java. Glossy colour thanks to Jerry Alexander. Thanks to all the contibutors for their fine words: Giles Milton, Tony Wheeler, Kylie Nam, Andrew Taylor, Alexandra Jordan, Asti Mulyana and Kusnandar. Huge thanks for homebase support from Lyndal Hall, Peter D'Onghia, Brendan Dempsey, Natasha Velleley, Donna Wheeler, Wendy Wright, Katharine Day, Martin Hughes and Rufin Kedang. Lastly, massive thanks to my family and especially to Rachel for love and support both on the road and at the table.

About the Photographer

Jerry Alexander is a highly credited food and travel photographer with extensive experience working in South-East Asia, particularly Thailand. When he's not travelling around the world – leaving behind a trail of crumbs from eating his props – Jerry lives in California and tends to his vineyard in the Napa Valley.

From Jerry: Although the credit line on photographs only states the photographer's name we know that we rarely make an image without help. I'm most grateful to those that helped me get to the right spots, translated for me and generally made my work much easier. To Surrinder, Adrianne, Siti, Emir and the whole gang at the Gaja Biru restaurant in Ubud, Bali. Wayan and his lovely family for guiding me and for the friendship. In Yogya to Mahdi and the crew at the Rama bookstore. They went the extra mile. Bill Dalton for his insightful tips. In Bandung; Asti, Didit and Nolly. For alot of things but for sure for their sense of humour. To Patrick Witton for his commitment, willingness and talents. My good fortune to work with him. And lastly the exceedingly capable crew at the Lonely Planet. They are both very professional and great fun!

From the Publisher

This first edition of *World Food Indonesia* was edited by freelancer Carolyn Papworth and designed in-house by Brendan Dempsey of Lonely Planet's Melbourne office with assistance from Wendy Wright. Natasha Velleley mapped, Katharine Day proofed, Lyndal Hall coordinated production and Donna Wheeler indexed. Rufin Kedang cast his keen eye over the manuscript in the role of official 'reader'. A big thanks to the entire LPI crew for coordinating the supply of photographs, captioning, cataloguing and doing all pre-press work. Peter D'Onghia, manager, dealt with big picture issues thereby releasing the team to work their magic.

WARNING & REQUEST

Things change – prices go up, schedules change, good places go bad and bad places go bankrupt – nothing stays the same. So, if you find things better or worse, recently opened or long since closed, please tell us and help make the next edition even more accurate and useful. We genuinely value all the feedback we receive. A well-travelled team reads and acknowledges every letter, postcard and email and ensures that every morsel of information finds its way to the appropriate authors, editors and cartographers for verification.

Everyone who writes to us will find their name listed in the next edition of the appropriate guidebook. They will also receive the latest issue of Planet Talk, our quarterly printed newsletter, or Comet, our monthly email newsletter. Subscriptions to both newsletters are free. The very best contributions will be rewarded with a free guidebook. We may edit, reproduce and incorporate your comments in all Lonely Planet products, such as guidebooks, Web sites and digital products, so let us know if you don't want your comments reproduced or your name acknowledged.

Send all correspondence to the Lonely Planet office closest to you:

Australia Locked Bag 1, Footscray, Victoria 3011
USA 150 Linden St, Oakland, CA 94607
UK 10a Spring Place, London NW5 3BH
France 1 rue du Dahomey, 75011 Paris

Or email us at: **talk2us@lonelyplanet.com.au**

For news, views and updates see our Web site: **www.lonelyplanet.com**

Contents

Introduction 8

The Culture of
Indonesian Cuisine 9
History 12
Indonesian Cuisine Today 21
How Indonesians Eat 22
Etiquette 25

Staples & Specialities 27
Beras, Nasi (Rice) 29
Mie (Noodles) 38
Fish, Fowl & Meat 39
Kedelai (Soybeans) 53
Telur (Eggs) 54
Soto, Sop (Soup) 55
Fruit & Vegetables 57
Sayuran (Vegetables) 57
Buah-Buahan (Fruit) 61
Spices, Sauces & Flavourings 71
Chilli 74
Jajanan (Snacks) 79
Bread & Pastries 82

Drinks of Indonesia 83
Non-Alcoholic Drinks 85
Alcoholic Drinks 97

Home Cooking
& Traditions 99

Celebrating with Food 109

Regional Variations 121
Java 123
Bali 135
Sumatra 141
Nusa Tenggara 149
Kalimantan 151
Sulawesi 154
Maluku 159
Irian Jaya 160

161 Shopping & Markets
163 Markets
170 General Stores & Supermarkets
171 An Indonesian Picnic
172 Things to Take Home

173 Where to Eat & Drink
175 Street Food
181 Rumah Makan (Restaurants)
189 The Menu & Bill
190 Road Food
191 Children
192 Where to Drink

195 An Indonesian Banquet

207 Fit & Healthy

215 Eat Your Words
216 Pronunciation Guide
217 Useful Phrases
225 English – Indonesian Glossary
241 Indonesian Culinary Dictionary

259 Recommended Reading

260 Index

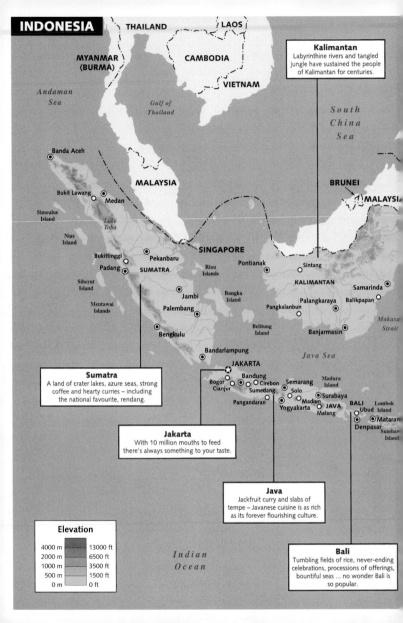

INDONESIA

THAILAND
LAOS
MYANMAR (BURMA)
CAMBODIA
VIETNAM

Andaman Sea

Gulf of Thailand

South China Sea

• Banda Aceh

MALAYSIA

BRUNEI

MALAYSIA

Bukit Lawang ○ ● Medan

Simeulue Island

Lake Toba

SINGAPORE

Nias Island

Bukittinggi ●
Padang ○

Pekanbaru ●

SUMATRA

Riau Islands

Pontianak ●

Sintang ●

KALIMANTAN

Siberut Island

Jambi ●

Bangka Island

Samarinda ●
Balikpapan ●

Mentawai Islands

Palembang ●

Pangkalanbun ●

Palangkaraya ●

Makasar Strait

● Bengkulu

Belitung Island

Banjarmasin ●

Bandarlampung ●

Java Sea

★ JAKARTA

Madura Island

Kalimantan
Labyrinthine rivers and tangled jungle have sustained the people of Kalimantan for centuries.

Bogor ○ ● ○ Bandung
Cianjur ○ Sumedang

Semarang
Cirebon ● ○ Solo
● ● Madiun

Surabaya ●

BALI Lombok Island
Ubud ○

Pangandaran ● Yogyakarta ● JAVA
Malang

● Mataram

Denpasar

Sumbawa Island

Sumatra
A land of crater lakes, azure seas, strong coffee and hearty curries – including the national favourite, rendang.

Jakarta
With 10 million mouths to feed there's always something to your taste.

Java
Jackfruit curry and slabs of tempe – Javanese cuisine is as rich as its forever flourishing culture.

Bali
Tumbling fields of rice, never-ending celebrations, processions of offerings, bountiful seas ... no wonder Bali is so popular.

Indian Ocean

Elevation

4000 m	13000 ft
2000 m	6500 ft
1000 m	3500 ft
500 m	1500 ft
0 m	0 ft

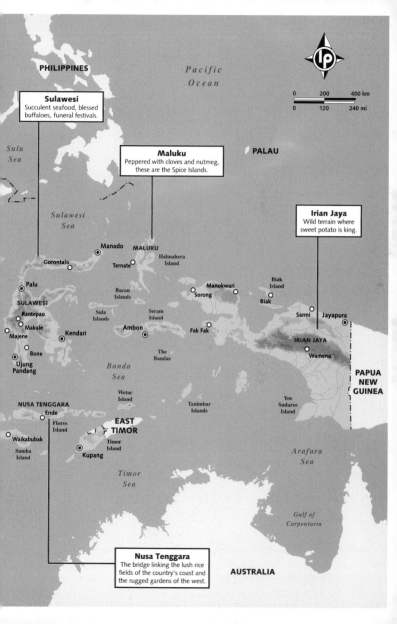

PHILIPPINES

Pacific Ocean

Sulawesi
Succulent seafood, blessed buffaloes, funeral festivals.

Sulu Sea

PALAU

Maluku
Peppered with cloves and nutmeg, these are the Spice Islands.

Sulawesi Sea

Irian Jaya
Wild terrain where sweet potato is king.

Manado

MALUKU

Gorontalo

Ternate

Halmahera Island

Biak Island

Manokwari

Palu

Bacan Islands

Sorong

Biak

SULAWESI

Sula Islands

Sarmi

Jayapura

Rantepao

Seram Island

Makale

Ambon

Fak Fak

IRIAN JAYA

Majene

Kendari

Wamena

Bone

The Bandas

Ujung Pandang

Banda Sea

PAPUA NEW GUINEA

Yos Sudarso Island

NUSA TENGGARA

Wetar Island

Ende

Tanimbar Islands

Waikabubak

Flores Island

EAST TIMOR

Sumba Island

Timor Island

Kupang

Arafura Sea

Timor Sea

Gulf of Carpentaria

Nusa Tenggara
The bridge linking the lush rice fields of the country's coast and the rugged gardens of the west.

AUSTRALIA

| 0 | 200 | 400 km |
| 0 | 120 | 240 mi |

Strapping the equator for 5000km, the islands of Indonesia promise an edible adventure. The archipelago is home to empires, rice, poverty, tea, dissent, soybeans, corruption, catfish all vital elements to discover, explore, embrace, avoid and ingest. Eat in Indonesia and you'll absorb its essence, for this nation is so well represented by its cuisine. The abundance of rice reveals Indonesia's fertile land, its spices recall times of trade and invasion (these, after all, are the Spice Islands) and the fiery chilli reflects the warmth and spirit of the people.

More than this, Indonesia's cuisine reflects the country's diversity. Just look at a map; here are 13,677 islands, home to at least 200 million people including 300 ethnic groups, countless cooks and a surplus of audacious stomachs. Difference is intrinsic to Indonesia's identity; the nation's slogan is 'unity in diversity' and the face of its cuisine changes depending on who you dine with and on which island.

By the same token, Indonesian food has its unifying attributes. Unlike that of its northern neighbours, for example, the cuisine here is not complex; flavours stay separate, simple and substantial. Nevertheless, Indonesian food is certain to surprise, enlighten, astound and keep you guessing: How was that fish kept fresh without the aid of a fridge? Where did that restaurant disappear to? And why does my dessert taste like avocado? All the clues lie within these pages, but to fully enjoy the nation's culinary make-up, you'll naturally want to taste the real thing; and this book will also help you do just that. Advice here includes how to choose the best place to try black rice pudding, how to order tea without an accompanying tonne of sugar and how to get a fix of jackfruit curry in the middle of the Muslim fasting month.

Considering that any one dish can appear in many variations, you could never try *everything* that Indonesia's fare has to offer – but just trying is reward in itself. **Selamat makan!** (bon appetit!)

the **culture** of
indonesian cuisine

Indonesian cuisine is really one big food swap. Colonists, traders, even Australian Aborigines have all influenced the inventory of ingredients and culinary practices appearing at the Indonesian table. Nevertheless, the cuisine here is nothing like that of its forebears, as even the most obviously imported of foods here have taken on a uniquely Indonesian personality, shaped by the archipelago's diverse geographies and cultures.

Cuisine in Indonesia is not something restricted to the kitchen. It is not tied up in rules and cooking schools. It is not the sole realm of chefs and connoisseurs. It is neither dusty nor dated. Rather, it is alive, flexible and approachable, symbolising a culture driven by interaction.

For better or worse, Indonesia has always been a centre of trade. In the name of commerce there have been kingdoms built, battles waged and cities destroyed. But underpinning the dealings and disasters has been a free exchange of foods and culinary practices. Rice, corn, curries and pineapples are just a few of the ingredients that first came to the islands aboard trading vessels. To the islanders the new foods looked as strange as the pantaloon-wearing people who brought them, but the exotic imports are now essentials in the Indonesian pantry. If Indonesians had closed their ports and been precious about what was allowed in the pot, their cuisine would be a diet-sized version of today's. This is not to say that Indonesians have abandoned their own culinary traditions for the new; for just as the religions of other countries were woven into pre-existing beliefs, new foods were always accepted and then gradually reworked into an identifiably Indonesian shape.

Geography has also had a great bearing on the diets of the archipelago. This is a living country; floods and active volcanoes regularly tear up the earth and as a result, much of the land is very fertile. Cassava grows wild on the slopes of Java's Mt Merapi, papaya trees sprout like weeds on Sumatra. And then there are the surrounding seas and inland rivers with fish, fish and more fish.

But here also is terrain not so characteristically Indonesian: the high-lands of Irian Jaya supporting little more than patches of sweet potato; the dry, craggy hills of Nusa Tenggara where corn is the staple; the chilled, European-style gardens of Brastagi where carrots are cultivated; the urban sprawl of Surabaya where fast-food franchises are a common sight. And, just to add to the mix, the people of this archipelago were not officially united as 'Indonesian' until the mid-20th century, when an imaginary line was drawn around a group of islands made of what remains a diverse range of people, cultures and cuisines.

When exploring Indonesian cuisine, you spend very little time in kitchens because, although functional, they aren't conducive to relaxing and socialising. In the Indonesian kitchen you won't find an **ibu** (mother; also polite form of address to older women) complaining to friends about the price of rice, nor will you find people leaving elaborate offerings to Hindu gods. You'll find the culinary life in public places: temples, side streets and markets, where food is central – sized up, sampled and savoured. Interaction keeps Indonesian food fresh and flavoursome.

Fishing in Jimbaran, Bali

History

In Jakarta, make sure you visit the National Monument. The view from the tower may be worth checking out, but the highlight lies in the basement: the history of Indonesia ... in diorama! The first model shows Indonesia at the time of Java Man (*Pithecanthropus erectus*), he who migrated to Indonesia via land bridges around a million years ago. As the diorama colourfully shows, Java Man was a hunter-gatherer living on a diet of taro, fruit, fish and game. His Indonesia was a land without rice, chillies, pineapples and tea – ingredients now so integral to nourishment in Indonesia.

Successive migration from South-East Asia from about 4000 BC saw the demise of Java Man and the rise of today's Indonesians, who are predominantly of Malay origin (the other major grouping is the Melanesians who inhabit much of eastern Indonesia). Beginning in Vietnam and southern China about 3000 years ago, the Dongson civilisation spread to Indonesia,

The rice terraces of Tabanan, Bali

bringing techniques of irrigated rice farming and other practices including the ritual buffalo sacrifice that still exists in the Batak region (Sumatra), Tana Toraja (Sulawesi), parts of Kalimantan and Sumba (Nusa Tenggara). (See Central Sulawesi in the Regional Variations chapter and the boxed text Death of the Party in the Celebrating chapter.)

By the 7th century BC well-organised societies had been established in the Indonesian archipelago. Their people tended irrigated rice fields and kept domesticated buffaloes, pigs, dogs and chickens. They were also noted seafarers, ever expanding on the bounty of the surrounding seas. Village pantries were stocked with such staples as breadfruit, bananas, yams and coconuts.

Java, with its hot, even temperature, plentiful rainfall and volcanic soil, was ideal for the wet-field method of rice cultivation. The level of organisation required for this complex method may explain why Java developed a more sophisticated civilisation than those of the other islands. Dry-field rice cultivation is much simpler and needs no elaborate social structure (see Rice in the Staples & Specialities chapter).

China, India, Persia & Arabia

Indonesia's strategic position on the sea lanes between India and China meant that trade between these two main Asian civilisations was firmly established here by the 1st century AD. Although Indonesia had its own products to trade, such as spices, gold and benzoin (an aromatic resin valued by the Chinese), it owed its growing importance to its position at the crossroads of trade. Along with rice, the Chinese gave Indonesia its soybeans, its noodles and its national drink: tea. (But the Dutch first imported the tea plant to Indonesia; see Tea in the Drinks chapter).

And it didn't stop with Chinese ingredients. China gave Indonesia the wok and stirfrying, now so integral to the cuisine: no stirfry, no **nasi goreng** (fried rice) – Indonesia just wouldn't be the same.

Merchants from Arabia, Persia and India brought goods to the coastal cities in exchange for goods from China and for local products, such as spices. Indonesia's **gulai** (coconut curry; also known as **kare**) owes its roots to Arab and Indian traders. The local version of curry may be different from its subcontinental counterpart, but the spices are all Indian originals: cardamom, coriander, cumin, ginger, onions, garlic. The **martabak** (crispy-skin omelette) is a *roti* relation that can also claim Indian and Arabian heritage; its dessert namesake is like a pancake on steroids (see Sweet Snacks & Desserts in the Staples & Specialties chapter).

Trade with India and China also saw the introduction of Buddhism, Hinduism and Islam, religions that changed the face of Indonesian culture forever. They did not, however, erase belief systems preceding them and religion in Indonesia remains a mix of old and new.

Park life in Bukittinggi, Sumatra

Indonesian Kingdoms

The Sumatran Hindu-Buddhist kingdom of Sriwijaya emerged in the 7th century AD and was Indonesia's first major sea power, controlling much of the trade in South-East Asia. The Buddhist Sailendra and Hindu Mataram dynasties flourished on the plains of Java from the 8th century. Sriwijaya's sea trade brought wealth, but these land-based states had far more human labour at their disposal and built magnificent structures including the ones that remain at Borobudur and Prambanan.

By the end of the 10th century the Mataram dynasty had mysteriously declined, paving the way for the rise of the Majapahit kingdom (East Java). Majapahit is thought to have controlled many coastal regions of today's Indonesia and even maintained diplomatic relations with China, Vietnam, Cambodia, Annam and Siam.

Islam spread across Indonesia from west to east, following the trade routes, and by the time of Majapahit's collapse in the 16th century, many of its satellite kingdoms had declared themselves independent Muslim states. Much of the states' wealth came from them being transhipment points for the growing spice trade. At this time, too, a new sea power emerged in the archipelago – Sulawesi's twin principalities, Makassar and Gowa. Renowned sailors, the Makassar visited the northern Australian coast in fleets over several hundred years. They introduced metal tools, pottery and tobacco to Australian Aborigines in exchange for sea cucumbers sought by Chinese traders for their culinary and aphrodisiac qualities. The Makassar had an influence on Aboriginal language, custom and kinship.

Prambanan temple, Java

Portugal, Spain & England

Marco Polo and a few early missionaries aside, the first Europeans to visit Indonesia were Portuguese, who came seeking to dominate the valuable spice trade in Maluku (cloves in Tidore, nutmeg in the Banda Islands). The Portuguese captured the Malay port of Melaka in 1511, arrived in Maluku the following year and controlled the spice trade out of Indonesia for a century, but – not counting cassava and pastries – the culinary legacy they left to Indonesia is minimal.

Soon other European nations (notably Spain and England) sent ships to the region in search of spices. Spain's ventures into the Americas had a massive impact on the Indonesian menu. Thanks to Spain's culinary dating service, Indonesia met and fell in love with the chilli; corn, peanuts and tomatoes are some of the other Spanish introductions. Thankfully, the English had little influence on Indonesian cuisine.

The Dutch

A disastrous 1596 expedition of four Dutch ships lost half its crew and a ship and killed a Javanese prince. Nevertheless, it returned to the Dutch Republic (the Netherlands) with boatloads of spices, making a profit for the expedition's backers; other expeditions soon followed. Recognising the potential of the East Indies trade, the Dutch amalgamated competing merchant companies into the United East India Company. This monopoly soon became the main competitor for the spice trade. Trading ships were replaced by heavily armed fleets with instructions to attack Portuguese bases. By 1605 the Dutch had defeated the Portuguese at Tidore and Ambon and occupied the territory themselves. A 1607 alliance with the sultan of Ternate in Maluku gave the Dutch control of the clove trade; their occupation of the Banda Islands gave them nutmeg.

RIJSTAFFEL

Borne of a time when Dutch planters had wide girths and extravagant tastes, rijstaffel is not Indonesian; rather, it is an experiment in indulgence. Rijstaffel ('rice table') is in practice a banquet of Indonesian-style dishes, the only constant being rice. The Dutch would put on mammoth spreads served by a legion of waiters, often one waiter to a dish. Such extravagance was, and is, well beyond the means of most Indonesians. They may put on an elaborate meal to celebrate a wedding, but they wouldn't call it rijstaffel, as that's considered – along with monocles and safari suits – something best left to history.

In 1610 the ruler of Jayakarta (present-day Jakarta) granted the Dutch permission to build a warehouse but at the same time granted the English trading rights. The Dutch warehouse became a fort, relations between the Dutch and the English deteriorated and skirmishes resulted in a siege of the Dutch fort by the English and the Jayakartans. The Dutch retaliated in 1619, seizing the town and renaming it Batavia. The 1641 capture of Melaka from the Portuguese completed Dutch mastery of sea trade in the region.

When the Dutch lost Belgium in 1830, the home country itself faced bankruptcy and any investment in the East Indies *had* to make quick returns. Thus began a concerted exploitation of Indonesia. Large areas of Java became plantations cultivated by Javanese peasants, their products collected by Chinese intermediaries and sold on to overseas markets. Up until WWII, Indonesia controlled most of the world's pepper, a quarter of its coconut products, and almost a fifth of its tea, sugar, coffee and oil. Indonesia made the Dutch one of the major colonial powers. Instead of paying land tax, Indonesian peasants were forced to either cultivate Dutch-owned crops on 20% of their land or work on Dutch plantations for nearly 60 days per year. To Javanese peasants this system brought extreme hardship. They were forced to grow such cash crops as indigo and sugar instead of rice and as a result, famines and epidemics swept Java in the 1840s. As well as cash crops such as coffee and sugar, the Dutch brought their breads, pastries, beer and cool-climate vegetables including carrots and potatoes.

Apart from the short period of British control and the WWII Japanese Occupation, Dutch control of Indonesia lasted right up until 17 August 1945. But their control was always tenuous and rebellions broke out frequently. The longest and most devastating war ran for 35 years until 1908 in Aceh (Sumatra) which retains an active independence movement.

Fields caught on canvas

THE SPICE RACE

Most of us have a dusty jar of nutmeg lurking at the back of our kitchen cupboards, brought out – if at all – at Christmas, when a few grains are stirred into mulled wine or festive pies. What few people realise is that nutmeg was once the most sought after (and fought over) commodity in the world. So rare and coveted was this spice that it was once worth far more than its weight in gold. The reason? Europe's 16th century physicians and quacks declared it the only certain cure for the plague.

Other spices, too, were held to have powerful medicinal properties: cloves cured earache and pepper stifled colds; relief from the embarrassment caused by farting came in an infusion of 15 spices including cardamom, cinnamon and nutmeg. Woe betide anyone who overdosed – spices were also held to be powerful aphrodisiacs.

And spices weren't just used as medicine. In days before refrigeration, spices served as powerful preservatives. Perishables were traditionally conserved by salting, drying or smoking. A sprinkling of nutmeg or pepper over the viands not only disguised the stench of rank meat, but also slowed the rate of oxidation and rotting.

Despite the huge demand from Europe's plague-ridden citizens, no one in Europe was sure how to lay their hands on large quantities of spices. Until the 16th century, Europe's merchants bought them in Venice and Venice's merchants acquired them in Constantinople. But the spices came from much further away, in the fabled Spice Islands or East Indies (today's Indonesia) where no European ship had ever sailed. With prices rocketing sky-high, and an ever-increasing demand, a fortune awaited the person who discovered their elusive source.

The 'spiceries' were not easy to locate. Unbeknown to the adventurers who put to sea, this large group of islands lay scattered over a vast area of ocean more than 1000 miles to the east of Java. Nutmeg, the rarest spice of all, grew only on the tiny Banda Islands. Even today, these specks of volcanic rock take time and effort to visit and are nearer Australia than Jakarta. To the spice dealers of Europe, they must have seemed as distant as the moon.

The Portuguese were the first to reach the Spice Islands or Moluccas (today's Maluku province) and stumbled across the source of nutmeg in 1511. They reaped enormous wealth from the monopoly they established and kept the islands a guarded secret. It was not until 1596 that the Dutch also reached the Indies and bought spices for a song.

The English followed in 1601 when the swashbuckling Sir James Lancaster set sail under the auspices of the newly founded East India Company. He discovered that spices cost almost nothing at source but fetched a fortune in England. Nutmeg sold at a profit of a staggering 60,000%. With three powers now competing for the priceless commodity, the spice wars really began.

Overleaf – Balinese carving made from sawokecik wood

The Dutch acted with a ruthlessness that horrified both native populations and European merchants. They attacked Portuguese forts and blasted their cannon at English vessels, capturing crews and imprisoning them. And, to secure their grip on the spices, they changed tactics from trade to conquest. They forced local spice merchants out of business and, in the Banda Islands, the governor general of the Dutch East India Company, Jan Peterszoon Coen, beheaded and quartered 44 native chieftains. Many islanders were sold into slavery.

Despite an heroic stand by the English on the Banda Islands, the Dutch ousted both them and the Portuguese from the Moluccas, tightening their grip on the archipelago. For a while they reaped a fortune but by the 19th century Europe's desire for spices had declined. The Dutch suffered a further blow when an English captain recaptured the largest of the Banda Islands and transplanted hundreds of nutmeg seedlings to Sri Lanka, Singapore and, eventually, the West Indies.

Today, most of the world's nutmeg comes from the Caribbean island of Grenada. This island also provides an important flavouring for one of Indonesia's most popular drinks. The ingredient is cinnamon and the drink is Coca-Cola.

Giles Milton is a London-based author who writes about the early history of exploration. He has written **Samurai William**, **Big Chief Elizabeth** *and* **Nathaniel's Nutmeg** *(about Jacobean adventurers in the Spice Islands).*

Nutmeg, star anise, cumin, chilli, cinnamon, cloves, cardamom, turmeric

CULTURE

Indonesian Cuisine Today

Indonesian cuisine continues to adopt ingredients and technologies, thanks mainly to the Indonesian people's open-minded attitude towards the new. There is no right or wrong ingredient for nasi goreng except rice. Americanisation is charging through the islands but, as always, Indonesians manage to give the new foods a local twist.

Waiting for a sale in Bukittinggi, Sumatra

At a McDonald's here a Big Mac comes with chilli and you can order McSatay. A tragedy for many, even Indonesia's 1998 monetary crisis sparked a culinary invention: **nasi krismon** (the monetary crisis meal), a meal made with any cheap ingredients. And as the policy of **transmigrasi** (domestic migration) is enforced in an attempt to reduce high-density living problems, regional culinary influence continues to spread throughout the islands.

INDONESIAN PROVERBS – Food for Thought

Ada gula ada semut.
  (Where there's sugar there are ants.)

Nasi sudah menjadi bubur.
  (The rice has already become porridge.)

**Karena nila setitik
rusak susu sebelanga.**
  (A drop of indigo ruins the pot of milk.)

Like bees to the honey pot.

You can't turn back the clock.

One bad apple spoils
  the barrel.

CULTURE

How Indonesians Eat

With a population of over 200 million, you'd expect a little variety in the way people fuel up during the day. One generalisation we can make is that **sarapan** (breakfast) is early – around sunrise. This is a nation of early birds, which makes sense since the morning is the coolest, freshest time of day; the best time for tending fields and walking to market or to school. But the breakfast meal varies with location, income and taste. In rice-growing areas such as central Java, you will see women sitting on the steps of their houses eating bowls of rice – perhaps with some soy and fried shallots – left from yesterday's dinner. In Maluku, a farmer's first meal of the day may be sago cake and a cup of tea. In Surabaya, taxi drivers find sustenance in a bowl of **bubur ayam** (rice porridge with chicken). In Jakarta, a business manager may start the day with a bowl of frosty crunchies or some other such cereal. And

such foreign foods are nothing new: President Soekarno, the father of Independence, often started the day with chocolate sprinkles on bread. Surprisingly, fruit is not a popular breakfast food. Some Indonesians say it's too much for the stomach first thing in the morning. The same goes for spicy foods. There is one time of the year when breakfast is always more grand: **Ramadan** (the Muslim fasting month; see the Celebrating chapter).

In the morning, cooks usually prepare a load of plain rice and three or four dishes, as well as a **sambal** (chilli sauce or relish). These dishes are left covered on the table for **makan siang** (lunch), **makan malam** (dinner) or any other time that hunger strikes. The cook is then free for the rest of the day and children coming home from school can help themselves rather than waiting for food to be prepared. The dishes on the table constitute the entire meal – Indonesian meals are not served in courses, or stages.

A spread of Padang food, Bukittinggi, Sumatra

Apart from rice, which is kept warm in a cooker or closed container, food isn't reheated; most Indonesian meals are eaten at room temperature. This may be disconcerting if you feel food is only safe to eat if it's cooked in front of you, but Indonesian cooking methods help to keep food edible for long periods. It's important to remember that the rice (or another starchy staple such as sago or sweet potato) is the filler, other dishes are the flavour. You may be surprised at the small size of, say, a serving of **rendang** (beef or buffalo coconut curry; see the recipe), but the meat is so tasty you don't need a huge slab and rice distributes the flavour well. Eat meat or any spicy food in industrial proportions and you're asking for 'Bali belly'. Filling up on rice also reduces the cost of feeding a family.

You'll soon discover that this country is well geared to eating out of the home; many Indonesians do just that for at least one meal of the day. Those who move to the cities for work, for example, don't have a kitchen at their disposal and so find nourishment throughout the day at a wide variety of eateries. A Balinese banker working in Jakarta may lunch on nasi goreng at her favourite **warung** (street stall), a busker could spend his takings on a refreshing **es jeruk** (citrus juice) from a **kaki-lima** (roving vendor) and a group of university students may break from their studies with a meal of **bubur kacang hijau** (mung-bean porridge) at the night market. Then there's the snack factor – more snacks than stomachs, snacks for any occasion, sweet snacks like **pisang goreng** (fried banana), savoury snacks like **tahu isi** (stuffed tofu) – you can't avoid them, and why would you? The locals don't. Indonesia is a snacking society.

WAYS OF COOKING

A quick lesson in some popular cooking techniques will help you to pick the street stall selling **ayam bakar** (grilled chicken) from the one selling **ayam goreng** (fried chicken) and the one selling ... you get the idea. Match the main ingredient with the cooking technique and you have yourself a meal.

bakar	chargrilled
gulai	coconut milk curry; also known as **kare**
goreng	fried
pepes	steamed or roasted in banana leaves; also **pais**
panggang	roasted
sate	chargrilled on skewers and served with peanut sauce
asam manis	'sour sweet'; served in a sweet & sour sauce
soto	soup; also **sop**

Etiquette

As a guest in someone's home, you won't be scolded for spilling your drink. In fact you could bury your head in your rice while singing 'Uptown Girl' without fear of retribution. Indonesians treat guests like royalty and any wrong footing of yours will be excused. Nevertheless a few tips on Indonesian etiquette will help make every meal more enjoyable.

Don't be surprised if, when invited home for lunch, you're the only one eating. This is your host's way of saying your stomach is considered the most important and you should have choice pickings. If you ask your host to join you, they'll probably say they've already eaten. But don't take this as a green light to eat big, as these lunch dishes are the same ones served at dinner. Fill up on rice, take a healthy spoonful from each other dish. Don't go ballistic on your favourite – leave enough for others. The spread before you is the entire meal.

Eating solo isn't always the way. You and your hosts could all be seated together, but more often each person fills their plate then sits in the living room. Either way, it's polite to wait until you're invited to start. Your host will give the go-ahead by saying **silahkan makan** (please eat) or **makan dulu** (dig in). Usually the eldest serve themselves first but as a guest you will probably get pole position. Remember – take more rice and less of other dishes, especially meat, which is expensive.

Indonesia isn't a nation of chopstickers; this is **garpu** (fork) and **sendok** (spoon) country. Many prefer eating rice *au naturale*; it is cooked to be sticky enough to hold together, perfect for scooping in your right hand along with some of the other dishes. Before you huff about hygiene, remember that you can only be sure of where your fingers have been. If you wash them before your meal (as you always should) there'll be no problem; a finger bowl is

---

DELICIOUS

If you're to learn one word in a local language, it should be 'delicious'. Your praise will be most appreciated.

Acehnese	**Mangat tat**
Balinese	**Je'en**
Indonesian	**Enak**
Javanese	**Ecol**
Makassar	**Malunra'**
Minang	**Lamak**
Sundanese	**Raos**

Mia, eating too much, Bukittinggi, Sumatra

often provided with meals or there'll be a basin nearby. Use your right hand for eating, passing things, anything – the left hand is for 'other duties'. If you're **kidal** (left handed), too bad, get used to it. We did.

No doubt your host will implore you to eat more than is humanly possible, and of course you should feel satisfied after your meal, but how to finish? A few theories flyabout: some say leave a mouthful on your plate so as to say 'I couldn't fit in another bite'; others say finish it off to imply 'the food is so good I cannot stop'. The best guide is to eat about as much as you would in a restaurant. And – not that you'll need prompting – be sure to praise the food.

Lighting up in Mataram, Lombok

Indonesians like to use toothpicks after a meal. To tooth-pick Indonesian style, cover your mouth with your left hand and get digging with the other. Smoking isn't taboo at the table here; people light up before, during and after meals. If that bothers you, you could politely ask a smoker to butt out and they'll probably oblige. Nevertheless smoke from **kretek** (clove cigarettes) smells nicer and keeps mosquitoes away.

staples
& specialities

The essentials of the Indonesian kitchen depend on location. An oppressive climate, a scarcity of refrigeration and cavity-ridden roads mean that transported goods aren't cheap and locals look to their regional produce for sustenance. There are, however, some constants across the islands that give form to the Indonesian plate.

The word **sembako** refers to Indonesia's nine essentials: rice, sugar, eggs, meat, flour, corn, gas fuel, cooking oil and salt. When any of these become unavailable or more costly, repercussions are felt right through to the presidency. **Sembako** is actually an abbreviation of three words: **sembilan bahan pokok** *(nine essential ingredients).*

Beras, Nasi (Rice)

No better place to start describing Indonesia's food than with the amazing grain. Wherever you turn, rice is there shaping the landscape, sold at markets, hidden in sweets and piled on your plate. And as this staple is so adaptable, there's no fear of tiring of it. Rice's multiple uses include **ketupat** (rice steamed in woven packets of coconut fronds), **lontong** (rice steamed in banana leaves), **intip** (rice crackers), desserts, noodles, **brem** (rice wine) and the national favourite, **nasi goreng** (fried rice; see the recipe). Despite its dazzling range, rice is most often eaten as **nasi putih** (plain rice), for – combined with just a little protein from side dishes – it's the most nutritionally complete food on the globe; the filler of a billion stomachs.

Threshing rice, Bali

Bubur (Rice Porridge)

In Hong Kong it's *juk*, in the Philippines it's *guinataan*; the English word for it is congee (from the Indian for 'boilings'), but in Indonesia rice porridge or gruel is called **bubur**. It can be sweet or savoury and is made with all kinds of rice and sometimes with other grains or pulses. There's the savoury **bubur ayam** (chicken porridge), in which strips of chicken, shallots and soy sauce are added to a steaming bowl of rice porridge. For a rich dessert, try **bubur ketan hitam** (black rice porridge with coconut milk). **Bubur kacang hijau** replaces the rice with mung beans, but it's still a sweet treat. Black rice and beans are often combined to make the wordy **bubur ketan hitam kacang hijau**.

Ulun Danu temple, Lake Bratan, Bali

Rice by Tony Wheeler

Rice is undoubtedly humanity's most important food (every day more rice is consumed than any other food). It's both nutritious and filling, but it's also the most beautiful crop on earth.

Whether it's dropping down a hillside in Sumatra, Java or Bali, each step of a rice paddy is an artistic masterpiece. The story of rice doesn't end with taste and looks; every step – from planting, through growing, harvesting, processing, trading and consuming – has its own interest and colour.

The origins of rice are sketchy, but evidence suggests it first sprouted around the border of today's Thailand, Myanmar and China. China's Yangtze River basin revealed evidence of rice consumption in the Neolithic period (6000 to 9000 BC). It's generally agreed that the technique of growing rice in flooded fields started in China and spread down throughout South-East Asia. The transition from hunter-gatherer to farmer commenced about 10,000 years ago, and rice farming was a vital factor in the development of Asian civilisations. The population of China during the Confucian era (around 500 BC) was 10 times that of the Athenian Greek civilisation.

High-yielding crops boosted rice's success, but adaptability is a key reason for its wide distribution. The warm, wet tropical regions of Asia may be rice's true homeland but it also grows beyond 50°N in Russia and beyond 40°S in South America. Surfers stumble their way through rice paddies on the way to the beach at Kuta in Bali; trekkers can see it growing high in the Himalaya.

Perhaps slightly more wheat is grown each year than rice's 500-odd million tonnes, but a significant portion of the wheat crop (about 20%) is fed to livestock. In contrast, rice is grown almost entirely for human consumption.

The two predominant species of rice are *Oryza sativa* and *Oryza glaberrima* but *O sativa* is by far the more common of the two, accounting for well over 90% of rice grown worldwide. Varieties abound in Indonesia and locals remark, like wine connoisseurs, on a grain's colour, shape, texture and taste.

Grains for sale, Yogyakarta, Java

Black rice, Bali

Red rice, Bali

STAPLES

The West Javanese town of Cianjur is said to produce Indonesia's finest rice, the pearly white grains sold at a higher price as **beras Cianjur**. Indonesia's rice of choice is the polished long grain, which is cooked until tender, never soggy. A more glutinous variety, called **ketan** or **pulut**, is made into such snacks as **lemper** (sticky rice with a filling of spiced and shredded meat). The misleadingly named **ketan hitam** (black rice – it's more a dark purple) is used to make the soul-enriching dish, black rice porridge; see Bubur earlier in this chapter.

There are no rice seasons in Indonesia, every stage from preparing the fields and planting, through to harvesting and beyond, can happen at any time. The size and shape of rice fields are equally unrestricted. They can be a jigsaw puzzle of interlocking pieces; they can be as small as a double bed and as large as a basketball court; they come in squares, rectangles and parallelograms and with edges straight, angled and gently curving.

Rice Legends

In Bali, crops grow year round so every stage of the rice cycle can be seen on the same day. In fact Balinese legend – in Bali there's a legend for everything – explains why the harvest is continual. A group of farmers promised to sacrifice a pig if the harvest was good. The harvest was indeed bountiful but as harvest approached there was not a pig to be found (a very strange occurrence in Bali but this, after all, is a legend). The unhappy farmers concluded their only option was to sacrifice one of their children. Then one of them had a brainwave: the sacrifice was promised for after the harvest; if there was always new rice growing, then there would never be an 'after the harvest'. Balinese have always planted a field of rice before harvesting another ever since.

Transplanting rice, Lombok

To prepare for rice, farmers plough their flooded fields repeatedly, raking them over and smoothing them out to get the same muddy consistency. Meanwhile the rice seedlings grow in a small nursery field free of weeds. The next stage sees the 15cm seedlings methodically transplanted into paddy fields. Nursing them to this stage gives seedlings a head start over weeds and means that herbicide shouldn't be needed. The price paid is the back-breaking labour in transplanting.

The next stage is easy: sitting back, watching the rice grow and keeping greedy birds at bay. Scarecrows loom over rice fields and offerings are made at field-side shrines to Dewi Sri, goddess of rice and the harvest. Although Dewi Sri is a Hindu deity, her powers are revered across the archipelago. Rice fields are dotted with shrines to her, some of them simple affairs the size of a birdcage, topped by a tin roof and standing on bamboo legs. In Bali, extra offerings are scattered derisively along the field edges to keep the demons from wandering on to paddies. And there is more life in the fields: dragonflies flit over paddies and between maturing stalks, children fish for tiny eels considered a delicacy in Bali, tadpoles wiggle among the shoots and frogs frogkick across the water. Lizards, birds and grasshoppers all make an appearance and catfish are reared here until they're big enough for the wok. The flooded fields of Bali are also home to flocks of ducks. Led out to the fields each morning and back each evening by a duck shepherd, they're a much-loved part of the Balinese rural scenery. All this animal life often features in Balinese paintings, wood carvings and stone sculptures, even if the real paddy frogs are rarely seen wearing crowns and toting umbrellas.

Channelling water for rice is politically charged. In Bali, the **subak** is a rice-fields council with responsibility not only for maintenance of irrigation channels and waterways but also for supplying farming tools and labour and for the equable and efficient distribution of irrigation water. It's thought that the best person to head the subak is the farmer at the base of the hill, as he has the most incentive to ensure that water flows all the way to the bottom!

It takes about three months for modern rice varieties to reach maturity. During that time the rice changes colour from the seedling's vividly fresh green through a darker green to a beautiful green-gold. At the same time, the growing grains – each cluster called a panicle – weighs down the stalks, producing that gentle curve that's as much an element of a rice field's seductiveness as its colour.

There is no across-the-board harvest season in Indonesia as dates, people and procedures all vary from region to region and even from field to field. But let's look at what happens in Ababi in eastern Bali. Soon after dawn, villagers from Ababi move on to I Made Geria's fields. Terracing right down to the road, Geria's holdings total 5500 square metres. He is joined by I Wayan Dauh, head of the local subak, and by more than 50 subak members. Every villager who owns as much as one **sawah** (rice field) must be a member of the subak and take part in its activities. The co-operative system encourages all members to help harvest other members' crops; on one hand, 10% of the harvest is distributed among harvesters but on the other, no-shows have to pay a fine.

Rice ready for harvest, Lombok

STAPLES

The harvest has been underway on Geria's fields for several days and a few hours of work this morning will finish bringing in the crop. Higher up the hill, rice stalks are rapidly scythed, bundled and carried to the large tarpaulin for threshing. Threshers whack the rice bundles against angled bamboo racks, sending grains flying onto the blue tarpaulin.

The harvest team, Lombok

It only takes a few hours to complete the harvest, at which point the paperwork begins. Geria calls a roll from the list in his exercise book, so that absentees can be charged. The subak head supervises bagging. It's been a good harvest and the morning's work yielded 22 bags, each weighing 40-45kg, so there will be nearly 100kg of rice to divide between the workers. Jero Mangku Diksa, the Ababi village priest, turns up for the 15% of the harvest that goes to the temple. The owner's bags are carted to the road to wait for a passing **bemo** (public minibus) to take them back to the village.

Already the threshing racks and the blue tarpaulin are being hauled uphill to the next batch of fields. The field owner, subak head and village priest squat under a shady tree to discuss the harvest. Ni Wayan Runi has already closed shop and headed uphill. In a **pondok** (the open-sided, grass-roofed shelters that dot rice fields), she had set up a small shop selling snacks, hot coffee, **kretek** (clove cigarettes) and other necessities. There's just a small girl and an old lady left in the field now. As each bundle of rice was tossed over a thresher's shoulder, a small contingent of hangers-on raked over the stalks for any grains still hanging on despite the threshing. These last two workers are busy filling their sacks with escapees.

The field, almost dry before the harvest, will be left to dry completely, burnt off, flooded and ploughed under. Then the whole process starts again.

Rice Tourism – Bali

Rolling fields of wheat in the American Midwest may be picturesque but nobody has ever built a hotel where views of wheat fields are the main attraction. And you've been drinking too much Guinness if you start dreaming of stunning views of a field of potatoes in Ireland. But Indonesia's rice paddies really are a tourist attraction. In Bali, a key part of the scenery of the astonishingly beautiful (and astonishingly expensive) Amandari Hotel is the view of rice paddies tripping down from the hotel to the Ayung River below. The nearby Four Seasons Sayan actually incorporates some artistically sited rice paddies into the hotel's garden design. Hotels along Monkey Forest Road in Ubud all look out over rice paddies and even advertise 'rice paddy views'.

In the late 1950s, it was widely feared that Asia's booming population was set to overtake the region's ability to produce its staple food: rice. Responding to this, the Ford and Rockefeller foundations established the International Rice Research Institute (IRRI) in 1962.

STAPLES

The post-harvest burn off, Lombok

Tools of the trade, Bali

Within a few years the institute had produced IR8, the first of the 'miracle rice' varieties that were: more productive (producing more rice per stalk); sturdier (in order to bear a heavier load of grains); faster-growing (so farmers could harvest more crops per year) and more resistant to disease. Farmers quickly adopted the new varieties and within a few years, rice production was increasing more rapidly than population. In 25 years world rice production had doubled; in some areas, like Indonesia, it had actually tripled. Today, new varieties make up 75% of all rice grown in Asia.

An early criticism of IRRI's rice strains was that productivity came at a heavy cost in increased need for fertilisers, herbicides and insecticides. These chemicals not only increased the cost of farming, they also poisoned soil and groundwater. Continuing research has not only produced rice varieties better able to withstand weed and pests, it has also identified strains possessing allelopathic properties; that is, they actually inhibit the growth of weeds in their vicinity. Similarly, nematodes (parasitic worms) can be controlled by crop rotation with such plants as peanuts and corn.

Herbicides and pesticides can have some surprising side effects. IRRI researchers discovered that using herbicides on field embankments to control weeds was often purely cosmetic. Destroying the weeds also destroyed populations of crickets that lived in the weeds and ate a variety of pests. Allowing these weeds to flourish protected the cricket populations and, in turn, deterred serious rice pests.

Another downside of 'miracle rice' is the increasing rarity of Indonesia's native rice species. These are slower growing and far more expensive than the modern species, but richer in protein and flavour; Bali's **beras merah** (red rice), for example, has a pleasantly astringent and nutty taste.

Rice Words

A food and word as important as rice is powerfully symbolic. Just as Tibetans have dozens of words for yak, Indonesians have many versions of our one word, rice. In its natural state, prior to the milling that removes its husk, rice is **padi**. This word has become the English term for a rice field: paddy. But a rice paddy in English is **sawah** in Indonesian —at least in its flooded state; a dry rice field is **ladang**. To Indonesians, rice is **padi** only while it's in the field. Once harvested but not yet husked and milled, the rice becomes **gabah**. After it's milled but still not cooked, it's **beras**. Cooked rice is **nasi**, as in the famed Indonesian dish, nasi goreng.

Nasi Goreng (Fried Rice)

When you think of Indonesian cuisine, the first thing that springs to mind is invariably nasi goreng. And why not? It is loved by Indonesians whether it's served by a **kaki-lima** (roving vendor) in Lampung or at a classy **rumah makan** (restaurant) in Jakarta. Part of its popularity is the fact that it's so versatile. Nasi goreng can be an inexpensive meal simply dressed with crispy shallots and chillies; it can be an extravagant dish studded with prawns and a garden of vegetables. Whatever the mix, if it contains rice and it's fried, it's fried rice. Of course other countries have their fried rice, notably China, who in fact introduced nasi goreng – and rice – to Indonesia. An authentic nasi goreng should include shallots, chillies, **kecap manis** (sweet soy sauce) and – the crowning glory – a fried egg.

Ingredients

3 cups	white rice, cooked and allowed to cool (it will go mushy if it's still warm)
3 Tbs	vegetable oil
5	shallots, chopped
3	cloves garlic, chopped
1-3	fresh red chillies, seeded and chopped
3 Tbs	**kecap manis** (sweet soy sauce)
2 Tbs	tomato paste
1	egg per person
1	small cucumber, sliced

Note: This recipe is vegetarian. Those with a taste for flesh can add a few cooked prawns (in fact feel free to add anything) just before serving.

Heat the oil in a wok. Add the shallots, garlic and chilli. When the shallots brown, add the soy sauce and tomato paste and fry for 5 minutes. Add the rice and stir continuously for about 10 minutes. Taste and adjust the flavour by adding soy sauce. In a separate pan or wok, fry an egg sunny-side up – one for each person. Serve hot with the egg on top and cucumber slices on the side.

Serves 4

Mie (Noodles)

Like rice, **mie** (noodles) came down through South-East Asia from China and are now an essential part of the Indonesian culinary lexicon. Rice noodles, wheat noodles and egg noodles are all found here, and any may be used in the night market staple, **mie goreng** (fried noodles). As with nasi goreng there is no one correct recipe; all it needs is a wok, some oil – and noodles. **Mie rebus** (noodle soup) is a very popular snack. Unfortunately, homemade noodles are being shunned for the convenience of the two minute packet variety, but a few fresh ingredients such as beansprouts, shallots and an egg are always added. There are many types of noodles available, including **mihun** (small rice noodles, also cellophane noodles), **kuaytau** (flat rice noodles) and **sohun** (mung bean noodles; transparent bean-flour vermicelli).

Chinese-style noodle soups are very popular throughout Indonesia and can include **pangsit** (wonton) and beansprouts. These are often served as a separate light broth that you can slurp separately or spoon over the noodles.

Fish, Fowl & Meat
Ikan (Fish)

Take a look at a map of Indonesia; the country is surrounded by water – swimming in it. There's the Java Sea, the Makassar Strait, the Banda Sea. So much water. And so many fish: tuna, sardines, snapper, mackerel, perch, shark, anchovies – just to name a few. This is the dietary constant across the archipelago. From Sabang to Merauke there'll be **ikan** (fish) to fry, and dry, and grill. Even inland there's fish to be found. The rivers, streams, flooded rice fields and lakes play home to carp, tilapia and catfish. Being cheaper and more widely available than meat, fish is the protein hit of the population.

But not only do fish offer sustenance, they are the livelihood of millions. Fishermen in Pangandaran export much of their catch directly to Japan, rice farmers in East Java supplement their income by setting bamboo traps to catch catfish for sale at market. You can see fishing boats spotlighting their catch at night as you fly into Jakarta. The search for the fishy dollar even

Fisherman with night lanterns, Jimbaran, Bali

STAPLES

sees fishing vessels try their luck in Australian waters – a venture sometimes ending with Australian customs confiscating vessels and burning them as a quarantine measure. But this is a hard habit to break; Indonesians have been fishing in Australian waters for thousands of years.

If you're buying fresh fish (you can often get your hotel to cook it for you), the gills should be a deep red colour (not brown), the eyes bright and clear, and the flesh firm to the touch.

So what to do with all these fine finned creatures? The most popular fishy dish is **ikan bakar** (char-grilled fish). It can be grilled straight over the charcoal or wrapped in banana leaves. **Pepes ikan** (spiced fish cooked in banana leaves; see the recipe) can be found all over Indonesia, the type of fish and spices depending on the region; the only constant is the banana leaf in which it is baked, giving the fish a smoky aroma. Most often fish is cooked with no more than lime and salt and served with a fresh sambal.

Deep frying is another popular treatment for fish, especially for **lele** (catfish), which is plunged into hot oil and served with **pecel** (spicy sauce made from chilli, peanuts and/or tomato). You'll find this dish, known as **pecel lele** at food stalls across the country.

What with so much heat and so little refrigeration, there's big business in drying fish. Once the catch is brought to shore, the fish are either sent straight to market, or they undertake a drying process where they are boiled in saltwater then left to dry for about half a day. The result is **ikan asin** (salted fish), and although not as good as the real thing, ikan asin is cheap and travels well. Another method of keeping fish fresh is to keep them alive, flapping in a bucket near the wok.

Makanan Laut (Seafood)

Although a wide variety of **udang** (prawn) and **cumi-cumi** (squid) is caught in Indonesian waters, much of it is earmarked for the international market, and what is sold locally is often too expensive for locals to be a daily dish. You will, however, find tiny, cheaper prawns lurking in a plate of **nasi goreng** (fried rice) or **kangkung** (water spinach). This is not to say larger prawns and squid are not available, it's just that you'll being paying more for the pleasure. Palembang in South Sumatra is home to massive river prawns as is Banjarmasin in Kalimantan.

Chinese-style restaurants do a healthy trade in **udang tiram** (prawns in oyster sauce) and if a fishing village is in a tourist area you'll be able to choose your dinner as it comes off the boat (see the boxed text). Other sea creatures liable to pop up at seafood restaurants include **kepiting** (crab) and **udang karang** (lobster), often served steamed with oyster sauce or deep fried.

The market at Mataram, Lombok

TITIN IN PANGANDARAN

Titin lives in Bandung, but her hometown is the fishing village of Pangandaran on the south coast of Java. We were planning a trip there since we had heard their seafood wasn't to be missed, so we asked Titin if she could suggest places to eat.

"Sure. I'll show you", she said, seemingly unconcerned that Pangandaran was six hours away.

"But it's six hours away."

"So let's get going."

And that was that. We organised transport, squashed into the very-mini-bus with our gear and headed off on the kind of road trip that reminds you of your mortality: beautiful scenery blemished by overturned trucks. Pangandaran was a welcome sight. The manic roads were replaced with black-sand beaches and swaying coconut trees. It was sunset and there were multicoloured boats being beached for the night, boats with names like *best friend* and *danger my bisnis*.

Titin sorted us a room then went off to find her family. Like her, most of Titin's siblings had left the small town in search of employment. Although this town was beautiful, there wasn't much work here unless you want a job in tourism or fishing.

In an hour Titin returned with her brother, sister-in-law and their robust baby son.

"So let's eat!" said Titin. "Nothing else to do in Pangandaran."

We knew this wasn't true – there were national parks, caves and reefs to explore – but undoubtably the food was what we were here for. Titin led us down some narrow streets, past a few inviting eateries, but she was on a mission. Soon we hit the east beach. We could hear the rolling waves ... as well as the sizzle of boiling oil. We were standing next to the **pasar ikan** (fish market), which consisted of a few open-air pavilions sheltering some tables and chairs, black sand creeping onto the floor. To the side of each shelter were rows and rows of plump red snapper, bulbous prawns and other marine treats.

The deal was to buy the fresh fish then explain how you wanted it cooked. Roasted? Deep fried? Sauteed? Just as we began pointing to our fish-of-choice, Titin turned around and told us to keep quiet. She would do the talking. As obvious foreigners we were prone to a mark-up, but for Titin this was her home. She and the seller talked the talk, caught up on the local gossip, who had left, who was back. Then, smoothly Titin moved into the realm of food, telling the seller she knew she'd get a good price here, plus we provided good business especially since trade was slow – times were tight and the seller could see us drooling, eyes out-weighing our stomachs. Titin suggested a meal of **udang tiram** (prawns in oyster sauce) and **ikan bakar** (grilled fish), plus stirfried water spinach and potatoes. We weren't sure that was enough, but she knew what we were in for and suggested we shut up, pick a table and get the beer. While waiting, Titin's brother told us how tourism was still slow. He spoke fluent Dutch and English but people were still staying away because of demonstrations hundreds of miles away.

"No unrest here", he said as his baby son clambered up his shirt and grabbed at his cigarettes.

Things were taking some time. Our stomachs were audible but we could see it was all happening in the kitchen area. Then it arrived. A few plates of vegetables, rice, a mountain of shining prawns and one massive red snapper. The spread looked too good to eat. Actually, that's a lie. For the next hour or so we turned the display of abundance into one of destruction. Prawn shells littered the table, the fish was stripped to its bones. We lost all sense of posture. The ocean sounds lulled us. We payed the bill and made for the hotel satisfied that Pangandaran's seafood had lived up to expectation.

"That was incredible", we told Titin in appreciation. She smiled and nodded knowingly.

"Didn't I tell you?"

Patrick Witton

STAPLES

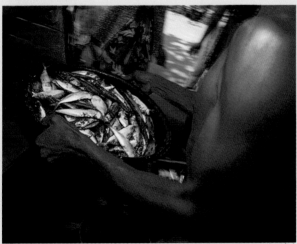

The morning catch near Mataram, Lombok

Ayam (Chicken)

Thin, fast and loud, the average **ayam** (chicken) is an integral part of Indonesia's culinary landscape. An village is just not a village without at least a couple of poultry bipeds pecking their way through scraps, clucking veraciously at dawn and being chased by aggressive toddlers. To visitors' eyes Indonesia's chickens are a tad on the scrawny side, often with a patchy plumage due to territorial disputes, and essentially don't look fit to eat. But remember this is real **ayam kampung** (village chicken), untouched by hormones and battery cages. And the proof of this is in the taste. These chickens may be skinny, but once you bite into a meal of **ayam bakar** (grilled chicken), **opor ayam** (chicken in pepper and coconut curry; see the recipe) or **sate ayam** (chicken sate), made with ayam kampung, you'll realise bigger isn't better.

One thing that may put you off your chook is the popularity of **cakar ayam** (chicken claw), which, unfortunately, is the tastiest part. We have seen adorable small children, slung on their mother's hip in a **selendang** (sling-like scarf), with a chicken claw protruding from their faces. If you see the word **cakar** on any menu item, prepare to meet the claw.

PAMPERED COCKS

A rooster is man's best friend

Bali's roosters are the most spoiled animals of Indonesia. Preened, groomed and dined; they are as pampered as Queen Elizabeth's corgis. Their owners look after them with unerring devotion: take them to meet friends, save them the choicest feed, place them in baskets near roads so they are entertained by passing traffic. Life may be rosy for the Balinese poultry, but death can be bloody. Cockfights are a feature of Balinese temple festivals. The birds are matched up, a spur is attached to their leg, then it's on. Blood and feathers. For the winner it's back to the easy life. For the loser, sate, soup or the grill.

DOG FOOD

You couldn't really call it a staple, in fact most locals shy away from the idea, but dog is indeed dinner in some areas of Indonesia, notably in North Sulawesi and the Batak region of Sumatra. They are, however, surreptitious about canine consumption and you'll never see the word **anjing** (dog) on a list of dishes. In the Batak region they call dog **B1** (pronounced *beh sah-tuh*, as dog in the local language is **biang**, which has one 'b'. They call **babi** (pig) **B2**. In North Sulawesi Fido is known as **rw** (pronounced *err-weh)*, in which 'r' stands for **rintek** (soft) and 'w' stands for **wu'uk** (fur).

Doggy can get done for dinner in other areas, and in Java the dish **oseng-oseng** (fried kangkung, yard-long beans and soy sauce) becomes **oseng-oseng jamur** with the addition of doggy, even though **jamur** means mushroom.

So why eat Rover? Well they say it's good for the heart and it's warming. They also say black dog is best. This all may be true, but the bottom line is the dog we tried was nothing special. It had no distinct taste and was an unappealing grey colour. Perhaps it was the collar.

STAPLES

Bebek (Duck)

Indonesia may well have the happiest **bebek** (duck) population on the planet. So many rice fields to swim in, so many insects to eat (something farmers are grateful for), life couldn't be better for these quackers. Too bad they taste so good. Ducks are found across the archipelago but, gastronomically speaking, they are their tastiest in Bali, where they are made into **bebek betutu** (duck stuffed with spices, wrapped in banana leaves and coconut husks and cooked in a pit of embers). In Sumatra ducks are called **itik** and are made into **gulai itik** (duck in coconut curry). Many Indonesians find the ruddier flavours of duck to be too strong and salt the flesh before preparation.

Taking the market duck home, Ubud, Bali

Sapi (Beef) & Kerbau (Buffalo)

Both these brawny animals are highly valued across the country, not only for their meat but also for milk, hide and as essential farming ability. **Sapi** (cows) are more often found on the drier islands of Madura and Nusa Tenggara, whereas the brawnier yet placid **kerbau** (buffalo) in areas of high rainfall, where the muddy ground requires more muscle to move. Even Bali enjoys their beef, as they are the only Hindus who permit eating of cows (although Hindu priests don't eat beef). In many regions, especially Sulawesi, Sumba and Sumatra, buffaloes play a large yet involuntarily fatal role in local culture (see West Sumatra and Central Sulawesi in the Regional Variations chapter and the boxed text Death of the Party in the Celebrating chapter).

As far as beefy meals are concerned, don't go past the Indonesian classic, **rendang** (beef or buffalo coconut curry; see the recipe). Don't be put off by the petite size of your rendang serve. The flavour and richness contained in that tasty tablet is easily enough to satisfy. What's more, eating a Texan portion will result in a feeling of fatigue at best. Let rice suffice, and rendang enrich. Traditional rendang is made with buffalo, however beef can also be used. In fact the rendang can be made with anything that won't dissolve into the liquid, such as chicken or jackfruit.

Another beefy favourite is to make it into sate and serve with rice and a spicy sauce. In Yogyakarta, buffalo is used to make **krecek** (buffalo-skin crackling), which is served as an accompaniment to **gudeg** (jackfruit curry; see Central Java in the Regional Variations chapter).

Ploughing the fields in Bali

Rendang
(Beef or Buffalo Coconut Curry)

This recipe was successfully road-tested in the kitchen of Ni Pen, who lives and works as a guide for Putu Bungsu Tours in Bukittinggi (West Sumatra). She also took us to the town's market where, amid the mayhem, we somehow bought all the ingredients needed (see the Shopping & Markets chapter). Rendang is traditionally made with buffalo, however beef is now more common as it takes less time to cook. Even so, beef rendang still takes about 4 hours.

Gaja Biru restaurant, Ubud, Bali

Ingredients

6 cups	coconut milk
2	salam leaves
2	lime leaves
1	turmeric leaf
3cm stick	cinnamon stick
10cm stick	lemongrass
15	cloves shallots
15	cloves garlic
3cm	piece of ginger
3cm	piece of galangal
1	nutmeg seed
2 Tbs	chilli paste
500g	prime rump beef, cut into 4 sq cm pieces (leave fat on)
	salt to taste

Heat the coconut milk in an uncovered wok over a very low flame. Add the salam leaves, lime leaves, turmeric leaf, cinnamon stick and lemongrass (don't cut these up). Crush the shallots, garlic, ginger, galangal and nutmeg to a paste. For this you can use a food processor or a traditional Indonesian mortar & pestle (see the Home Cooking & Traditions chapter). Add this paste, the chilli paste and the salt to the coconut milk. Once the ingredients are heated through, add the beef and leave to cook very slowly for about four hours. Once the coconut milk has been reduced to an oily paste that sticks to the meat it is ready.

Rendang is rich so it's best served (one piece of meat per person) with lots of rice and other dishes.

A SATE TOUR

Meat on a stick is by no means a patentable invention, it was probably the Neanderthal cooking method of choice, but skewered meat cooked over coals and called **sate** is an Indonesian institution. Any meat can be used: goat, chicken, mutton, rabbit, pork, entrails or even horse and snake can find their way on to a sate skewer. Cooking the sate over coals produces aromas delicious enough to lure a vegetarian. Sate is nearly always prepared 10 to a serve with spicy peanut sauce and rice or **lontong** (rice steamed in banana leaves). Here are a few of the more well-known sate stations:

In Jakarta, Jl Sabang is famed as the sate capital of Indonesia. Dozens of sate hawkers set up on the street in the evening and the pungent smoke from their charcoal braziers fills the air. Most business is takeaway – some very expensive cars pull up here – but benches are scattered along the street for a sit-down meal.

The road between Bandung and Lembang, and in Tawangmangu (both in Java) you'll find eateries serving up **sate kelinci** (rabbit sate).

Sate served with lontong and a smooth, spicy, yellow-coloured, turmeric-heavy sauce is a West Sumatran speciality and is sold all over Indonesia as **sate Padang**.

Balinese sate, **sate lilit**, is made with minced, spiced meat that's pressed onto skewers

The Madurese are famous for their sate, served with rice and a sweet and spicy soy sauce. It may not differ much from other sate varieties, but **sate Madura** is still an experience. It is traditionally sold at night from boat-shaped carts plying the streets in search of the hungry. And when the shadow of a Madurese sate boat floats by, the bells on its bow jingling with each ebb and flow, it's hard to resist a late-night meal of spicy sate Madura.

The regional government office in Bandung is known, because of its peculiar spire, as Gedung Sate (the Sate Building).

Sate for sale, Jalan Veteran, Jakarta

Babi (Pork)

As much of Indonesia is Muslim, and Islam prohibits the consumption of pork, you won't find too much **babi** (pork) on your plate. But in non-Muslim areas where pork is accepted, it is accepted with fervour. Places wandering pigs should avoid include Bali, where they are turned into such dishes as **babi guling** (spit-roast pig). The Chinese-Indonesian population also enjoy pork, as do others such as the Batak of Sumatra and the Toraja of Sulawesi (see the Regional Variations chapter).

Blessing a new house with a pig offering, Sulawesi

IBU OKA

Say the name Ibu Oka to any Balinese and they start drooling profusely. People make wide detours so they can visit her, they queue up just to get close, and her name is known as far away as Surabaya. So what is it that makes people love Ibu Oka so much? Well, to be honest, it's not her but her speciality, **babi guling** (spit-roast pig).

Ibu Oka lives and runs her restaurant in the centre of Ubud. Her restaurant opens at midday and it was then that I first set my eyes on Ibu Oka. She was managing the busy restaurant with aplomb: taking and giving orders. When I caught her attention she looked at me sternly. When I asked how she prepared the pig I thought she was going to let loose. How dare I ask such a question! But she simply glanced up the road and said "Come to my house tomorrow".

"Really?"

Her expression didn't change. "6am." And she turned to much more pressing matters.

The next morning I arrived at Ubud Tengah, the village compound where Ibu Oka, her husband, children and their spouses live and work. The back of the village was set aside for Ibu Oka's business: a large, covered concrete space, blackened by the smoke of a thousand fires. Their day had well and truly begun. Ibu Oka was sitting on the porch overlooking her domain while her sons were fanning the flames and preparing the pigs. In fact five of the eight pigs she had bought from Klungkung village had already met their maker. One was being set onto a spit, one was being stitched up and three more were being rotated over a fire of coffee wood. The other three were in their pens, looking somewhat solemn.

But Ibu Oka wasn't just watching. She was busy preparing ingredients for the stuffing. She told me to sit down, and she cleared a bag of chillies so I could do so.

"This was my parents' business, they taught me how to make babi guling the same way they were taught by their parents. At sunrise we wake up and kill the pigs, then shave and clean them with hot water. The insides we keep for sausage."

She pointed to a coil of intestines, a bucket of blood and a wide tray of goop.

"Next we stuff the pig with a spice mix" and she glanced to where her daughter was pounding a mixture in a massive mortar.

"Chilli, garlic, shallots, kencur, ginger, turmeric, coconut oil, salam leaf, salt and mango leaf."

While she talked, Ibu Oka prepared tomorrow's spice mix, cutting the chilli and garlic.

"Always fresh. Only the very best ingredients … and no MSG, it hurts my throat!"

Lunch is served at Ibu Oka's, Ubud, Bali

Ibu Oka's daughter had finished pounding the mixture and, while her brother stuffed it into the cleaned pig, she moved on to prepare the sausage. For this she minced the liver and other grizzlies, mixed that with blood, spices and shredded coconut, then funnelled the resulting gunk into the pig intestines. I watched as the gunk stretched through the intestines, turning it a burgundy red. She then coiled the filled intestine on a large bamboo pole and placed it at the back of the fire.

Ibu Oka had things to do, so I ventured down to where her sons were turning the creaking spits by hand. It was there I met Made, not Ibu Oka's son but a family friend from Klungkung who was now working for the Oka clan. Made, like many of the other men working the spits, was covered in tattoos. This, along with the smoke, flames, creaking spit and smell of flesh gave the scene a touch of Hieronomous Bosch, however the workers were cracking jokes while a breakfast of ice lemon water and pig liver was distributed. Made and I shared stories, and soon I was turning the spit while he pricked the pig skin so it wouldn't explode. A woman came down to the cooking area and placed a Hindu offering of rice and flowers next to each spit.

One of Ibu Oka's sons (the one with the mullet) was doing the rounds while chewing on pork liver, making sure the spits were straight and the fire wasn't too hot. He would strategically douse the flames with water so the skin didn't cook too fast. The pig looked done to me. Glistening red, it looked like a meal straight out of Asterix. But no.

"Three more hours", said Made. "Five hours for a large pig, three for a smaller one. That one's ready."

From the fire next to ours came out a smaller pig, deep red and dripping with juices. A moment later we were tucking into the first cuts of the day: a serve of white rice, **urab** (long bean and coconut salad), rich-red crackling, oret (which tasted like a spicy liverwurst) and warm, tender yet spicy roast pork. Heaven on a spit.

I thanked the Oka mob and left the village a happier, porkier man. Down the street there was already a crowd gathering at Ibu Oka's restaurant. They were sitting patiently, waiting for their orders to be taken: **biasa** (normal serve) or **spesial** (bigger, better cuts). If I wasn't so full I would have joined them for one more serve of spit-roast pig, Ibu Oka style.

Patrick Witton

Kambing (Goat)

Not used much for their milk, too small to do any work, too large to be easily transportable, the **kambing** (goats) of Indonesia have two primary uses: to eat that which no other animal would and to fill the pot. Goat is used in a number of dishes including **gulai kambing** (goat in coconut curry) and **sate kambing** (goat sate). For the uninitiated, goat meat is similar to mutton but has a higher fat content. So if you want a cholesterol hit, gulai kambing is the prime choice.

Kelinci (Rabbit)

Yup, 'fraid to say Flopsy ain't safe here. On the road to Lembang and in Tawangmangu (both in Java) you'll see the big-eared bunnies sitting in their hutches on the side of the road. The cute little rabbits will be sitting there, happily munching on greens, awaiting the trip to restaurants further up the road where they'll be made into gamey **sate kelinci** (rabbit sate). Thumper beware.

BLOOD & GUTS

Bag of claws to go, Yogyakarta

If you find offal awful, if liver makes you livid, then beware while you're dining in Indonesia. Here every part of the animal is fair game. You'll find chicken liver sate in Java, stuffed buffalo intestines in Sumatra and chicken feet soup in Kalimantan. The Batak of Sumatra, the Torajans of Sulawesi, the Dayaks of Kalimantan and the Balinese all make use of every part of the pig, including the blood. And a fish head left on a plate is the best bit wasted. The liver holds special meaning for Indonesians who believe it is the cradle of one's emotions, just as westerners regard the heart. So if you want to avoid the innards, then be sure to ask what part of the body an unidentified piece of meat comes from (easily done by pointing to parts of your own body). As the Indonesians say, **hati-hati** (literally, liver-liver; take care).

Kedelai (Soybeans)

Vegans rejoice, as the protein-rich soybean, introduced from China, is an essential in the Indonesian kitchen. In fact it was Indonesians who invented **tempe**, the soybean product now eaten across the globe. In Indonesia, versatile soybeans are not thought of as a 'meat substitute', but a tempe or tofu dish will cost half that of a meat dish. And those who think tofu has no taste obviously haven't bitten down on **tahu Sumedang** (tofu from Sumedang; see West Java in the Regional variations chapter). Other soybean products include **kecap** (soy sauce) and **susu kedelai** (soy milk).

Tempe

High in protein and holding a rich, nutty flavour, tempe is a soybean 'cake' used in a multitude of dishes including **tempe kering** (sweet and crispy fried tempe; see the recipe), **bacem** (tempe, tofu or chicken cooked in stock; see the recipe) and **tempe penyet** (deep-fried tempe steak). To make tempe, the beans are washed, soaked until their skins fall off, halved, then boiled. Once drained they are sprinkled with a yeast starter, then wrapped in tubes of either banana leaf or perforated plastic. The starter grows rapidly around the beans, breaking down the properties indigestible to humans and, in two days, creating a vitamin-packed and protein-rich foodstuff.

Tahu (Tofu)

Also called beancurd, tofu is made by soaking, grinding and cooking soybeans to form a soft cake. Although the resulting tofu can be marinated, dried, fried, baked, put in soup, whatever, here it's most often deep fried to make **tahu goreng**. For a tasty snack, try **tahu isi** (tofu stuffed with beansprouts and other vegetables then deep fried).

A late night snack of deep-fried tempe and tofu

Telur (Eggs)

Eggs feature both in and on dishes, or constitute the dish itself. **Nasi goreng** (fried rice) is often served crowned with a fried egg, and **mie rebus** (noodle soup) often comes with **telur setengah matang** (literally half-cooked egg), which you mix into the dish. Restaurants prepare **ceplok** (fried egg) and **dadar** (omelette), both smothered in chilli sauce. But the best use of egg is in a **martabak** (crispy-skin omelette). This night market speciality is a meal in itself, fried until crispy in a shallow wok with fresh ingredients such as cucumber, garlic, shallots and – less usually – with meat.

Eggs are also cooked as part of the Javanese speciality, **gudeg** (jackfruit curry; see Central Java in the Regional Variations chapter).

Eggs for sale in Yogyakarta's Demangan market, Java

Soto, Sop (Soup)

Traditional Indonesian soups are meat based, with all parts of the animal used in the stock, what else goes in to the broth depends on where you are. The cooks of Bandung make **soto Bandung** (beef and vegetable soup with lemongrass). In Madura they are as equally creative with their names, making a soup called **soto Madura** with beef (any part thereof) lime, pepper, peanuts, chilli and ginger. In fact most towns have a signature soup as well as their own **sayur asam** (sour vegetables in clear broth).

Chickens can be found scurrying around anywhere in Indonesia and, unfortunately for them, so can **soto ayam** (chicken soup; see the recipe), which usually contains garlic, shallots and turmeric. This soup, as well as others will be served with a dish of rice which you can spoon into the soup, or visa versa. If you see the word **soto**, expect a well-seasoned broth, whereas the word **sop** describes a clearer, lighter broth. Many soups come with sambal and wedges of lime for you to flavour your meal. The lime adds a sharp edge to the homey stock.

STAPLES

Bakso (Meatball Soup)

This is the national comfort food. A homesick Indonesian wouldn't crave **gado-gado** (salad of vegetables and peanut sauce); they'd crave a steaming bowl of bakso, perhaps with noodles, perhaps water spinach or a few beansprouts. Whatever else ends up in the bowl depends on the bakso seller. Some add fried shallots, some deep-fried **pangsit** (wonton). Some add **cakar ayam** (chicken feet), just look for the word **cakar** on the signage. Every Indonesian has their favourite bakso seller, the one who makes 'the best bakso in Solo ... Sumbawa ... Indonesia'. Bakso has stirred people to write songs, such is its simple beauty.

> Bakso bulet seperti bola ping pong
>> Bakso shaped like a ping-pong ball
>
> Kalo lewat membikin perut kosong
>> If you pass by, your stomach will stay empty
>
> Jadi anak janganlah suka bohong
>> So don't act like a stupid child
>
> Kalo bohong digigit nenek ompong
>> If you're stupid you'll be bitten by grandmother (!)

Fruit & Vegetables

Wander through any produce market and you'll quickly realise how fertile the Indonesian soil really is. Even in provincial markets where everything on sale is grown locally you'll be spoiled for choice: carrots in Brastagi, mangoes in Maumere, pineapple in Ujung Pandang ... much of the produce you'll find here was introduced from as far afield as the Americas, but they are now essentials in the Indonesian kitchen.

In the villages, and where space permits, people supplement market goods with their own produce: beans, bananas, papaya, cassava (good for the tuber and the leaves). Even the grounds of universities have corn growing between the faculty buildings. Every available piece of land is put to use.

Sayuran (Vegetables)

As well as the vegetables listed, you'll find **wortel** (carrots), **kol** (cabbage), **bunga kol** (cauliflower), **asparagus** (asparagus) in many markets, especially those in higher altitudes such as Bukittinggi and Brastagi (Sumatra), and Lembang (Java).

Bawang (Onion & Garlic)

When Indonesians think of onions they think of **bawang merah** (shallot), as this is the most common type of onion used in Indonesian cooking. For an easy and tasty garnish, pre-fried shallots can be bought at any food store, and make for a crunchy addition to **nasi goreng** (fried rice). **Bawang putih** (garlic) is a main player in sambal and is also used to flavour stirfries and curries. Larger onions are known as **bawang bombay**.

Corny fashion trends, Sumatra

Jagung (Corn)

An American introduction, corn is most popular as **jagung bakar** (grilled corn). To make this, the corn is often left in its husk. They are so tasty, no butter is needed, but sellers slather it (or sometimes butter substitute) on anyway. Also look out for **perkedel jagung** (corn fritters). In the eastern reaches of Nusa Tenggara, corn replaces rice as a staple.

Market fare, Denpasar market, Bali

STAPLES

Kacang (Beans & Nuts)

Both of these protein-rich foods are known as **kacang**, and both are used in sweet and sour dishes. As for beans, you'll find **kacang buncis** (green beans) and the spirally, rougher skinned **kacang panjang** (yard-long beans), both of which are chopped up into salads such as gado-gado or stirfried on their own. Also look out for **pete**, a large tasty bean that grows in what looks like a massive pea pod. The bean can be sliced and fried or roasted in the pod. Although tasty, pete are notorious for leaving you with shockingly bad breath. Don't order pete on a romantic night out.

As far as nuts go, you can't go past **kacang tanah** (peanuts). These versatile fellas are eaten plain as a snack, are ground and made into sate sauce, and are made into **rempeyek** (peanuts cooked within rice-flour crackers; see the recipe), which can be sweetened with the addition of palm sugar. They also feature in the textural sensation, **ikan bilis goreng kacang** (fried peanuts and anchovies).

Tauge (beansprouts) are used in salads, as a garnish on stirfries and soups or as a filling for **tahu isi** (stuffed tofu). **Kacang hijau** (mung beans) are used more as a sweet treat, finding their way into **bubur kacang hijau** (mung bean porridge) or used in the delicious **onde-onde** (sesame balls with a sweet mung bean filling).

Kangkung (Water Spinach)

If you're missing your greens, look no further than the iron and vitamin-rich **kangkung** (water spinach). Despite being so nutritious, kangkung actually tastes damn good. So good, in fact, that Indonesian children would consider 'eat your greens' a treat, not an order. Kangkung is best when simply and quickly fried with sliced chillies and a dash of soy.

Kangkung and kids near Mataram, Lombok

Kentang (Potatoes)

This starchy staple is served up in many restaurants as **kentang goreng** (fried potatoes), however they aren't cut in a slender, French-fry style, rather they are fried as chunky cubes. Potatoes are also mashed and formed into **perkedel** (fritters), often with a filling of spiced and shredded meat.

Ketimun (Cucumber)

Cool, crisp cucumbers can provide relief if you've exceeded your chilli intake. A plate of **nasi goreng** (fried rice) is usually crowned with a few slices of cucumber. They also feature in many Indonesian salads and even feature in the sweet drink **es ketimun** (iced cucumber), a refreshing concoction.

Sago

Sago is the starchy trunk of a palm, which is stripped, powdered, washed and strained to produce the staple in the drier areas of Indonesia – such as Nusa Tenggara and Irian Jaya (see Nusa Tenggara and Irian Jaya in the Regional Variations chapter).

Singkong (Cassava)

As it is such a hardy plant, cassava can be seen growing anywhere and everywhere, its wide, hand-like leaves reaching out from gardens and road-sides. Every part of cassava is used, the tuber is made into chips, roasted potato style, and made into cassava meal. Singkong is also made into **tape**, a strange-tasting speciality made by peeling, boiling and fermenting the tuber in yeast. Eating fermented tape doesn't have any alcohol-like effects, although we couldn't prove this as the taste verges on rancid. The only rule for eating cassava in any form is that it must be cooked; in its raw state it contains hydrocyanic acid – not so tasty.

Taro

This versatile root vegetable has been grown here longer than rice. Taro is treated like a potato: boiled, fried or mashed. The leaves are also eaten. It is more a staple in eastern Indonesia where rice production is minimal.

Terong (Eggplant)

Eggplant was introduced to Indonesia through Indian trade and is now here to stay. Indonesians don't use eggplant extensively, but when they do it's with astounding success. **Terong belado** (eggplant with chilli sauce; see the recipe) is Indonesia's tastiest eggplant dish. Perhaps it's the addition of lime, or the combination of eggplant and chilli. Who cares? And what's more it's simple to make. Not every restaurant offers terong belado, so when you do see it make room in your stomach.

Terong Belado (Eggplant with Chili Sauce)

Ingredients

2	large eggplants (or 4 small ones), halved
5 Tbs	coconut oil
4	shallots, chopped
3	garlic cloves, chopped
2cm	ginger and/or galangal, chopped
4	red chillies
400g	tomatoes, chopped (or a can of peeled tomatoes)
2	juice of 2 limes
	salt to taste

Halve the eggplants and brush them with 3 tablespoons of oil. Place them on a tray and bake at 180°C (350°F) for about 40 minutes or until they soften. Grind the shallots, garlic, ginger (and/or galangal) and chillies into a paste with a mortar & pestle. Heat the remaining oil in a wok, add the paste along with the tomatoes and salt and stir until heated through. Stir in the lime juice. Place the eggplant in a bowl and pour over the sauce.

Serves 4 with rice or cut the eggplants and serve as part of a banquet.

Tomat (Tomato)

Tomatoes are easily found, but not used for a great number of dishes. They are, however, often used as a base for many types of sambal. **Saus tomat** (tomato sauce) is becoming more common at the restaurant table, but wouldn't be missed if it disappeared. As long as there's sambal.

Ubi (Sweet Potato)

This is another American import, but its arrival preceded Columbus, giving credence to the theory that South Americans made the voyage to Polynesia well before the region was discovered by Europeans. Although found across Indonesia, **ubi** (sweet potato) reaches a peak of culinary importance in Irian Jaya, where it is the staple food of the highlands (see Irian Jaya in the Regional Variations chapter). For a tasty snack try **ubi goreng** (deep-fried sweet potato), which is essentially a big tasty chip.

Salad

Don't come to Indonesia expecting a green salad. You can get one if that's what you really crave, but expect watery tomatoes and floppy lettuce. A far better option would be to sample one of the local salads. Our favourites include **karedok** (Sundanese salad; see the recipe) and the famously popular gado-gado.

Buah-Buahan (Fruit)

As well as the varieties listed here, you'll also find **apel** (apple), **markisa** (passionfruit), **semangka** (watermelon) and **delima** (pomegranate).

Mangosteen, passionfruit and papaya

Apokat (Avocado)

This American import is both plentiful and cheap here, however Indonesians regard them as a sweet fruit and make them into **jus apokat** (avocado juice; see the recipe). Nevertheless no one will stop you spreading fresh avocado on a cracker with a little salt and lemon; but they may look at you strangely.

Belimbing (Starfruit)

The starfruit is a cool, crisp, watery and slightly tart-tasting fruit. Although they can be eaten raw, they taste fresher when peeled (also good for hygiene). Look at the starfruit head on and you'll immediately see where the name comes from.

Belulut (Palm Tree Fruit)

At the top of the palm tree grow bunches of belulut, which when opened look like lychee and rambutan but are harder and not as sweet. They are used mainly to flesh out **es campur** (mixed ice; see Es Campur in the Drinks chapter).

STAPLES

Durian

This large, spiky fruit has a serious public image problem. Durian devotees call it the 'king of fruits' but its detractors point out that many of history's kings were evil bastards. Hotels and airlines in Asia often ban the durian, so it's hardly surprising that it takes some time to become a durian aficionado. But let's take a closer look at this split-personality fruit. The durian's spiky skin looks like something from the Spanish inquisition. It's almost as if nature is saying 'best you don't get any closer'. But the truth is in there. Cracking a durian open releases its all-pervasive odorous power. Writers have been inspired to produce colourful prose upon smelling durian flesh: a superb raspberry blancmange inside a revolting public toilet ... onion sauce, brown sherry and other incongruities ... hell incarnate. But it's not over yet. If you look closer (many would have given up by now) you'll see five segments of custard-like flesh surrounding large seeds. These are the jewels in the king's crown. Some say the glory of the taste overrides the stench, others say keep running and don't look back. Let's just under-state the issue and say durian is an acquired taste. You don't have to buy a whole durian to sample the flavour as it can be bought by the segment. It is also the feature of **es durian** (ice durian) served with sugar syrup on a bed of ice.

Water apple, oranges, bananas and star fruit

Jambu (Guava)

There are many varieties of guava: small, large, round, full of seeds, few seeds. And guavas change as they grow: when young and crisp you'll find them in **rujak** (fruit served with a spicy sauce; see Sweet Snacks & Desserts later in this chapter). When older they soften, become more fragrant and can be eaten as is.

Jambu Air (Water Apple)

This fruit is shaped like a small, red-pink pear. Its flesh is only subtly sweet but very juicy, making it extremely refreshing.

Jeruk (Citrus Fruit)

There is a wide variety of citrus fruit available here. The main varieties include the huge **jeruk muntis** or **jerunga** (pomelo). It's larger than a grapefruit but with a very thick skin, a sweeter, more orange-like taste and segments that come apart very easily. Regular oranges are known as **jeruk manis** (sweet jeruk). The small tangerine-like oranges, which are often quite green, are **jeruk baras**. Lemons are **jeruk nipis** or **limon** and limes are **jeruk perut**. Indonesia's citrus fruits are usually too tart to be eaten plain. More often they are used in cooking or made into **es jeruk** (citrus juice).

Kelapa (Coconut)

Ah the versatile coconut; used for making brooms, baskets, packaging, decorations, oil. They even eat them for crying out loud. Coconuts are classic beach dwellers, enjoying the sea air and light soil. Inland they are grown in regimented rows on massive plantations. Here are but a few uses for the crafty kelapa:

Coconuts for sale, Bukittinggi, Sumatra

- Drink **air kelapa muda** (coconut water) fresh from a vendor – and you know it's fresh, 'cause you watched him open the nut. Some vendors spike the water with cordial and ice.

- Use the water to make **nata de coco**, a jelly-like dessert made by mixing coconut water with sugar, an acid bacteria and leaving it to solidify. The resulting jelly is cleaned, cubed, pasteurised in syrup and sold as a refreshing snack.

- Soak and strain the flesh of older nuts to make **santan** (coconut milk), which is used extensively in cooking.

- Boil the coconut milk down to make coconut oil

- Sample **kelapa kopyor** (coconut that has loose flesh – it grows on an ordinary palm but is made into a sensational ice cream)

- Destroy vast tracts of rainforest, plant coconut palms to the end of the horizon and make a bundle o' cash.

Opening a coconut takes some skill and a big knife, not something you're probably carrying around. At home you may want to try cracking a kelapa yourself but, remember, even the coconut farmers probably had failures before they got it right. It can be a mess, it can be dangerous (count your fingers) but using fresh coconut does make a difference. However canned coconut milk is no poor substitute

Overleaf – Elder woman in Yogyakarta, Java

Mangga (Mango)

If there is a heaven on earth it is within the skin of an Indonesian mango. This sweet yet not too sweet, refreshing, gloriously sticky fruit is a native of South-East Asia, and nowhere will you find more delectable varieties. Perhaps it's coincidental, but it makes sense that the word **mangga** also means 'you're welcome' in West Java. You'll see the welcome sight of mangoes for sale at markets, mixed into **es mangga** (mango shake) and, while still young and tart, cut into **rujak** (fruit served with a spicy sauce; see Sweet Snacks & Desserts later in this chapter).

Mangosteen

Manggis (Mangosteen)

One of the most delicious of tropical fruits, the mangosteen has a purple-brown exterior that you crack open to reveal tasty pure-white segments. These have a sweet, perfumed flavour; a little like lychee. Mangosteen do not travel well, so are rarely found outside of tropical Asia. Queen Victoria once offered a reward to anyone able to bring a mangosteen back to England which would still be edible on arrival.

Nanas (Pineapple)

Yet another American import – more kudos to Columbus – pineapples have made a comfortable home in Indonesia. They don't grow right across the country, but durable as they are, Indonesia's small and sweet pineapples can be found in markets across the archipelago. On Bali's beaches you'll see pineapple sellers offering up their succulent products. Of course they'll sell them with a mark-up, but watching how they swiftly skin and carve up the fruit is worth the extra rupiah.

Bagging pineapple at a rujak stand

Rambutan

Meaning 'hairy', it's easy to see how rambutan got its name: this fruit is bright red and covered in soft, black, hairy spines. Break one open to try a delicious white fruit that's closely related to – and tastes like – lychee.

Papaya

These green and orange fruit are as common as apples are in the west. The Dr Seuss-designed trees, with their bulbous fruit and mops of leafy hair, grow absolutely everywhere, year round. Such is the ordinariness of papaya, that we once asked if we could buy one from a woman whose papaya tree could be seen poking out of her garden plot, and she promptly cut the whole bloody thing down. Some people are put off by the smell of the flesh – especially that of a more mature papaya – saying that it has the smell of, well, vomit. Not wanting to put you off here, but papaya does in fact contain papain enzyme, which aids digestion and is found in the stomach. Papayas are another native of South America and were brought to the Philippines by the Spanish. From there they spread across South-East Asia and into the fruit-filled markets of Indonesia.

Papaya

Pisang (Banana)

There are over 40 types of banana grown in Indonesia, but only a few of these are grown commercially, most are grown at the back of peoples plots for personal use or sprout wherever conditions allow, making tempting pickings for school-bound children. Those sold at market are harvested green, so they are not overripe when it comes to purchase.

Bananas would have to be one of the most versatile fruits around, as they are made into chips, pancakes (backpacker fodder), **pisang goreng** (fried banana) and **pisang bakar** (grilled banana). The banana-palm heart is supposedly good food for pregnant women, and is cooked up in a coconut sauce. Even the leaves are widely used in cooking, as packaging and as plates.

Bananas sold to ripen at home, Lombok

Sirsak (Soursop)

The warty green skin of the sirsak covers a thirst-quenching interior with a tart, slightly lemonish taste. You can peel it off or slice it into segments. You can tell a soursop is ripe when its skin has begun to lose its fresh green colouring and has become darker and spotty. It should feel slightly squishy rather than firm when it's ready to eat.

NANGKA (Jackfruit)

First night alone in a city full of men, or so it seemed. I felt like I was at a meat market but meat was not what I was after. I hankered for the local cuisine. I jumped on a bus not knowing where I was going and told the money collector/drivers assistant/spruiker/porter that I wanted to go to a restaurant. I saw what I was after, the restaurant, shimmering in the distance with it's beautiful fluorescent lights, grimy laminex tables and classy pink plastic chairs.

I told the waiter I don't eat meat, ordered iced tea and sat down. As I sat I realised I didn't know where I was, I couldn't remember where I was staying and it was dark. I started to sweat ... even more. Then, placed in front of me was a steaming bowl of ... meat.

Jackfruit curry

Srikaya (Custard Apple)
This fruit looks more like an artichoke than its cousin, the soursop. Nevertheless the taste is similar, although its texture is a little more granular. When ripe, each segment of the custard apple can be pulled out and the flesh eaten, however with so many seeds there's more than a fair bit of work involved.

"Excuse me", I said to the waiter, trying to be polite, "I don't eat meat". He looked confused so I repeated myself, "Sorry, I don't eat meat". He looked bewildered. Had I said it wrong? I thought my Indonesian wasn't that bad. Then he cracked a big smirk.

"Ahhhh", he said loudly, "this isn't meat, this is nangka".

Nangka, I was thinking as everyone in the restaurant broke into fits of giggles, what is nangka? Nangka, I was thinking back to the shopping-at-the-market lesson. Then it clicked, nangka, jackfruit. I sat down and marvelled at this fruit that was as fleshy as a plate of meat. Admittedly, I had not eaten meat for quite some time but it sure had me fooled.

I tried to eat my way though it as everyone who came in was told the story of me, the nangka girl.

Since then, I have become a professional nangka eater. I have eaten it as **gulai nangka** (jackfruit in coconut curry) in Padang restaurants (one of my faves), as **gudeg** (jackfruit curry) in Yogyakarta and in a soupy broth with other vegetables in Lombok. When it is ripe it is most delectable – a tropical smell, bright yellow/orange, juicy with a taste that fills your mouth with pleasure.

While exploring Indonesia you'll probably come across what looks like a bag-bearing tree. This is in fact a jackfruit tree. The yellow-green fruit is bagged so as to speed up the ripening process. And once you taste the slightly rubbery, bright-yellow segments inside the fruit, you'll realise why the growers are so impatient. Due to its enormity, jackfruit is sold in markets already divided. Also, the oil contained in the fruit is ridiculously sticky, hard to wash off and will stain your clothes. Best leave the cutting up to the experts, or your enemies.

One of the most amazing things about this knobbly fruit is its size, which can range from the size of one football to three. In one village in Lombok farmers grow them along the side of the roads so the tree can see the other trees. The farmers talk to the trees and threaten them saying, "look at that one over there, it's got loads of big fruit. You've got hardly any, you're no good, I am going to chop you down". The farmer puts a chop into the tree and says, "OK I won't chop you down today but when I come back you'd better have some jackfruit for me or else!"

Kylie Nam was born in Australia and now lives in Yogyakarta

Salak (Snakeskin Fruit)

As the name suggests, the skin of the salak resembles that of a snake. And this fruit has bite, especially when still on the tree. We visited a salak plantation near Banjarnegara (Java) and found ourselves ducking from the spikes protruding from the salak plant. Once peeled the taste of the flesh is cooling and crisp and has texture almost like a peeled almond. Eating salak can leave your mouth feeling dry, but this can be avoided by peeling the thin opaque skin off of the interior flesh. At the fruit's centre is a beautifully smooth seed about the size of a date. Some friends in Banjarnegara gave us a box full of salak as a gift. Unable to refuse this generous and cumbersome offering, we feared we wouldn't get through them before they turned (salak are quite perishable). But no problem.

A salak stall in Bandung, Java

Sawo Manila (Sapodilla)

It looks like a potato, but its grainy flesh tastes like pear and is easily separated from the firm skin and large seeds. Sapodilla are only ever eaten fresh as they don't travel well and can't be sliced without falling apart.

Sawokecik

This small, plum-shaped fruit has white, grainy flesh and as many as five seeds. Its skin comes in a wide variety of reddish shades and can even be striped. The wood of the sawokecik tree is used for making the Balinese carvings so popular with tourists.

Sukun (Breadfruit)

This dark green, smooth-skinned fruit has a white starchy flesh that is essentially cooked like a potato. The similar but rough-skinned **timbul** (breadnut) has a similar taste – or lack thereof.

Spices, Sauces & Flavourings

Indonesian cooking does not suffer the flavouring complexities of other cuisines. Believe it or not, many Indonesian dishes aren't even very spicy. But that's not to say Indonesians don't like chillies, good God no, their desire for them is insatiable. It's just the real kick, in the form of sambal, is added to the meal once it's served. You'll find more complex use of spices in areas that historically had more contact with Arab and Indian traders, such as Sumatra.

Many dishes, such as **gulai** (coconut curry) and **soto** (soup), will start with a **bumbu** (paste of freshly crushed spices) that is then diluted with coconut milk or a soup stock. Made with a mortar & pestle, the bumbu can include **jinten** (cumin), **bawang putih** (garlic), **bawang merah** (shallots), **ketumbar** (coriander seeds), **kapul** (cardamom), **kunyit** (turmeric), **jahe** (ginger), **sereh** (lemongrass), **kayu manis** (cinnamon) and **cabe** (chilli). Here are some other, less-familiar bumbu candidates:

Asam (Tamarind)

In Indonesian, **asam** is the name given to tamarind as well as the taste: sour. This is the pulp surrounding the pod found on the tamarind tree. Indonesia's love affair with tamarind has stood the test of time and distance: Indonesian traders who visited the northern coast of Australia planted tamarind trees that still stand today.

Tamarind is usually sold in dried form and is mixed with water when used in curries and fish dishes. To make tamarind water, break a tamarind pod off of the block and soak it in 3 tablespoons of boiling water for 5 minutes. Break it up with your fingers and throw out any left over chunks.

Cengkeh (Cloves)

These are the buds of the clove tree, but, as the unopened buds are the most flavoursome part of the plant, the tree is rarely left to flower. Once only grown in the Maluku islands, cloves were the catalyst for an intense trade war (see the boxed text The Spice Race in the Culture chapter). The clove monopoly has long since been broken and you'll see cloves drying on the side of the road as far west as Sabang, which is as far west as you can go in Indonesia. In fact Indonesia imports cloves to keep up with demand. Nevertheless you won't taste cloves much in Indonesian cooking, but you will smell them burning everywhere as they're the prime ingredient in **kretek** (clove cigarettes).

Daun Jeruk Perut (Kaffir Lime Leaves)

These aromatic, tart-tasting leaves are used much the same way as bay leaves are: added into a stock or curry then taken out before serving.

Daun Salam (Salam Leaves)

These leaves are also called Indonesian laurel or Indonesian bay leaves, but neither name does the leaf justice. It is an aromatic ingredient added to savoury dishes.

Gula (Sugar)

The primary sweetener in Indonesian cooking is **gula merah** (palm sugar), which is made by extracting and boiling sap from the **jaka** (palm tree). Unlike granulated cane sugar, palm sugar is sold as a solid block. You can see palm sugar for sale in markets, where it is piled high like a brick wall. When it comes to using the sugar, it is chipped off or even grated into the mix. Cane sugar is also grown here and is readily available. It's what makes **teh manis** (sweet tea) so sweet.

Kemiri (Candlenut)

The fleshy interior of these nuts is used to add a nutty flavour and creamy texture to dishes. The nut is in fact an Australian native, however it has made its home in the Indonesian pantry. Although the raw kernel looks good enough to eat, don't. Candlenut is toxic in its raw form.

Laos & Kencur (Galangal)

This rhizome has the same shape and function as ginger, but is bright orange and has a more bitter taste. Also popular is **kencur** (sometimes known as lesser galangal), which has more kick than cousin laos.

Minyak (Oil)

The most widely used oil is **minyak kelapa** (coconut oil) as it burns at a high temperature, making it perfect for deep frying. Other types of oil include **minyak kacang** (peanut oil) and **minyak jagung** (corn oil). But coconut oil, also called **minyak sawit**, is the number one oil used for all types of cooking.

Pala (Nutmeg)

It's ironic that the ingredient all of Europe scrambled for (see the boxed text The Spice Race in the Culture chapter) isn't used extensively in the Indonesian kitchen. The fruit of the nutmeg is made into a preserve called **manisan pala** and both the seed and the mace (nutmeg's shell) are dried and sold whole or as a powder.

Daun Pandan (Screwpine)

This plant, named for its twisted stems, is used in traditional cooking from India to Australia. Screwpine is used in sweet dishes for its delicate fragrance and green colouring.

Terasi, Belacan (Shrimp Paste)

You'll know when you come across shrimp paste because it has an aroma that is far from subtle. This fishy, pungent paste is made from small shrimp that are rinsed in sea water, dried, salted, dried again then pummelled to a paste. It is left to dry for about two weeks before being shaped into blocks. As you would expect, the paste adds a fishy, salty flavour to dishes.

STAPLES

Mataram, Lombok

Chilli

Known as **cabe** when fresh off the bush and **sambal** when mashed into a paste, chillies are what make Indonesians tick. They'll chew them raw between bites of **tahu goreng** (fried tofu), they'll crush them into sambal and add that to almost anything. Perhaps not ice cream, but they would think about it.

Maybe it's the exotic, high-seas history that makes Indonesia's romance with the chilli so heated. Before the 16th century, Indonesia's cuisine was far from fiery. But with the discovery of the New World and the produce therein, it wasn't long before such foods as pineapple, papaya and chillies were being hauled off the boat at the port of Banten. The spicy fruit soon found adoration across the archipelago, most notably the small, red **cabe rawit** (bird's eye chilli), which is reputed to be the nation's hottest. Concerning spice, the general rule of thumb is the smaller the hotter. Mind you we picked some unidentified, more bulbous chillies while visiting Dieng Plateau (Java) and they blew our heads off. If you ever fall victim to a deceptively hot chilli, do not try to extinguish the fire with water as it'll only make it worse. Instead, eat some plain rice, which will smother the flames. In the Indonesian film *Daun di Atas Bantal* (Leaf on the Pillow), chillies are used as a weapon, spat into the face of an abusive father.

Bird's eye chillies

Sambal

The Mexicans have salsa, the Indians chutney, but here the essential condiment is **sambal** (chilli sauce or relish). A table set without at least a bottle of sambal, at most a freshly crushed version, isn't set properly. We once made mashed potatoes, 'a taste of the west' for friends in Cimahi (Java). Our friend took one mouthful, hesitated, quietly apologised and went for the sambal. Sambals come in many varieties but the base for any sambal will be chillies, garlic, shallots and salt. Here are some of the more popular varieties, but every sambal is as different as every cook.

Sambal Badjak

Chilli sauce made with shallots, sugar, tamarind, galangal and shrimp paste. Fried to a caramel consistency. Mild by Indonesian standards (see the recipe).

Sambal Badjak (Dark Chilli Sauce)

Ingredients

10	red chillies
2 tsp	shrimp paste
5	shallots
5	cloves garlic
1 Tbs	palm sugar
3 Tbs	coconut oil
2	kaffir lime leaves
1	salam leaf (optional)
5 Tbs	tamarind water
1 tsp	ground galangal
	salt to taste

Combine the chillies, shrimp paste, shallots, garlic, salt and sugar in a mortar & pestle and grind them to a coarse paste. Heat the oil in a wok and fry the paste along with the lime and salam leaves for 3 minutes. Add the tamarind water and reduce back to a paste. Leave to cool. Sambal will keep, covered in the fridge, for about a week.

Use as a condiment to curries and stirfries

Sambal Jeruk

Chilli sauce made with lime juice, lime peel, salt & vinegar.

Sambal Terasi

Chilli sauce made with lime and roasted shrimp paste.

Ulek
Chilli sauce made with vinegar and lots of chillies. Very spicy.

Pecel
This sauce is similar to sambal but the spice is lessened with the addition of peanuts and tomato. Pecel is coupled with a freshly fried **lele** (catfish) to make the popular meal, **pecel lele**.

A sambal assortment

Saus Kacang (Peanut Sauce)
This is one of Indonesia's most famous culinary exports. The reason being that peanut sauce is so versatile: it can be used as a condiment, as a dip, or as the flavour for a main meal. It's most famous for its appearance in gado-gado. (See the Saus Kacang recipe in the Banquet chapter.)

Kecap (Soy Sauce)
Every restaurant in the country provides their diners with a bottle of soy sauce (made from soybeans fermented in brine). Most provide two: **kecap asin** (salty soy sauce), which is the same as soy sauce found throughout the world; and **kecap manis** (sweet soy sauce), which is thicker and sweeter. Beware that some varieties of kecap manis are too treacly and overpowering, but the most popular brand, ABC, produces a kecap manis that provides perfect sweetness.

HOT LOVE

Whilst I was planning a trip to Indonesia, a Malaysian friend warned me not to become too addicted to chilli. Easier said than done as here, the sambal rocks. It's everywhere, each batch is different and nearly each seems 'the best one yet'. In Flores, Romi and his mates from the Maumere moto shop whipped me one up with fresh mango and fried papaya. In Jakarta, Tinni gave me a sambal lesson in the sparkling kitchen where she reigned as maid. In Bajawa (Flores) Ishye gave an equally good demonstration between kids and kittens on her bamboo fire at home in the hills.

Sometimes fried and sometimes fresh, the main ingredient of course is chilli. Then there's onion, garlic, ginger, galangal-like roots I don't know the name of, and other bits and bobs depending on the cook. Sambal goes with most things; chicken, goat, vegies, soup, but nowhere is it more perfect than with **ikan bakar** (grilled fish) or **pecel lele** (deep-fried catfish). All that is needed is the fish, rice, a few fresh green things and the sambal. The sambal however, is imperative. I strongly suggest protesting loudly should it happen that the sambal is not offered to you out of respect for your delicate western taste buds.

The super-best sambals though, *are* dangerous, as one becomes seduced into eating nearly equal proportions of sambal to rice. Particularly tempting are the fresh-looking ones with sumptuous chunks of tomato and shallots, seeming no more nasty than a good pasta sauce. People gasped in horror at the ladlefuls I took in the stalls in Yogyakarta (I did think it was a vegetable dish). After one breakfast session with such a sambal I had to just sit and drink tea for a good five minutes. Forget vegemite for a pick-me-up.

Now I miss the stuff and should have paid more attention to Tinni. It seems my only alternative remains to return ASAP and have her cook it for me directly.

Alexandra Jordan had marmalade on butter on bread for breakfast, important preparation for a dance in her Melbourne kitchen

Jajanan (Snacks)

Both sweet and savoury snacks fall within the realm of **jajanan** (snacks). The best are made to order, right before your eyes, by kaki-lima. Here are some of our favourites:

Savoury Snacks

The majority of Indonesia's savoury snacks are of the deep-fried variety. Look for those that are hot from the wok.

- **bakwan**: deep-fried vegetables such as cabbage and carrot (also called **bala-bala**)
- **lemper**: sticky rice with a filling of spiced and shredded meat steamed in a banana leaf
- **perkedel**: fritters; often made with corn or potato
- **tahu isi**: tofu stuffed with beansprouts and other vegetables, covered in batter and deep fried
- **tahu Sumedang**: plain, deep-fried tofu from Sumedang (see West Java in the Regional Variations chapter).
- **tempe goreng**: deep-fried slices of tempe
- **ubi goreng**: deep-fried sweet potato

Emping, Kerupuk, Intip (Crackers)

Emping is Indonesia's favourite snack. Resembling lumpy chips, emping are made from the seeds of melinjo tree fruit, which turn an iridescent red when ripe. To make emping, the seeds are roasted, opened and the kernels are flattened. These are then dried and fried in oil. Packets of emping, either plain or coated with a sweet chilli sauce, can be bought at any supermarket or grocery. They have a slightly bitter taste, making them a perfect match for a chilled glass of beer ... and a breezy verandah. Oh so colonial.

Basically anything that can be sliced thin enough and fried in oil will be made into chips: bananas, fish skin, cassava. But our favourites include the aforementioned emping and the sweet purple ones made out of cassava.

Larger deep-fried treats such as **kerupuk** (prawn crackers) and **intip** (rice crackers) are usually served as an accompaniment to gado-gado or nasi goreng. In many restaurants you'll see glass-fronted containers filled with these squiggly shaped crackers. On the containers will be written profound words such as **subur** (fertile) and **fajar** (wisdom). Help yourself, but be sure to tell the proprietor how many crackers you had when it comes to settling the bill. They're cheap, but they're not free. Many people make their own intip with leftover rice: you'll see stacks of the crackers drying on roofs and in front of houses.

Packing the crackers in Pasar Demangan, Yogyakarta, Java

STAPLES

Sweet Snacks & Desserts

The concept of following a meal with something sweet is a strange one for Indonesians. Why wait until the end to get your sugar hit? Try some of these sweeties anytime:

- **kelepon**: a rice-flour dumpling coloured green with pandan, rolled in shredded coconut with a treacly palm sugar centre.

- **onde-onde**: a sesame ball with mung bean filling. These are usually about 5cm in diameter but the best ones we had were half the size and cooked in front of us.

- **pisang goreng**: a banana coated in batter and fried

- **putu**: a cylinder of steamed coconut with a palm sugar centre. The little cylinders are placed over a hole in the lid of a steamer. We have even seen the steamer strapped to the back of a bicycle, and one of the holes doubled as a whistle to attract customers.

- **serabi**: pancakes made with rice flour, coconut milk and pandan leaves and topped with chocolate, banana or jackfruit. A Solo speciality (see Central Java in the Regional Variations chapter).

To quell that sweet craving, many restaurants in tourist areas offer the backpacker favourite, banana pancake, whether it be a simple affair, or spruced up with chocolate sauce. If you're after something a little more authentic, look no further than the **martabak**. Thick, hot, sweet and served with toppings such as banana, chocolate sauce, condensed milk and nuts; the martabak is a pancake on steroids. It is an Indian import, similar to yet far chunkier than roti, and variations of it can be found from Nusa Tenggara to New Delhi and beyond. In Indonesia you'll find martabak sold at any night market. Look for the stall with six burners on the go and a salivating queue. Martabak sellers also make a savoury version more akin to an omelette (see Eggs earlier in this chapter).

Sweet snack stall in Gianyar, Bali

Cutting up the fruit for a serve of rujak, Jakarta, Java

Naturally speaking, fruit is the best answer to the dessert conundrum. Any market will have a wide variety of fruit to choose from, all you need is a knife and somewhere to wash your sticky hands. You'll also see fruit sold at stalls on the streets or, even better, growing on trees. Most people will be happy to sell you a papaya directly from their garden. Fruit lovers should look out for **rujak** (fruit served with a sour, spicy sauce made with peanuts, sugar and chilli) sold by kaki-lima. The fruit is kept fresh on a bed of ice and chopped up to order. Rujak sellers are so adept with a machete and can peel a pineapple in seconds. They can even segment the fruit while it's in the carry bag, thwacking it with the blunt end of the knife, cutting the fruit but leaving the bag intact. The fruit in rujak is usually very young and crunchy, making it an experience in both taste and texture.

Permen & Biskit

Every food store and supermarket will sell **permen** (lollies, candy) and **biskit** (biscuits). Most of these are pretty run of the mill, however you will find some strange-flavoured sweeties, such as tamarind, ginger or durian jubes. Sometimes the small sweets are used to make up change in a transaction, so don't be surprised if you're given a mango sweetie instead of Rp25.

Bread & Pastries

The Dutch left Indonesia with the art of baking, however not to the same quality or capacity as the French left in their realm of Indochina. Bakeries can be found in all larger towns, serving up sweet bready treats. Even a loaf of bread will be pumped with sugar. Indonesians have, of course, added a tropical twist to a lot of pastries, adding coconut and peanuts to cakes, slices and buns. A popular late-night snack is **roti bakar** (white bread with a filling of jam, chocolate and/or cheese fried on a hot plate).

drinks
of indonesia

As you would expect of a tropical country, Indonesia has a surfeit of choice in thirst quenchers. Here, they make delicious use of fruit, drink tea to form social bonds and grow some of the finest coffee on the globe. After something harder? As well as beer, Indonesia produces unique alcoholic drinks. Glass of palm sap wine, anyone?

Non-Alcoholic Drinks
Teh (Tea)

Blanketing huggable hills, folding into clouds and camouflaging meticulous pickers, Indonesia's tea vies with rice for the title of world's most beautiful crop. It's as if the sensation of a good cuppa has been imbued by the landscape, high (at least 900m) above the cacophony and heat of the towns. Indonesia produces some green tea, but the vast majority is black. More than three quarters of the total harvest is marked for export, but even so, there's enough left over to satisfy the craving for the national beverage of choice.

The first tea plants arrived in Indonesia in the 1600s but weren't used for drinking; the Dutch just thought they looked nice. It wasn't until 1728 that tea was grown as a cash crop, and then another century before it became a real money maker for the Dutch, who forced Indonesians to replace subsistence crops with tea, under their Compulsory Planting Policy. Tea estates are now run by private companies and the Indonesian government, and some of the original Dutch tea plants are still being used.

A beautiful landscape, a cool breeze and a conical hat do not erase the fact that tea picking is a laborious job. On the Puncak Pass in Java you'll see lines of labourers painstakingly working their way across the slopes, filling the bamboo baskets on their backs with around 50kg of the loose leaf in a 10-hour day. Once collected, the leaves are sorted according to quality and left to 'wither' to around a third of their original moisture content. They are then 'curled' in a heated room of 100% humidity. Curling releases the remaining moisture in the leaves and the tea begins to ferment. At this stage, the flavour, aroma and caffeine content are developed; so too the variety of tea. Orange pekoe, Earl Grey, Russian caravan – all come from the same plant species: *Camellia sinensis* – tea. Once the desired flavour, colour and aroma have been achieved, the fermentation process is stopped and the tea dried, ready for the pot.

So what do you get when you order tea in Indonesia? The most popular brew is black, with varying amounts of sugar. In West Java they like no more than a teaspoonful, in Central Java they don't like too much tea with their sugar. If you want tea without sugar, ask for **teh pahit** (bitter tea) and if you want milk, buy yourself a cow. At many eateries, weak, sugarless tea is served free of charge. For a different take on tea, you'll find sweet **es teh** (iced tea) available at any store or restaurant.

The standard cuppa comes in a glass, often with a lid to keep it warm. Indonesians like to take their time over a cup of tea, and the lid helps them to do just that. On an eight-hour train ride, we noted a traveller who took the whole trip to get through his cup of tea: occasionally lifting the lid, slurping a droplet, then falling back into his chair.

Tea plantation in Lembang, Java

Kopi (Coffee)

Indonesia produces a lot of coffee; in fact it's the third largest producer in the world. There was a time, after the Dutch set up their coffee estates in the 18th century, that Indonesia was number one, but disease all but wiped out the arabica plantations. Today the inferior robusta bean constitutes 90% of the nation's coffee crop. Nevertheless, the arabica beans still produced here are percolatable heaven, prized by caffeine freaks around the world.

Indonesian coffee beans often have a mottled appearance and may be roasted for long periods to hide such imperfections. A shorter roast is a better roast; the appearance of the beans may not be as uniform, but the flavour is better.

You can visit many of Indonesia's coffee plantations and processing plants, where the aroma of the roasting beans envelops you. Ask to taste the ground beans. Just a pinch on the middle of the tongue and the flavour rings through your body and gets your heart pumping as only caffeine can. Whether you want your beans whole or ground, this is your chance to buy them direct from the source. You can visit plantations in the vicinity of Jember and Kalibaru (East Java), Munduk (Bali), Bukittinggi (West Sumatra) and Rantepao (Central Sulawesi).

Katut Darna enjoying Balinese coffee

KINKY COFFEE KITTEN – HELLO KITTY!

The process required to turn a ripe coffee cherry into a roastable bean can be long and laborious: there's picking to be done as well as sorting, washing and ageing. But in Indonesia Mother Nature has stepped up to the challenge with an all-in-one coffee processor: the civet, known in Indonesian as musang, in Javanese as luwak and in Balinese as lubak. She's a wild feline with large ears, agile feet and a weakness for ripe coffee cherries, which she chews off the bush. After her meal, the undigested beans are expelled, ready for the roaster. Rampant development has seen the decline of the cat's habitat. But many locals still remember collecting civet droppings and turning them into a full-bodied brew.

So how to drink coffee, Indonesian style? Black, sweet and gritty is the nation's preferred pick-me-up. Known as **kopi tubruk**, ground coffee goes straight into the glass with sugar and boiling water. It's chewy, but that's what you get.

There are other coffee options to be had. **Kopi jahe** is coffee brewed with ginger. Sumatrans like to start the day with **kopi telur**, coffee mixed with sugar and an egg yolk. In Tana Toraja (Sulawesi), things can get really strange; coffee is sometimes roasted with garlic. Coffee-flavoured lollies or sweets are popular, especially the Kopiko brand.

Java

The Dutch first brought arabica coffee to Java in the early 18th century and they thrived until rust disease hit in the 1860s. The robusta variety was brought in around 40 years later. These days, with the international demand for it, arabica has been reintroduced and is grown on original highland estates such as Balwan and Jampit. Many of these estates are government owned and the coffee they produce is called Government Estate Java. Non-government coffee is called Private Estate Java. Most coffee produced here is wet-processed, which results in a lighter body and higher acidity than coffee from Sumatra or Sulawesi. If you prefer a sweeter, less acidic brew, look for Old Java, which is aged for up to three years.

Bali

Growing high in the hills of Bali are both robusta and arabica beans. The town of Munduk ('town' being one stretch of shops) is a great base from which to explore coffee plantations, and the town itself produces **kopi bubuk Bali asli**, which has a warm aroma and taste, perfect for Munduk's almost chilly clime (locals think it cold; they wear leather jackets).

DRINKS

TOKO AROMA

Mr Widyapratama starts his day with seven cups of coffee.

"Small cups for tasting" he explains, his manner suggesting otherwise, as he speaks at a rapid pace with lucid enthusiasm about his family business, Toko Aroma ('Aroma Shop'). Located in an art deco building on Jl Banceuy 51 in the heart of Bandung, almost everything about the shop remains as it was when Mr Widyapratama's father started the business in the 1930s. The weights and coffee canisters are the originals; even the cash register is configured in Dutch guilders.

"I buy coffee from all over Indonesia. From Aceh, Sulawesi, Timor", Mr Widyapratama leads us through the roasting room, where his father's bicycles – once used for deliveries – hang on the walls. Through another door is a big room, stacked to the rafters with sacks of coffee.

"Arabica beans, aged for eight years", he says, disappearing into the darkness between piles of coffee. Next thing he's bracing himself between sacks and climbing to the roof. He must be at least 60, but he can still carry a sack of beans down from the top of the pile.

Mr Widyapratama, owner of Toko Aroma, Bandung, Java

An antique scale weight still in use at Toko Aroma

"You have to be strong to work here."
No kidding.

The whole place smells like freshly ground beans – it is, after all, called Aroma. Perhaps the caffeine in the atmosphere makes Mr Widyapratama so hyper. He shows us the old coffee posters and the ancient safe, the code for which only his wife knows.

"She controls the money. I don't know the code so I can't run away", he says with a cheeky smile. About the only modern thing in the shop is the large photo of his three daughters, the youngest of whom wants to take over the business. Mr Widyapratama sells direct to restaurants and individuals; nothing too complicated.

"I could make more money, but it would mean I have no time to enjoy life."

We buy 4kg, thank Mr Widyapratama and leave the shop feeling like we've just imbibed a fresh cuppa. The alluring smell of coffee from our bags fills the car.

DRINKS

Dutch Toko Aroma poster

Sulawesi

Tana Toraja in Central Sulawesi produces some of Indonesia's best coffee beans. The beans here are usually dry-processed, and render an earthy brew with a sweetness akin to maple syrup. Coffee from the Torajan town of Rantepao is left to swell in the cherry before processing and may be aged for over three years, further accentuating the flavour. Small-scale production and a hungry Japanese market give Sulawesi's arabica beans a high, yet well-deserved price tag.

Sumatra

In Sumatra, the word to remember is Mandailing. This is not the name of a region, but of an ethnic group living in the coffee-producing regions of central-north Sumatra. Most coffee (and the best quality) produced here comes under the Mandailing umbrella; the difference lies in the quality of bean and the way it's processed. For the best brew, look for dry-processed Mandailing, which has more character than its wet-processed counterpart. The dry-processed beans may not look as uniform in shape or colour, but their herbal aroma, hefty body and deep flavour make them far superior.

Harvested coffee, Bukittinggi, Sumatra

DRINKS

Bandrek (Ginger Tea)

In tropical Indonesia, you wouldn't think there would be a need for a warming ginger beverage. But high-altitude areas as Dieng Plateau, Brastagi and Lembang are surprisingly chilly and a steaming glass of **bandrek** (ginger tea; see the recipe) provides respite from the cold. On the hill trails around Bandung stand bamboo shelters where a weekend walker can rest, take in the views and down a soothing glass of bandrek. Here, bandrek is brewed by an **ibu** (mother or older woman), who spikes the drink with pepper.

Air Minum (Water)

You'll be needing to drink a fair amount of this while under the tropical sun. Although tap water is a no-no (nasty amoebas abound), there are plenty of other options at hand. At any store or stall you'll see bottles or sealed cups of **air minum** (drinking water) for sale. Keep a small bottle in your bag.

When offered a glass of water, rest assured it's OK; Indonesians always boil their water before drinking. Other names for drinkable water you'll hear include **air rebus** ('boiled water'), **air botol** ('bottled water'), **air putih** ('white water') and **aqua** (a popular brand of bottled water).

Bandrek (Ginger Tea)
This brew has added pepper for extra bite.

Ingredients

6 cups	water
3cm	piece ginger, sliced
5cm	cinnamon stick
2 tsp	palm sugar
10cm	piece coconut flesh (or 1 tablespoon shredded coconut per glass)
1 tsp	black peppercorns

Combine all the ingredients except the sugar and coconut flesh in a saucepan and boil for 3 minutes. Add the sugar and stir for 1 minute. Place the coconut in glasses and strain the liquid over.
Makes 4 glasses

DRINKS

Minuman Es (Ice Drinks)

Indonesia's ice drinks are not only refreshing, they are visually stimulating, kaleidoscopic even, with red syrups, orange fruit, green jellies and more, all in the one glass. Even the contraption used to make the ice shavings is worth checking out: a vice that rotates a block of ice on a blade, it looks more like a drill press than a drinks machine.

Es Campur (Mixed Ice)

Served in a bowl, es campur is more dessert than drink, and a great pick-me-up should lethargy strike while you're out exploring. Ice shavings are combined in a bowl with fruit, rice-flour jelly pieces and sugar syrup. With a few mouthfuls of es campur, the heat and chaos of the streets slip from your mind. If a few fruits are included the drink is called **es buah**; if one fruit is the feature, the drink is named after that fruit, as in **es nangka** (jackfruit ice drink) and **es durian** (durian ice drink).

Es Cendol or Es Dawet

This dessert-drink contains droplets of green rice-flour jelly, coconut milk and palm-sugar syrup.

Es Cincau

This dessert-drink contains **cincau** (dark green jelly made from the cincau plant), sugar syrup and ice.

Ingredients for Es Cendol

Es Jeruk

Jeruk means orange, but don't expect a freshly squeezed refreshment. Indonesia's oranges are tart and thus a fair load of sugar is added to the glass of ice and squeezed juice.

Es Ketimun

Shredded cucumber with sugar syrup and ice. Yes indeedy, shredded cucumber. Albeit strange, this concoction is refreshing and tastes a little like honeydew melon.

Stopping for a drink in in Gianyar, Bali

DRINKS

Jus

Indonesia's juice drinks are real taste treats. Just take one or two varieties of tropical fruit, add crushed ice and pass through a blender. You can produce mind-blowing combinations of banana, mango, pineapple, jackfruit, orange and papaya or whatever is available. Avocado juice would have to go down as Indonesia's most eccentric edible invention. Take an avocado, blend with ice and condensed milk or chocolate syrup and you have yourself a **jus apokat** (avocado juice; see the recipe). Indonesians don't consider this strange; for them the avocado is just another sweet fruit.

Stroop (Cordial)

A lot of Indonesia's cordial is produced in the fertile region of Brastagi, where it's made from **markisa** (passionfruit).

DIVINE COCONUT

Eastern Nusa Tenggara is notoriously hot and dry. Despite this fact I one day spontaneously decided, with serious disregard for my personal water supply, to walk to the top of a local smokin' volcano.

Friendly seaside villagers gave me plenty of directions on getting to the top of Ile Api, which in my mind simplified to 'keep heading *up*'. So wander *up* the trails I did, heading in the general direction of *up*. Upon bumping into some gardeners on their way *down* with a load of bananas, I hung out for a bit and chatted. I was feeling pretty comfortable with the whole situation: tropical setting, coconut trees, chatty gardeners, hot sun.

Predictable it may be, but at the time I was somewhat shocked to realise that, after heading *up* long enough to have finished all my bottled water, the hillside was now devoid of everything except for me and forests of silent coconut trees. Apparently nobody was so silly as to work in the hillside gardens in the afternoon and had all gone down to the village below to avoid the midday sun.

Still heading *up* and getting close to the top of the canopy, a second realisation dawned: I was entering a pretty desperate state of affairs on the dehydration side of things. Now, local gardeners don't need to lug bottles of water about because the liquid from young coconuts is so super-dooper. But I couldn't even *steal* a coconut because, unlike everyone else, I wasn't carrying a big fat machete.

'Lost' wouldn't be a totally accurate description of my situation but, upon deciding that I needed to head *down* to avoid desiccation, the path that I thought I was previously following clearly wasn't there at all. So, in somewhat of a state, I started stumbling *down*, headed in the general direction of *down*.

Air Kelapa Muda (Coconut Water)

As long as you can open the nut, you can slurp coconut water straight from a still-green coconut. If you don't happen to have a machete handy, buy your coconut from a vendor. Just look for a fella wielding a machete and surrounded by green coconuts – he's your man. Some vendors doctor the coconut water with cordial and ice.

Susu (Milk)

Cow's milk is not a common drink in the tropics, although you can buy it in supermarkets. Sometimes in the evenings you'll see stalls selling **susu panas** (hot, sweet milk), catering to the low local chill threshold. More popular here is sweet **susu kedelai** (soy milk), which comes packaged in bottles, cartons and cans.

> To reiterate, I was in somewhat of a state, so when I stumbled upon a couple of huts – obviously quite separate to the seaside village at the foot of the volcano – I was very surprised to say the least.
>
> In an instant I was embarrassed by my trespass but, being so very very very thirsty, I managed to overcome any feelings of self-consciousness to call out to the ibu and the couple of young lads quietly working on some afternoon chores in the shade of the huts. They didn't seem too impressed by my clumsy entrance but at my apologetic requests for fluids the lads clicked into action and shot up a coconut tree. As I sat feeling like an inconsiderate whitey klutz, an old bloke came out talking nicely to me in what might have been the local dialect, senile ramblings, or a mix of the two; he apparently didn't understand my Indonesian (the young lads could). None of the others even blinked as he wandered off, still talking. We apparently had zero verbal understanding, so I was humbled by his sweet and totally generous gift to me of bananas – so sweet!
>
> The lads came back with three young coconuts.
>
> Thwack. Thwack.
>
> Skilled and efficient thwacks with long-handled machetes. I gulped down the liquid until my stomach didn't want to hold any more. When you're this thirsty you can't drink enough to feel satisfied. The lads offered to trim some remaining nuts to give me some handy travel pack coconuts – very cool, but you still need a knife to open them, so I filled my aqua bottle instead.
>
> They reluctantly asked for a paltry payment. I gave them double and headed off in the general direction of *down* with shaky legs and a bellyful of air kelapa muda sloshing *up* and *down* inside.
>
> *Andrew Taylor likes Melbourne's swamps and vegan fried food*

DRINKS

Alcoholic Drinks

Anti-alcohol Islam being the predominant religion, alcohol is not integral to a good time in Indonesia, and many festivities take place without a drop of booze in sight. Nevertheless, a range of alcoholic drinks is available, some of which have been brewed on the islands since well before the arrival of Islam.

Tuak (Palm Sap Wine)

The sap of the coconut palm is not only the base for palm sugar, it's also made into a sweet wine called tuak. Clusters of fruit produced by the palm are cut off and the resulting sap collected. Leave this sap for a day and it begins to ferment, leave it longer and the alcohol content rises (but remains relatively low) and sweetness subsides. Leave the sap for three days and you have yourself a lovely glass of vinegar. This is the reason why you can only sample real tuak at its source. It is white or pinkish in colour and almost slimy in texture.

Arak (Spirits Distilled from Palm Sap or Rice)

There is a way to stop tuak turning into vinegar, and that is to boil and then distil it. Whether or not the resulting spirit, **arak**, is drinkable is another question; it tastes deplorable and gives you one ugly hangover. Mix arak with lemonade or orange juice and you have yourself an **arak attack**.

Arak is also made from rice, as in **brem**, the Balinese speciality. In fact, much of Indonesia's spirit production happens on Bali, where the people are predominantly Hindu.

Brem

A type of arak distilled from rice, brem is a Balinese speciality made by cooking, steaming, cooling and adding a yeast culture to a mixture of white and black rice. After a few days the mash is pressed and the liquid left for another two weeks. The resulting sweet, vaguely sherry-like alcohol is taken straight (chilled) or mixed with lime juice. Brem is also left at temples as an offering; the gods are partial to a stiff drink too, it seems.

Anggur (Wine)

When it comes to inventing new tastes, you couldn't accuse the Indonesians of lacking a sense of adventure. They'll give anything a try; if it doesn't work, they can always bottle it, label it 'a taste of the tropics' and sell it to tourists. Take Lombok's banana wine ... actually don't. Drinking this stuff is like trying to swallow putrid cough medicine. More success has been had in northern Bali with a rosé and a sparkling wine made from Isabella grapes.

Service with a smile in Jimbaran, Bali

DRINKS

DINING UNDER THE INFLUENCE

Closing time comes too quickly at the bar. As doors are banged shut and rickshaws are snapped up, someone shouts "masih sore!" (it's still afternoon!): yes the night *is* young and we restless souls head into it in search of sustenance.

Where at home a kebab would satisfy, here we have three choices. The first and best is a feast at a **lesehan**, a streetside eatery with no more than grass mats for us nocturnal diners to spread out on. The night market lesehan are great places for a late feed, and at one on Malioboro in Yogyakarta we share stories and nasi goreng with street kids and post-gig musicians.

If there's no lesehan around we head for a **warung kopi**, a stall recognised by its coal burner and dim kerosene lamp. The fare is simple: ginger tea, coffee, fried tempe. We speak in soft tones, as this is the domain of tired taxi drivers and local insomniacs. But new faces – even haggard ones and white ones – are always welcome.

The last choice is a tiny **kios** (kiosk), Indonesia's answer to a corner store. Its windows are crowded with cigarettes, sweets and – to our detriment – bottles of Anker and Bintang Beer, the local brews. Kios owners do a roaring trade; they know we'll be back – they also sell headache tablets.

Bir (Beer)

As with coffee, bread and pastries, we can thank the Dutch for beer in Indonesia. Two domestic breweries, Bintang and Anker, produce clean, slightly sweet lagers that when ice cold are refreshing accompaniments to local cuisine. In recent years, Guinness has been pushing into the market, successfully it seems – Anker now brews stout. Tourist restaurants always have beer; restaurants geared for locals generally do not. Beer is, however, available at many supermarkets and general stores, if not always cold. If you're fridgeless you may have to settle for a warm brew or – sacrilege! – adding some ice bought at a general store. (See also Where to Drink in the Where to Eat & Drink chapter).

home cooking
& traditions

Indonesian kitchens may well be entering the modern age, but some traditional implements and processes aren't so easily discarded. You could be in high-rise Jakarta and still see someone scraping coconut by hand; likewise an electric blender can turn up in the remotest of village kitchens. Convenience is a preference, but flavour comes first.

Using a cobek & ulek-ulek, Bandung, Java

In Indonesian homes the kitchen remains a woman's realm. You'll rarely see a fella pottering around the kitchen at home unless he's making a celebratory meal that will earn him public praise. Even then there's usually a woman standing by, making sure the fried chicken doesn't turn into burnt bird. It's a classic story; she would have learned how to cook at her mother's side, her mother at her grandmother's and so on – from working out exactly how many chillies to use, to folding a banana leaf perfectly for steaming. These days, recipe books abound (both in Indonesia and beyond), but home cooks here use their experience and practical judgement; rarely do they follow recipes to the word. Anyway, historical culinary texts tell more of opulent banquets and 'sweetmeats' than they do of everyday meals.

Many middle-class households and all wealthy ones employ a **pembantu** (live-in housekeeper; servant) to take care of household duties, including cooking. Unlike traditional European butlers and maids, the pembantu is usually an intrinsic part of the family structure.

The 'kitchen' could refer to a benchtop-lined room, as it does in the West, or a smoke-stained lean-to, or the front porch – even the coffee table in front of the television (especially if a sinetron (soapie) is screening). But the implements used are similar no matter where the kitchen is. The usual suspects are cleavers, chopping boards, spatulas and wire ladles for deep-frying. Many are still handmade, and you can see coconut-shell ladles for sale at almost every market. As you'd expect, a **kuali** (wok; also called **wajan**) is an essential item. One thing you won't always find is a fridge; food is traditionally prepared to keep at room temperature for a day, with the aid of fly covers.

A lot of Indonesian kitchens still feature a traditional terracotta fireplace. These are in the shape of a tapered, squat cylinder (wider at the base and only 50cm high) with an open front so fuel can easily be added. The type of fuel that's used depends on where you are: near the coast it may be coconut husks, in the hills it could be coffee wood. In any case the cook will have to squat on her haunches for long periods (as only Indonesians can) to fan the flame and stir the wok. If the family can afford one, a **kompor** (stove burner) is used, but an oven is a rarity since most roasting is done on open coals.

The real proof of the authentic Indonesian kitchen is its **cobek & ulek-ulek**. We could call this a mortar & pestle, however it's quite different than most. The ulek-ulek is shaped like an upended fat cigar and is used to push ingredients along the cobek, a shallow circular grinding stone. Both are made from heavy volcanic rock. The cobek & ulek-ulek is used to make **bumbu** (spice mixture, paste or sauce) and **sambal** (chilli sauce or relish); it grinds the ingredients well, but leaves some texture, so the finished product is more chunky than smooth. To see how a cobek & ulek-ulek should be used, look over the shoulder of a vendor who's preparing **rujak** (fruit served with a sour, spicy sauce of peanuts, sugar and chilli – they are the fastest grinders in the archipelago.

Sister and brother in Bali

HOME COOKING

SOLO CYCLE TOUR

For years now the people of Solo have been offering visitors to their city a chance to learn about village life first hand. This is done on a bicycle tour that takes you from Solo's city limits, across quieter (but bumpier) back roads, through rice fields and into the daily goings-on of the village of Bekonang. Many people here have set up cottage industries, some do it to supplement their income, for others it's a full-time job and ventures have expanded to employ family members and neighbours. The tour also takes you to batik and gamelan workshops but we, being gastromeo-pathic, insisted we spend more time at the food-focused places.

Yoyo, a sociology graduate, was our guide. Yoyo also ran a private English school in the centre of town and it was from there we cycled out, over the Solo River and into the verdant village terrain. First stop was a dark, hot bakery, where about 20 people were at work. Some were kneading the mountain of dough, some were shaping it into swirls and pretzels; some were tending the cavernous ovens, some were sealing plastic packages of rolls by melting the edges of the packages with a candle; some were taking breakfast. I asked the 13-year-old lad who had stopped for a smoke whether he liked the rolls. He said he preferred rice.

Next, we stopped at a cottage and watched as a woman, her husband and her 689-year-old mother made tempe to sell at the local market. First, they boiled the soybeans to separate the skins, then they placed the beans in banana-leaf packages along with **ragi** (yeast) powder. Over a few days the ragi forms a mould and bonds the beans into a slab of tempe, ready to be fried into any number of delicious dishes.

From there it was back on the bikes, down lanes and past schools and garden plots to a backyard **ciu** (sugarcane spirit distillery). The owner had just started cooking lunch when we arrived, but she was happy to show us the process. There were about 30 plastic drums around the shelter, all of them filled with sugarcane juice and a starter. The fermenting liquid was bubbling away. It takes about a week before the bubbles subside and the liquid is boiled through the contraption that looks like it was used in the Spanish Inquisition. The end product was a clear spirit with a taste not unlike boiled pyjamas. Later, Yoyo said "the people who drink this are usually the ones who like to eat dog".

Next on the Solo cycle tour was a **karak** (rice cracker) factory in Desa Bulak. Inside the massive bamboo shelter the air was hot and heavy. There were large pots of rice on the boil and about six fellas draining the well-cooked rice, mixing it with salt and yeast, then pressing the glug into long, rectangular moulds. In the shade next to the cooking room sat six women, chatting as they sliced the moulded glug into wafers. Two younger girls were placing the wafers on bamboo racks then taking them outside to add them to the field of drying karak. Once dry, the karak are

Transport to the rice harvest, Bali

Folding banana leaves for food packaging at Gudeg Yu Djum, Yogyakarta, Java

deep fried, bagged and sent to market or restaurants. While we were there, a fella rode up on a bike with panniers the size of industrial garbage skips. These he filled to overflowing with karak, then set off on his karak crusade. One of the women gave me a slab of just-cooked karak glug. It tasted like salty rice pudding (which is what it is).

The final leg of the tour took us past a pig sty. I was surprised to see pigs in a Muslim area, and Yoyo explained that they are bred for the Chinese community, and aren't killed here but at a slaughterhouse in town. Beyond the sty lay a soggy, dark factory. Inside the soggy factory, dressed in soggy clothes, were two men and women busy producing slabs of tofu while Indonesian pop blared from a radio. Soaked soybeans were first blended in a constantly chugging machine, then they were cooked, drained and poured into rectangular moulds. The tofu was then left to set in the moulds until firm enough for the wok.

We took a different road back into Solo, skirting the walls of the giant kraton (sultan's palace). Near the kraton we stopped for a lunch of **mietoprak** (beef noodle soup with tempe, peanuts and spinach) and Yoyo dropped us at our hotel, stomachs and minds fully satisfied.

Solo cycling tours can be arranged at any of Solo's travel agents or tourist cafes

HOME COOKING

A 'natural' addition to the Indonesian kitchen is **daun pisang** (banana leaf). Banana leaves are used to wrap food for steaming or grilling; also for wrapping soybeans and yeast to make tempe. What's more, the leaves can be used to wrap a packed lunch, and even as a plate.

Although prepared coconut milk and flesh are widely available, fresh coconut is preferred so a coconut scraper is a kitchen regular. Cooks use either a manual scraper (which looks like a mounted back-scratcher) or a motorised grater (which looks like a small satellite dish with a rotating scraper protruding from the centre).

Now to rice. There are numerous ways to cook rice, and numerous implements with which to do it. Of course all you need is a pot and water, but in Indonesian cooking tradition, rice is only par-boiled then drained and placed back over the boiling water in a conical bamboo steamer and steamed until soft and fluffy. A pot complete with detachable colander makes this an easy process. But you can forget about steaming and timing now; Indonesia has embraced the electric rice cooker. It's less labour intensive and keeps rice warm for long periods, but no-one has yet invented a rice cooker that prevents the rice from becoming somewhat sticky.

Misanam with her child, Segenter Village Kitchen, Lombok

Soto Ayam (Chicken Soup) Asti Mulyana's Recipe

Spice Paste

4	shallots
5	cloves garlic
3-5	fresh red chillies
2cm	piece ginger
2cm	piece turmeric
2cm	piece galangal
8cm	lemongrass
	salt to taste

To Serve

3	hard-boiled eggs, sliced
200g	sohun (transparent bean-flour vermicelli), dipped in hot water
1 cup	beansprouts, dipped in hot water
1	spring onion (scallion), chopped
1	tomato, chopped
	kerupuk (crackers – shrimp or any other flavour), deep fried
	sambal ulek or hot chilli sauce

Soup

¼	whole chicken (or 2 thigh pieces with breast)
1.5L	water

In a mortar & pestle grind the shallots, garlic, ginger, turmeric, galangal, lemongrass and chillies to a paste. Salt to taste. Bring chicken to the boil in a pot with the water, then add the spice paste and simmer until the chicken is tender. Take the chicken out and slice it thinly. Add the spring onion to the remaining broth. To serve, put some chicken, egg, tomato, vermicelli and beansprouts in each bowl. Shower with the chicken broth and kerupuk. Enjoy with hot chilli sauce.
    Serves 2

SUNDAY SOUP

It's early Sunday morning but the sun shining into my room has forced me to get up, as has the music coming from my brother's bedroom. Outside my room the music is blasting, and I can see my brother sorting his tapes and CDs. He greets me with a line from a song by a popular local band

A girl who wakes up late will find it hard to find a soul mate.

I lean against the door, still not completely awake.

He says, "Hey, what can we eat? I'm starting to feel hungry now". Then I remember that mum and dad had to go out of town and I am responsible for feeding my brother and I. Last night mum gave me Rp15,000 to buy food.

After washing my face I make a strong cup of coffee, hoping it will freshen me up. I enjoy it while watching television. I open the curtains, the window and the door so the sun shines through the house. Luckily I see a door-to-door grocery seller walk by. I decide to buy some food from him. Five of my neighbours have already surrounded him and are buying produce. They ask me where my mother was going and they're pretty excited when I tell them that I'm cooking today. Then they all complain about how lazy their daughters are when it comes to cooking. I kind of like getting attention and compliments from my lady neighbours in the morning. Thank God, I have already washed my face and had a hit of caffeine; I look awake enough. Just.

Bargaining with the grocery man is kind of fun, even though it takes a while. I am impressed by the spirit of my neighbours as they do some collective bargaining. With help from them I get a reasonable price. The chicken and vegetables look fresh; the fruits also look juicy enough, but I don't have enough money for them. Finally I get everything I need: a quarter of a fresh chicken, some sohun, spring onion, lemongrass, tomatoes and some red chillies to make it spicy. The total price comes to only Rp12,500, so I still have Rp2500 for buying kerupuk. Everything I need to make soto ayam.

In preparation for the cooking I make a deal with my brother: I cook the soto ayam and he cooks the rice.

I clean the chicken, removing the fat. Getting my brother off the phone is a battle, but he cleans the rice quickly and puts it into the rice cooker with some water. Actually, he's a little disappointed as he was hoping to buy a fast-food meal with the Rp15,000 mum gave me. He starts to make fun of meals I have made that have given my family horrible memories. On Mother's Day, I almost killed my whole family because I put too many chillies on the nasi goreng. They all ate with tears streaming from their eyes. Worst of all, mum told everyone to keep eating because she felt sorry for me.

HOME COOKING

We argue about standard ingredients for making the fried rice. My brother keeps criticising my over-creativity. I admit that it's my hobby to try some new ingredients when I'm making food, so as to create a specific cuisine that I could become famous for. But my brother says it will be famous because it could kill people.

I boil the chicken, and while waiting for it to finish, I prepare all the spices, and blend the shallots and garlic. We keep on laughing about my cooking accidents until the chicken is ready. Then we cut it into small pieces. I'm surprised that my brother is willing to help. When I ask him why he replies, "I'm just making sure that you won't try to poison me while mum and dad are out of town and that the inheritance will still be divided into two".

Once everything is prepared, we fry all the spices together and put them into the water that the chicken was boiled in. We also cut tomatoes and some spring onion that will be put with fried soybeans when we eat the soto ayam.

I didn't realise that my body was so sweaty because I'm standing near the stove for quite a long time. While waiting for the stock to be ready, I take a quick bath. I return to the kitchen feeling a lot fresher, and there it is, the soto ayam is ready to be served. The aromas coming from the pot are making me feel hungry. I grab a cup of hot water to soak the sohun for five minutes. It feels like a lifetime.

My brother is placing the rice into two plates. I put the sohun into two bowls and shower them with the stock. The chicken slices looked very tender. In go the tomatoes, spring onion and some fried soybeans. I add a little bit of sweet soy sauce and chilli sauce, as it gives a click on my tongue. It tastes yummy, salty but not too salty, and has the exact balance of ingredients. My brother turns to me and says, "Hmm … not bad. Once you've poisoned me you will probably have a successful career as a chef in prison".

He smiles at me with his mouth full of soto ayam. It's dribbling down his cheek.

Asti Mulyana lives in Bandung and loves both travelling and cooking whenever she can

celebrating
with food

Indonesians celebrate with food and celebrate because of food. Not only are there the personal observances such as weddings, there are also religious practices and traditional customs such as harvest festivals. And just because there's no specific religious or personal occasions taking place doesn't mean the celebrations stop. Indonesians, like anyone, love to party.

Whether for a marriage, business launch or just for visiting friends, food – lots of it – is an essential part of any Indonesian celebration. A meal with a lot of food for many people is called a **selamatan**. Such a meal can include any combination and variety of dishes, but for special occasions a **tumpeng** will be the centrepiece. This is a pyramid of yellow rice, the tip of which is ceremonially cut off and offered to the eldest present. Meat is always served at celebrations, often a speciality such as Sumatran **rendang** (beef or buffalo coconut curry; see the recipe) or Balinese **babi guling** (spit-roast pig). Once formalities are over (Indonesians love speeches) it's time for guests to help themselves to the food and to mix, mingle and enjoy themselves.

Each of Indonesia's main religious faiths (Islam, Hinduism, Christianity, Buddhism) are interwoven by customs and traditions that predated their arrival in the archipelago. Consequently, Hindus from India will see many differences between themselves and Balinese Hindus. Similarly, the Minangkabau of West Sumatra are devout Muslims yet their social structure is matriarchal. And although many Floresians profess the Catholic faith, they still celebrate new harvests by sacrificing a pig.

For the 90% of Indonesians who are Muslim, the largest celebrations are Ramadan (which ends with Lebaran) and Idul Adha. Ramadan is the month of fasting, the ninth month of the Muslim calendar. During Ramadan, in order to develop empathy for the poor and the hungry, able-bodied Muslims are forbidden to eat or drink between sunrise and sunset.

Each day for the duration of the month of Ramadan, Muslims rise before subuh (sunrise prayer) to eat a breakfast big enough to keep them going until after maghrib (sunset prayer). In Tapaktuan, Aceh, we awoke to a bowl of **gulai kambing** (goat in coconut curry), not a bright and breezy way to start the day, but in this deeply Muslim region they know what's needed to survive while the sun's up. During Ramadan many eateries are closed (or their windows curtained at least) throughout the day, in respect for those fasting. Eating or drinking in the open is a definite no-no. It may sound like a bad time to be in Indonesia but – ironically – Ramadan does hold its attractions for the culinary-minded visitor. You may have to plan your meals, you may have to go without lunch, but when sunset comes the locals' appreciation of a good meal is contagious.

As with the commencement of **puasa** (fasting) at sunrise, breaking the fast is publicised by the beating of drums and the call to prayer. You would expect the faithful to dive straight into a bowl of rice, not so; the first thing Indonesians eat is usually **kolak** (fruit in coconut milk), a gentle way to re-acquaint the body with food. Then, after prayers, the evening meal begins and eating takes on a new energy. In some areas, such as in Bukittinggi's Pasar Atas (Upper Market), cooks set out food on street stalls and wait for

Praying at Ulun Danu temple, Lake Bratan, Bali

Temple ceremony in Besakih, Bali

the hungry to be lured by the aroma. During Ramadan, eating is rarely a solitary pursuit; people gather to savour and enjoy their food as a community.

The end of the fasting month is called Lebaran or Idul Fitri. Many Muslims journey to celebrate with their families, therefore any travel during this time can be a circus. Don't expect to get very far in the days leading up to Lebaran. The celebrations start with early morning prayers, followed by two days of visits to family and friends to ask for forgiveness for wrongdoings, and to join the feasting. During Lebaran, **ketupat** (rice steamed in woven packets of coconut fronds) are hung everywhere, just like Christmas bells and holly.

70 days after Lebaran is Idul Adha, the Muslim festival commemorating Abraham's devotion. Allah ordered Abraham to sacrifice his son, however once the boy was on the block Allah spared him, as Abraham's devotion was now obvious. In the boy's place a ram was sacrificed; this sacrifice is repeated across the Muslim world during Idul Adha. In Indonesia a sheep or goat is the usual victim, and you know Idul Adha is approaching as you'll see the unfortunate animals everywhere – in cars, on the backs of bikes – on their way to meet their maker, and to make some meat.

The Balinese calendar is peppered with family celebrations and festivals including **Kedaso** (the tenth full-moon festival) and **Penampahan**, a festival of purification in which sacred images are cleaned and pigs sacrificed to the gods. Such celebrations are always observed with a communal meal of national and regional dishes (see Bali in the Regional Variations chapter). In some areas people share from one massive banana leaf piled with various dishes. Specific festivals aside, every day in Bali can seem like a celebration. In doorways, beside rice fields, at bus stations, in buses, in offices, in markets, on staircases and in gardens – wherever a god or spirit may reside (which is anywhere) there will be **banten**

(offerings) placed for their pleasure.

Balinese offerings are artworks in themselves – they can be intricately woven banana-leaf pockets holding a spoonful of fresh rice or they can be mammoth towers of fresh fruit and iridescent **jaje** (fancily shaped rice and tapioca cakes). Smaller offerings are made daily to ensure the gods are pleased and that evil spirits are placated; larger offerings – often studded with whole chickens and a garden of produce – are made to celebrate special occasions such as **odalan**, the birthday of a local Hindu temple.

As Bali is home to thousands of temples, there will be an odalan happening somewhere on Bali every day. During such times you'll undoubtably see processions of immaculately dressed Balinese women balancing the towering offerings on their heads as they make their way to temple. After the gods have devoured the essence of

Preparing Hindu offerings, Bali

the offerings, the earthly leftovers can be devoured by all and sundry. Bali's offerings are usually made by female-only collectives called **anyaman**. These collectives also double as social groups, and members get together not only to make banten but to discuss the issues of the day. At an odalan, men will prepare an **ebat** (five-dish feast) that includes such Balinese specialties as **lawar** (salad of chopped coconut, garlic and chilli with pork (or chicken) meat and blood).

BALINESE BIRTHDAY

Krishna is racing around the house like an unguided missile. In one hand is an inflatable Pikachu doll and in the other a half-eaten banana fritter.

"She drives me crazy", Wayan, her father, says with a smile as she scurries past chasing the dog.

It's not hard to know where Krishna is because the silver bracelets on her wrists and ankles are jangling. These were put on during her **sambutan** (when she was three months old according to the Balinese calendar), signifying the move further from the gods and closer to humans. Before then, her feet weren't even allowed to touch the ground.

Now she's a gutsy little human being. In fact the time has come to take her bracelets off, as Krishna's **telung oton** (third Balinese birthday) has arrived. As she tears across the room her parents and uncle begin to prepare the celebratory feast.

First up is **pepes ayam** (spiced chicken steamed in banana leaves) and for this dish Krishna's uncle chops up a whole chicken but sets aside the skin and pancreas.

"The skin is too fatty and this …" he holds up the small, yellow pancreas, "… too bitter". He screws up his nose.

He chops lemongrass, shallots, garlic and chilli. Ketut, Krishna's mother, has already ground the galangal and ginger, and she brings it outside to where we're sitting on a large bamboo mat. Here, we mix the chicken and spices, fold the mix into banana leaves along with a salam leaf and place them in the steamer. The little green packets catch Krishna's attention for a second, but she's soon distracted by Wayan, who is preparing lawar. He has already boiled the chicken and is now shredding the coconut. For extra flavour the coconut flesh is lightly grilled and the smell of this has warmed our nostrils. In a large bowl Wayan mixes the coconut and chicken with a fried paste of garlic, chilli, and the lawar essential, pig's blood.

"Some people use raw blood", Wayan says with a smile, "but we don't want you to get Bali belly."

I'm pleased … I guess.

From the corner of my eye I notice that Krishna is moving steadily toward the tray of hot coals that have been set up in the garage. But before I say anything, Ketut has hoisted the protesting Krishna up into her arms. Krishna's uncle prepared the coals to make **sate lilit**. This sate is made with minced pork mixed with coconut oil, chilli, garlic, salt, palm sugar, pepper and shrimp paste. The resulting mix is pressed onto flat sate sticks, and this process gives the sate its name.

"You lilit the paste onto the stick", explains Wayan.

While the sate is grilled, Wayan makes **urab**, a salad of diced long beans, coconut milk and flesh, chilli, shrimp paste, salt, shallots and garlic.

So the pepes ayam is in the steamer, the sate is on the grill, the lawar and urab are ready, Krishna's uncle is clearing the mat, Ketut is bringing out plates and Krishna is poking her dad with the leftover sate sticks.

"We're not making **babi guling** (spit-roast pig) today", says Wayan. "That's only for the bigger festivals."

To be honest I'm not disappointed. The four dishes and rice easily suffice. We dig in as Krishna bashes the dishes with a spoon. The flavours are sharp and clean. The salam leaf in the pepes ayam gives it a tangy edge, the lawar and urab are both crunchy and juicy. The chilli in the sate is starting to make me cry, but the peppery flavour is too good to give up.

"Isn't Krishna eating?" I ask.

"Too spicy – she's not brave enough yet", Wayan says and grabs Krishna's hand before she can plunge it into the rice bowl.

Patrick Witton

Krishna & mother wearing Hindu blessings

Making sate lilit for a Balinese birthday

Apart from those for young children, birthdays aren't a big deal in Indonesia, and when celebrated it's usually the celebrator who pays for their friends' meal. Bigger than birthdays is the Javanese Mitoni celebration of the seventh month of pregnancy. Mitoni involves a feast that includes a tumpeng surrounded by six smaller ones (or seven dishes) and often also seven hard-boiled eggs, one of which is stuck on a skewer in the middle of the central tumpeng. No prizes at guessing what the lucky number is. If the feast looks beautiful, it will be a girl. If it looks ordinary, a boy's in the making.

There are a few celebrations that occur in the first stages of life. When a child is 35 days old their head is shaved and a meal of rice (usually tumpeng) is prepared along with dishes of beef (representing the child's ability to walk), fish (to swim) and chicken (to fly).

There are also some celebrations that instill fear. Indonesian Muslims, like Muslims everywhere, practise male circumcision; and here it's done sometime between the age of six and eleven. This rite of passage is marked by prayers and a banquet for the lad's friends and family. We once saw a boy sitting in a hot tub to 'tenderise' the flesh in preparation for the chop, a look of sheer terror on his face.

What with 300 ethnic groups you'd guess there's a little variety in how Indonesians celebrate marriage (or anything else for that matter) and you would be right. Some Indonesian weddings include an animal sacrifice, others include karaoke. Some probably have both. But the common denominator is a meal of monstrous proportions.

Food to celebrate the seventh month of pregnancy

LIVING TRADITIONS

Indonesians may have adopted new religions, but traditional rituals and celebrations, including these ones, continue to colour the country:

In Lombok on the 19th day of the 10th month of the Sasak calendar (usually February or March) locals gather on Kuta Beach, build fires and see out the night outdoing each other in **pantun** (rhyming couplets). Dawn marks the start of the **nyale** fish season, and once the first of these worm-like fish are caught, teenage boys and girls head out to sea in separate boats and gleefully chase each other around. The nyale are thought to be an aphrodisiac, and the teenagers have licence to mingle freely. However if a girl publicly accepts a gift from a boy, she has essentially agreed to marry him.

At the Wektu Telu temple, West Lombok, Hindus celebrate the start of the wet season (sometime between October and December), pelting each other with ketupat.

Ketupat: rice steamed in woven packets of coconut fronds

In Bali, villages are given a fresh coat of paint and festooned with colourful flags to celebrate successful rice harvests. In honour of Dewi Sri, the goddess of rice, small straw dolls are placed around rice fields and villages.

At the junction of the Opak and Gajah Wong rivers, near Wonokromo, Java, villagers perform a water ritual to ask for a successful harvest. In other areas, animals are blessed and comforted in rituals that seek to ensure livestock remain healthy.

In Sumba, in February or March, priests gather on the beach to examine the behaviour of the nyale fish in the first catch, thus to forsee how the harvest will be. This heralds the start of the Pasola Festival, in which colourfully dressed horse riders engage in mock battles, often ending in injury or even death. Traditionally, spilt blood satisfies the spirits, who then guarantee a good harvest.

Temple ceremony in Besakih, Bali

In Javanese weddings, the bride feeds the groom by hand, symbolic of her new responsibilities. Some weddings last for several days and include visits to the parents' houses, to the place of worship and to the reception. And during this time, those involved should be well nourished, as there's nothing worse then starving those who play a part in blessing your commitment. At the reception the food served can be anything, as long as there's lots of it. A spit-roast goat or pig is a popular item. The reception is a mix-and-mingle affair; guests help themselves to the food, buffet-style. The lucky couple, glittering in their regalia, sit on thrones at the front of the room receiving well-wishers and watching people eat. Maybe that's why they always look so solemn.

A funeral is obviously another occasion that varies depending on where you are and the mourners' religious denomination. In some regions, such as Central Sulawesi and Sumba, funerals are massive occasions involving the whole community, as well as some unlucky animals (see also Central Sulawesi in the Regional Variations chapter).

DEATH OF THE PARTY – A Funeral in Sumba

"Where did you come from?"

Well may she ask, since it's her grandfather's funeral. And how did I end up here, at a festival in a yard in the hills of western Sumba? Well, when a truckload of machete-wielding Sumbanese insist I come, it's hard to say no.

The splendour of a party, feasting ... a funeral? My machete-wielding friends mixed and mingled. I tried but, well, a whitey not packing a machete like everyone else? I was unblendable.

The granddaughter, Mariana, wore a bright blue sarong – pretty racy for the occasion – and there were droplets of blood on her raven hair. This didn't phase her much, especially as we were standing ankle-deep in the doings of a makeshift abattoir. My machete-wielding friends were slaughtering buffalo and cooking their meat on a bed of coals.

Killing the water buffalo for a funeral

"Your grandfather was an important man." Said I, stating the obvious.

"Yes, many buffaloes are being killed today", says Mariana, picking at a plate of buffalo. "He needs a feast to reach the next world. If he doesn't have enough he'll haunt us here."

A group passed us carrying a concerned-looking pig. It was sniffing the air, now thick with the smell of blood.

"Are pigs sacrificed too?" My carnivorous streak was being tested.

"Yes, six pigs, and 24 buffaloes. The spirits will be happy."

"But wasn't your grandfather Christian?" There was a cross on their front door.

Sumbanese in traditional dress near Waingapu, Sumba

"Yes ... there's the priest." She pointed to the verandah and there he was, dining on a plate of pork whilst eulogising to his flock, who were busy preparing the next course. Religion here in western Sumba is a cocktail of traditional beliefs with a Christian chaser.

"Aren't you Christian?", Mariana asked between mouthfuls.

"Err ... yes." My sandals were feeling pretty sticky now. I could feel pig skin between my toes. I was thrust another serve of cracklin' buffalo by an elder who smiled a red mouthful of betelnut.

"This is his wife, please give her a gift."

It felt weird, giving money to the widow. But she happily pocketed it and splashed back through the blood.

Mariana explains, "The funeral has been very expensive, but his spirit is satisfied".

"Aren't you unhappy?"

"Of course. I won't see him again. But he is here." And she beamed. Her grandfather was of the spirit world now. He could influence weather, crops, people's health – I felt like converting. I would buy a machete, marry Mariana, then impatiently wait for death and the subsequent feast. I thought I knew how to party, but then I saw how the Sumbanese mourn.

Patrick Witton

regional
variations

With 13,677 islands encompassing rivers, swamps, beaches, jungles, farms, volcanoes, mountains and metropoli, it makes sense that ingredients vary from place to place. Add some 300 ethnic groups speaking 365 languages or dialects and you have the makings not only of a diverse cuisine but also of an eclectic approach to eating. The difference between Sundanese and Sumbanese is as great as that between, say, Swedes and Sicilians, and never more evident than at the dinner table.

REGIONAL VARIATIONS

REGIONS

VIETNAM — South China Sea — PHILIPPINES

THAILAND — PALAU

MALAYSIA — BRUNEI — Sulu Sea

Bukittinggi — SINGAPORE — MALAYSIA — Sulawesi Sea — Pacific Ocean

I N D O N E S I A

Banjarmasin

JAKARTA — Bandung — Java Sea — Banda Sea — PAPUA NEW GUINEA

Yogyakarta — Ubud

EAST TIMOR

Indian Ocean — Timor Sea — Arafura Sea

AUSTRALIA

Aceh & North Sumatra	East Java	North Sulawesi
West Sumatra	Madura	Central Sulawesi
South Sumatra	Bali	South Sulawesi
West Java; Jakarta	Nusa Tenggara	Maluku
Central Java	Kalimantan	Irian Jaya

A wonderful thing about Indonesia's **masakan khas daerah** (regional cooking) is that often you don't have to travel to a location to try its speciality. Indonesians have migrated extensively throughout their own country, thus introducing home flavours to a wider audience. You could be wandering the laneways of Denpasar and find a warung selling Acehnese **gulai itik** (duck in coconut curry) or you might be lost in Jakarta when you smell the aroma of **sate Madura** wafting from a kaki-lima.

And it's usually easy to identify the origin of a dish or cuisine by its name, as in **tahu Sumedang** (Sumedang-style tofu); **soto Lamongan** (Lamongan soup) and **pempek Palembang** (Palembang fish and sago dumplings).

Java

You would be hard-pressed to find a land more dynamic than Java. It's one of the most crowded islands yet its lushness is soporific, it's the economic nucleus of the country yet ancient culture and traditions still underpin daily activity, and the urban sprawl still pales beneath the backbone of volcanoes that carve the rivers and enrich the soil. Over half of the county's people live on Java, but it has less than seven percent of the nation's landmass, and with so many people there's a hell of a lot of cooking going on.

Gudeg, the speciality of Yogyakarta

REGIONAL VARIATIONS

Night life in Yogyakarta, Java

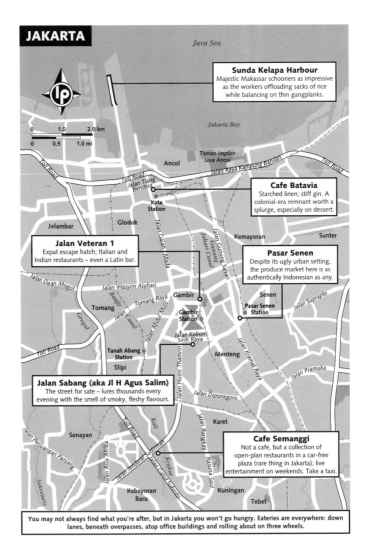

JAKARTA

Java Sea

Jakarta Bay

Sunda Kelapa Harbour
Majestic Makassar schooners as impressive as the workers offloading sacks of rice while balancing on thin gangplanks.

Jakarta Bay

Ancol

Taman Impian
Jaya Ancol

Cafe Batavia
Starched linen; stiff gin. A colonial-era remnant worth a splurge, especially on dessert.

Jalan Raya Kampung Bandan

Jalan Tiang
Bendera

Kota
Station

Jelambar

Glodok

Kemayoran

Sunter

Jalan Veteran 1
Expat escape hatch; Italian and Indian restaurants – even a Latin bar.

Pasar Senen
Despite its ugly urban setting, the produce market here is as authentically Indonesian as any.

Jalan Daan Mogot

Jalan Hasyim Asyhari

Gambir

Senen

Tomang

Tomang Raya

Pasar Senen
Station

Jalan Suprapto

Gambir
Station

Jalan Kebon
Sirih Raya

Tanah Abang
Station

Menteng

Slipi

Jalan Sabang (aka Jl H Agus Salim)
The street for sate – lures thousands every evening with the smell of smoky, fleshy flavours.

Jalan Diponegoro

Jalan Pramuka

Karet

Senayan

Cafe Semanggi
Not a cafe, but a collection of open-plan restaurants in a car-free plaza (rare thing in Jakarta); live entertainment on weekends. Take a taxi.

Kebayoran
Baru

Kuningan

Tebet

You may not always find what you're after, but in Jakarta you won't go hungry. Eateries are everywhere: down lanes, beneath overpasses, atop office buildings and rolling about on three wheels.

Jakarta

There are three reasons why Jakarta is also known as Kota Kompor (stove-burner city). Firstly, the heat hits you here like nowhere else – it clings to your face and digs into your pores. Secondly, this is where emotions are highest, where revolutions simmer and demonstrations run riot. And it's plain to see why people want reform: the division between rich and poor here makes your stomach turn. At every intersection you'll see smog-cured children pressing against the tinted glass of imported cars, asking for change. Thirdly, and most literally, Jakarta *is* a city of stove burners. Its 10 million residents have to eat – and the streets are so crammed with stalls, restaurants, and kaki-lima that you're liable to trip over a kitchen when you're crossing the road.

Within the 661 sq km of this town, you'll find every cuisine you may want to try, from across the nation and across the world. And along with this goes a a great choice in style or category of eating environment. The nation's elite dine on oysters kilpatrick in surrounds of starched linen and polished silver, just over the road from traffic-stained stalls serving up chicken soup to a benches full of road-weary bus drivers. Then there are food centres, roving vendors, shopping mall food courts, American fast-food imports and hotel restaurants, all ready to fill your stomach.

Despite the choice, eating in Jakarta is hard work. If you're after something specific, it'll probably be found across town and if you want to find a specific restaurant, it may well have closed down. But as long as you remain flexible, you'll find something to fill the hole. Walk out onto the street and see what your neighbourhood has to offer. If nothing takes your fancy, jump into a taxi or a **bajaj** (Jakarta's three-wheel, two-stroke, smog-producing auto-rickshaw – like a Thai *tuk-tuk* only evil) and head to another area of town. You may even see an appealing eatery en route and, if you can be heard over the engine, cut the trip short. Stay open to change. Don't plan your stay in Jakarta. Jakarta is not a planned city.

For an authentic taste of Jakarta, look for places serving Betawi cuisine. The Betawi are the original inhabitants of the region, and their food is known for its richness and meatiness. Although found across the country, **gado-gado** (salad of vegetables and peanut sauce) is a Betawi original. A similar dish, **ketoprak** (salad of noodles, beansprouts and tofu with soy and peanut sauce) is named after the Javanese musical style that supposedly sounds like someone chopping up ingredients. The local soup, **soto Betawi** (soup with every part of the cow, including the marrow) is made creamy with the addition of coconut milk. For a full and hearty meal, look for places serving **nasi uduk**, (rice cooked in coconut milk served with meat, tofu and/or vegetables).

West Java

Indonesians say you can always recognise a Sundanese as they're the ones eating from trees and shrubs as they walk past gardens. And the inhabitants of West Java won't deny this; they love their greens too much. Meals are usually accompanied by a plate of greens whether you want it or not. You'll recognise things like cucumber , but perhaps not the less familiar flora, such as **leunca**, which looks like a green pea but is a bitter-tasting fruit. Big **pete** beans are another Sundanese staple despite the fact that they leave you with baneful breath. A texturally interesting speciality of the region is **karedok**, a salad made with yard-long beans, beansprouts and cucumber with a spicy sauce (see the recipe). There's also a wide range of **acar** (pickled vegetables) and **lalapan** (salad of raw vegetables served with sambal).

BANDUNG

Bandung Indah Plaza
Street food, chic dudes in the premier shopping district.

Bandung Station
Board a minibus to Lembang for fresh air and fine food.

Jalan Watu Kencana

Jalan Merdeka

Jalan Aceh

Toko Aroma
Holy grail for the caffeine crusader.

Jalan Kebon Kawung

Governor's Residence

City Hall

Jalan Sumatra

Jalan Kalimantan

Jalan Manado

Bethel Church

Catholic Church

Jalan Jawa

Bandung Station

Jalan Suniaraja

Jalan

Jalan Tera

Jalan Braga
Sundanese restaurants, European bakeries, sleazy bars all on the one street.

Jalan Kebonjati

Jalan Pecinan

Cikapundung

Jalan Braga

Jalan Lembong

Museum Mandala Wangsit

Jalan Tamblong

Jalan Sunda

Jalan Duliatip

Jalan Oto Iskandardinata

Jalan ABC

Jalan Veteran

Jalan Jen Sudirman

Jalan Naripan

Jalan A Yani

Jalan Cibadak

Jalan Dewi Sartika

Jalan Asia Afrika

Jalan Karang Anyar

Jalan Dalem Kaum

0   200   400 m
0   200   400 yd

River

Lengkong Besar

Pasar Baru
This market pumps with produce, products and people.

Alun-Alun
Where the food vendors converge.

Fame Station
Live music and lager at the top floor club.

The Sundanese love their greens, Bandung, Java

West Java's regional capital of Bandung, with its cooler air and pockets of colonial charm, is a good location to try the local flavours, although it now has traffic jams like any city. The town is ringed by the fertile Parahyangan mountain range, produce from which supplies the city's markets and kitchens. And heading north into the foothills from the city centre, it's not long before the metropolis gives way to a bucolic landscape rich with gardens of cassava and corn.

Lembang, Dago and Ciumbuleuit are easy-to-reach areas to explore, and the backroads and walking trails, especially around Maribaya and between Ciumbuleuit and Lembang, are peppered with food stalls. These are great places to lose an afternoon, especially when they provide bamboo mats to stretch out on while looking out over the foothills. As well as snacks, these warung usually come with big, black, kettles used to serve **bandrek** (ginger tea with coconut and pepper; see the recipe) and the regional warmer, **bajigur** (spiced coffee with coconut milk).

Further east via a strikingly green landscape is Sumedang, home of the world's best tofu. Why Sumedang's tofu tastes so good is a mystery, but even those who thought tofu was tasteless fodder for vegetarians are not likely to stop at one piece of **tahu goreng** (fried tofu). Sumedang's tofu sellers are recognisable by their hats; made of loosely woven bamboo, they often double as packaging for large orders.

For an easy complete meal, the Sundanese look to **nasi timbel** (rice cooked in banana leaves and served with sambal, chicken, tofu, salted fish and/or tempe). Other Sundanese dishes include two meaty soups: **mie kocok** (beef and egg noodle soup) and **soto Bandung** (beef and vegetable soup with lemongrass). A kaki-lima favourite in West Java is **ketupat tahu** (pressed rice, beansprouts and tofu with soy and peanut sauce). Many Sundanese restaurants serve salty and strange-looking **gepuk** (flattened and fried spiced beef).

Sundanese sweet specialities, **colenak** (roasted cassava with sweet coconut sauce) and **ulen** (roasted brick of sticky rice with peanut sauce), are best eaten when still warm, at the place they're cooked. On rural roads you'll see colenak stalls decorated with curtains of cassava, luring hungry travellers. One last sweetie worth mentioning is **dodol**, a chewy, toffee-like sweet made of rice, coconut milk and palm sugar. It's from Garut, 'the Switzerland of Indonesia'. Yes, locals think it's cold.

Sundanese and Javanese meld in the hot port-town of Cirebon, where specialities include **empal genton** (beef and turmeric soup), **tahu gejrot** (fried tofu swimming in spiced soy sauce) and **nasi lengko** (rice with tofu, tempe, beansprouts, cucumber and peanut sauce).

Roasting colenak in Lembang, Java

Central Java

Central Java is a land of bubbling volcanoes, ancient temples and royal courts, a land where tradition permeates all levels of life, and remnants of Hindu-Buddhist kingdoms mix and weave into modern Indonesia. It's a powerfully patient place; social and political changes come slowly to Central Java, yet when they do, Jakarta listens.

The city of Yogyakarta (Yogya) is the beating heart of Javanese culture. The city is shadowed by volatile Mt Merapi, which may have the power to destroy the region, but is also the source of fertile volcanic soil that feeds Central Java's 30 million. Smack in the centre of Yogya is the kraton (sultan's palace). Although stripped of most of its former power, it remains an important centre of culture, where Javanese arts are nurtured and promoted. You can visit the kraton and its museum, which is dedicated to the late Sultan Hamengkubuwono IX. In a painting in the museum, the Sultan's family tree is a pomegranate, with men represented as fruit, women as leaves, and those who died at birth as blossoms. Among the Sultan's personal effects, you'll notice a few peculiar possessions: some spices, a jar of MSG, even a pair of oven mitts. Indeed the great man had some kitchen know-how, and it's said he used make a fine **sop buntut** (oxtail soup).

Surrounding the kraton is one of the most densely populated areas in the country. Houses front onto lanes too tight for cars, people cook on their front steps and children duck and weave around the wheels of roving kaki-lima. These are great areas to explore, to see life carried out at a patient, Javanese pace.These are great streets to explore and to see the serene manner of the Javanese's daily life of the Javanese.

Cutting through the centre of town is the main road and commercial centre, Jl Malioboro. At Jl Malioboro's southern end is Beringharjo Market, a mix of souvenirs, clothes and produce. The back of the market is where the fish, spices and other comestibles are sold, and out the front there's always a crowd of kaki-lima selling food to starving shoppers. During the day this road is the place to buy trinkets and batik, but by night the souvenir stalls are cleared and Jl Malioboro becomes the domain of **lesehan**, makeshift eateries with grass mats for seating. Some lesehan are decked out with low tables and paper napkins, others provide no more than a plate for your food. In the early hours, the lesehan of Jl Malioboro are great places to share stories and fried rice with street-kids, students and post-gig musicians.

Ask any Indonesian to describe the food of Central Java and they'll say one word: sweet. The people here use palm sugar more than anyone else in Indonesia. They shovel it into their tea and pour it into their sauces. And nowhere else is this more apparent than with **gudeg** (jackfruit curry). Many dishes take the name of their city of origin, but the homage is reversed for

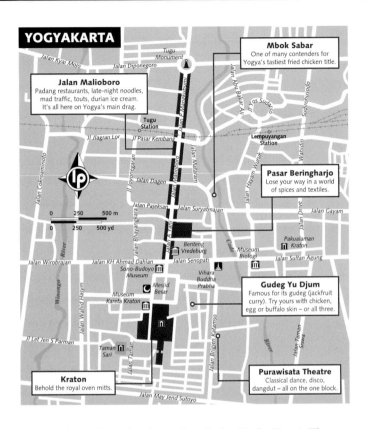

YOGYAKARTA

Mbok Sabar
One of many contenders for
Yogya's tastiest fried chicken title.

Jalan Malioboro
Padang restaurants, late-night noodles,
mad traffic, touts, durian ice cream.
It's all here on Yogya's main drag.

Tugu Monument

Jalan Kyai Mojo
Jalan Diponegoro

Tugu Station

Jl Jlagran Lor   Jl Pasar Kembang

Lempuyangan Station

Pasar Beringharjo
Lose your way in a world
of spices and textiles.

Jalan Dagen

Jalan Cokroaminoto

0   250   500 m
0   250   500 yd

Jalan Pajeksan   Jalan Suryatmajan

Jalan Gayam

Jalan Bhayangkara

Jalan Wirobrajan   Jalan KH Ahmad Dahlan

Benteng Vredeburg   Jalan Senopati

Pakualaman
Kraton

Jalan Sultan Agung

Sono-Budoyo Museum

Museum Biologi

Vihara Buddha Prabha

Gudeg Yu Djum
Famous for its gudeg (jackfruit
curry). Try yours with chicken,
egg or buffalo skin – or all three.

Museum Kareta Kraton

Mesjid Besar

Jl Let Jen S Parman

Jalan Wahid Hasyim

Taman Sari

Taman

Kraton
Behold the royal oven mitts.

Jalan May Jend Sutoyo

Purawisata Theatre
Classical dance, disco,
dangdut – all on the one block.

Jalan Brigjen Katamso

Jalan P Mangkubumi
Jalan A Yani
Jalan Abu Bakar Ali
Jl Yos Sudarso
Sudirhusodo
Wahidin
Jalan Mataram
Jalan Hayam Wuruk
Jalan Drive
Winongo River
Jalan Taman
Jalan Taman Siswa
River
Code

Yogya, which is often referred to as Kota Gudeg (Gudeg Town). The taste of this speciality is sweet and fleshy. To make gudeg, young jackfruit is very slowly cooked in coconut milk with coriander seeds, candlenut, galangal, palm sugar, garlic, shallots and salam leaves. Often people add jatih leaves to turn the dish a dark red. A similar stock is used to cook the accompanying chicken, egg and **krecek** (buffalo-skin crackling). You can order your gudeg with any or all of these tasty morsels from restaurants and warung all over Yogya. In the morning and in the evening you'll see old women selling gudeg from pots on street corners, filling banana-leaf packages with rice and their sweet, fleshy gudeg. Other Yogya specialities include **ayam goreng** (fried chicken), variations of which are found all over Indonesia but taste best here (see the boxed text Featherweight Feast in the Where to Eat & Drink chapter). And for dessert deviants, there are **kelepon** (green rice-flour balls with a palm sugar filling) and **geplak** (sticky rice sweets with palm sugar and coconut).

Colourful becaks in Yogyakarta, Java

REGIONAL VARIATIONS

An hour northeast of Yogya by train, past sweeping rice fields and the huge temple complex of Prambanan, lies the city of Solo (also called Surakarta). While Yogya is coloured by an influx of students from around the world, Solo remains a more refined, traditional Javanese city. It is home to two kratons and a rich arts scene (some of the best batik comes from Solo) yet it receives very few visitors. Solo is surrounded by fertile fields that support a healthy village culture, and it's from Solo that you can take a bicycle tour to see Indonesian agriculture and food production first hand (see the boxed text Solo Cycle Tour in the Home Cooking chapter). In the centre of town, especially at night around Jl Teuku Umar and Jl Brigjend Slamet Riyadi, you can sample Solo specialities. The most famous of these is **nasi liwet**, rice cooked with coconut milk, **labusiam** (a kind of pumpkin), unripe papaya, garlic, shallots and **kumut** (solids from cooking coconut milk). It's served with chicken or egg. The sugar mad should frequent the stalls selling freshly cooked **serabi** (rice-flour pancakes made with coconut milk and pandan leaves and topped with chocolate, banana or jackfruit). Another Solo sweetie is **gempol pleret** (discs of spiced rice flour made with coconut milk).

There is a sultan's banquet worth of Central Javanese specialities to be tasted on your travels. A number of local dishes use spicy peanut sauce, among them **pecel** (peanut sauce with spinach and beansprouts), **lotek** (peanut sauce with vegetables and pressed rice) and the fun-filled, fleshy **rujak cingur** (peanut sauce with cow skin and lips).

Oseng-oseng is a dish of fried kangkung, yard-long beans and soy sauce. It can also be with meat: **ayam** (chicken) makes **oseng-oseng ayam**. And be warned, **oseng-oseng jamur**, doesn't mean it comes with mushrooms … Fido beware. (see the boxed text Dog Food in the Staples & Specialities chapter). A local stirfry dish is **orak-arik** (vegetables fried with pepper; beaten egg is added at the end).

Two coconut curries to try are **tengkleng** (goat curry with coconut milk and all parts of the goat) and the very popular **opor ayam** (chicken in pepper and coconut curry; see the recipe).

A few dishes of Central and East Java make use of **kluwek**, a seed used to add an earthy flavour. Kluwek also darkens the colour of dishes, and this is no more noticeable than with **rawon** (beef stew with kluwek) and **brongkos** (beef and bean stew with kluwek).

Numerous towns have signature soups, including Kudus' **soto Kudus** (chicken and egg soup), Pekalongan's **soto Pekalongan** (tripe and soy soup) and Tegal's **soto Tegal** (beef and noodle soup). Tegal is also known for clay-pot dishes such as **garang asam** (chicken offal, spices, starfruit and coconut milk cooked in a clay pot) and warming **teh poci** (jasmine tea with rock sugar brewed in a clay pot).

The Javanese word for drink is **wedang**, and you'll find such dessert drinks as **wedang kacang** (coconut milk drink with nuts) and **wedang dongo** (coconut milk drink with black rice-flour jelly drops).

DON'T MISS – Java

- Java's jackfruit curry (pictured)
- Exploring fertile fields on the slopes of volcanoes
- The fresh flavours of Sundanese cuisine
- Streetside dining in Yogyakarta or Solo
- A late-night snack of sate Madura

East Java

The eastern portion of Java stretches out into a terrain of serpentine rivers and traditional rice-farming villages, occasionally broken by rugged volcanoes, plateaus and national parks. The scenery changes dramatically around the capital of Surabaya, an extremely hot port city, second in size only to Jakarta.

As well as sharing the Javanese language, there is a lot of crossover between Central and East Javanese cuisine, so in East Java you'll easily find dishes like rawon and pecel. In fact the best pecel is said to come from the town of Madiun.

The northern coast provides East Javanese cooks with a range of fish and shellfish so they can cook up such dishes as **sate kerang** (clam). Fish also spawn from the rivers or are propagated in the rice fields. Such is the case with **lele** (catfish), which you'll see flipping in buckets next to stalls serving **pecel lele**, deep-fried catfish served with rice and **pecel** (spicy sauce made from chilli, peanuts and/or tomato; not to be confused with the nutty dish of the same name).

Much of East Java was used by the Dutch to grow such cash crops as coffee and cloves, and their influence can be seen in the hill town of Malang. Although it has the congestion of any Indonesian city, the temperature here is cooler and the markets, Dutch-style buildings and tree-lined streets make it a pleasant place to hang. Malang specialities include **bakwan malang** (meatball soup with fried wonton and noodles) and **arem-arem** (a mix of pressed rice, tempe, sprouts, soy sauce, coconut and peanuts).

The town of Lamongan is famous for its **soto Lamongan** (chicken soup with noodles, soybean leaves, turmeric and lemongrass). It is served with rice and potato fritters for you to mix into the soup.

The Mt Bromo National Park, with its spectacular volcanic landscape, may be East Java's premier tourist attraction, but there are plenty of other regions worth exploring. Both Jember and Kalibaru are fresh hill towns surrounded by superb scenery and a number of coffee, clove and cacao plantations that you can visit.

Madura

There are three million Madurese living on the hot craggy island of Madura, however there are around ten million living in other areas of Indonesia. The Madurese have a reputation for being forthright and entrepreneurial, and whether it's true or not, the Madurese have successfully introduced the rest of the country to two very popular dishes. One is **soto Madura** made with beef (any part thereof), lime, pepper, peanuts, chilli and ginger; the other is **sate Madura**, sate served with rice and a sweet and spicy soy sauce (see the boxed text A Sate Tour in the Staples & Specialities chapter).

Bali

Lush, green Bali is often held up as an example of tourism gone wrong, of a paradise lost and a people corrupted by the foreign dollar. But it doesn't take long much to see that all the reasons for Bali becoming so popular are still here to be found. Yes the rampant development and dollar hunt is apparent, but so is the stunning scenery, self-assured people and rich culture that lured sailors from their homeward journey in empire days and still lures visitors today.

For many visitors, Bali *is* Indonesia. In fact Bali is in many ways a country unto itself. The Balinese are predominantly Hindu, and although there are pockets of Hindu communities in other parts of the country (such as Java, where a few isolated communities remained in the mountains when Islam took over) it is in Bali that Hinduism thrives, colouring every facet of daily life. You'll see lines of women walking to temples carrying towering fruit offerings on their heads, you'll see bamboo pockets of rice, flowers and incense placed at the front of houses for protection, you'll even see buses blessed with a sprinkle of water before they hurtle down the road.

Balinese specialities are often difficult to find as it's presumed that tourists won't like the spicier and unashamedly fleshy flavours. Even when specialities are dished up they are often tempered for foreign palates; ghoulies such as blood are omitted from dishes like **lawar** (salad of chopped coconut, garlic, chilli, along with pork or chicken meat and blood). A more popular dish with visitors is **bebek betutu** (duck stuffed with spices, wrapped in banana leaves and coconut husks and cooked in a pit of embers). Other dishes that use banana leaves in the process are **tom** (duck, chicken or their livers cooked with spices in a banana leaf) and **pepes ayam** (spiced chicken cooked in a banana leaf). The local version of sate, called **sate lilit**, is made with minced, spiced meat that's pressed onto skewers (see the boxed text Balinese Birthday in the Celebrating chapter).

The grandest Balinese dish is **babi guling** (spit-roast pig), which is stuffed with chilli, turmeric, garlic and ginger, the skin smothered in turmeric. This is a long and laborious dish made for special occasions, however there are restaurants that make one babi guling and serve it throughout the day. Gianyar is famous for its babi guling, as is Ubud's Ibu Oka (see the boxed text Ibu Oka in the Staples & Specialities chapter). And wherever you find pig in Bali (which is pretty well everywhere) you'll also find **oret** (sausage) made with offal, blood and coconut.

In Denpasar, vegetarians should keep a look out for **serombotan**, (a mix of beansprouts, yard-long beans, and coconut). But over in the north of Bali, things get hard for the vegetarian. In Singaraja they love their lawar as well as the piggy favourite, **siobak** (minced pig's head, stomach, tongue and skin cooked with spices). Above Singaraja in the beautiful hill town of Munduk

Hindu offerings, Bali

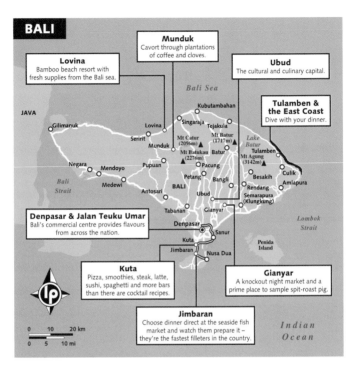

BALI

Lovina
Bamboo beach resort with fresh supplies from the Bali sea.

Munduk
Cavort through plantations of coffee and cloves.

Ubud
The cultural and culinary capital.

Tulamben & the East Coast
Dive with your dinner.

Bali Sea

JAVA

Gilimanuk
Lovina
Singaraja
Kubutambahan
Tejakula
Seririt
Munduk
Mt Catur (2096m)
Mt Batur (1717m)
Lake Batur
Tulamben
Mt Batukau (2276m)
Batur
Mt Agung (3142m)
Culik
Negara
Mendoyo
Pupuan
Pacung
Besakih
Amlapura
Petang
Bangli
Rendang
Bali Strait
Medewi
Antosari
BALI
Ubud
Semarapura (Klungkung)
Tabanan
Gianyar
Lombok Strait
Denpasar
Sanur
Penida Island
Kuta
Jimbaran
Nusa Dua

Denpasar & Jalan Teuku Umar
Bali's commercial centre provides flavours from across the nation.

Kuta
Pizza, smoothies, steak, latte, sushi, spaghetti and more bars than there are cocktail recipes.

Gianyar
A knockout night market and a prime place to sample spit-roast pig.

Jimbaran
Choose dinner direct at the seaside fish market and watch them prepare it – they're the fastest filleters in the country.

Indian Ocean

0   10   20 km
0   5   10 mi

they make a sharp-tasting chicken soup, **timbungan bi siap**, made with minced chicken, tamarind, brown sugar and starfruit leaves for a bitter touch. If you have a cold, this soup will knock it out. Munduk is also a great place to explore rice, clove and coffee plantations; all homestays in the area can arrange guides.

As well as providing rice, Bali's rice fields provide locals with eels and frogs. Dragonflies are another rice field-dweller up for grabs – they're caught with sticky sticks and then roasted.

The Balinese make a wide range of rice-flour snacks, including **lak lak** (a small pancake with palm sugar and coconut) and **alam** (rice flour, sugar and pandan leaf cooked in a banana leaf cylinder). (For more Balinese specialities see the boxed texts Balinese Birthday and Balinese Offerings in the Celebrating chapter.)

It can't be denied that the foreign influx has changed the face of Bali, but every country that looks to tourism for sustenance has an ugly side, replete with neon and pushy people. Where there was once a rice field there's now a guest house, and where there was once a guest house there's now a hotel complex. Anything you want can be found here: tickets, Rolex watches, hair braids, massage and more. And regarding food, well what do you feel like? There is a surfeit of bamboo restaurants serving pizza and smoothies, steaks and latte. There are sushi bars, spaghetti houses and Ronald on a surfboard. And for drinking, there are more bamboo bars than there are cocktail mixes. There is, however, an element of Kuta that hasn't changed since when it was a fishing village. Squeezed between a surf bar and a music store you'll notice a warung dishing out rice meals to local traders on their break, at the back of a cafe you'll notice one of the staff folding together coconut leaves to form a **sampyan** (decorative offering). Dodging traffic on Poppies Lane you'll see a **bakso** (meatball soup) seller making a five-bowl delivery (follow him to the source; it must be top bakso). Behind a sunglasses stall you'll see a girl in a sarong and yellow sash sprinkling water on a Hindu altar.

And you don't have to walk far from Jalan Legian (the main drag) before the tourist restaurants give way to authentic Indonesian eateries. Southward along Jalan Raya Kuta there's a glut of choice, or betake yourself to the stretch of restaurants along Jl Teuku Umar, between Kuta and Denpasar. Stretched out on either side of the road for a kilometre or so are regional restaurants serving their regional best. You'll find West Javanese restaurants dishing up **karedok** (Sundanese Salad; see the recipe), Betawi restaurants providing the meat lovers **soto betawi** (soup with every part of the cow, including the marrow) there are Madurese food stalls, Palembang places, Lombok eateries and numerous Padang restaurants. Sorry to say this isn't a picturesque stroll; the traffic here is manic and not every business is food focused, nevertheless Jl Teuku Umar is a fine place to familiarise yourself with the nation's cuisine and suspect traffic laws. Just follow your stomach, but make sure it looks before crossing the road.

DON'T MISS – Bali

- The colour and beauty of Bali's Hindu culture
- Spit-roast pig with all the trimmings
- Wandering the wondrous rice fields
- The cultural and culinary delight of Ubud
- Seaside dining at sunset

Squeezed between Kuta and the airport is the fishing district of Jimbaran. A while back one of Jimbaran's fisherfolk must have looked south to the airport, north to Kuta, down at his feet sinking into the white sand, across to that day's catch of snapper, prawn and other sea delicacies, and realised there was a rupiah to be made. These days the foreshore of Jimbaran is peppered with seafood restaurants, where you can look over buckets of seafood (snapper, barracuda, prawns and lobster for starters), make a choice then watch as it's deftly scaled, split, basted with garlic, lime and oil then roasted over a tray of burning coconut shells. Just before it's

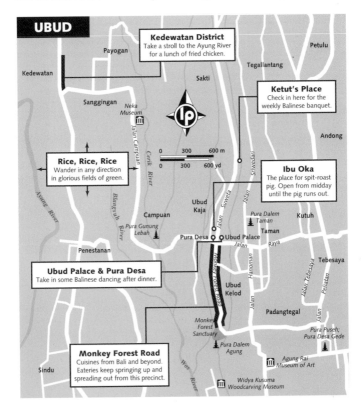

UBUD

Payogan

Kedewatan

Sanggingan

Kedewatan District
Take a stroll to the Ayung River for a lunch of fried chicken.

Sakti

Tegallantang

Petulu

Neka Museum

Ketut's Place
Check in here for the weekly Balinese banquet.

Andong

Rice, Rice, Rice
Wander in any direction in glorious fields of green.

Jalan Campuan

Cerik River

0   300   600 m
0   300   600 yd

Sriwedari

Ibu Oka
The place for spit-roast pig. Open from midday until the pig runs out.

Ayung River

Blangsuh River

Campuan

Ubud Kaja

Jalan Suweta

Pura Dalem Taman

Kutuh

Pura Gunung Lebah

Pura Desa   Ubud Palace

Taman

Penestanan

Jalan   Raya

Tebesaya

Ubud Palace & Pura Desa
Take in some Balinese dancing after dinner.

Monkey Forest Road

Ubud Kelod

Jalan Hanoman

Jalan Tebesaya

Jalan Peliatan

Padangtegal

Sindu

Monkey Forest Sanctuary

Pura Dalem Agung

Agung Rai Museum of Art

Pura Puseh; Pura Desa Gede

Monkey Forest Road
Cuisines from Bali and beyond. Eateries keep springing up and spreading out from this precinct.

Wos River

Widya Kusuma Woodcarving Museum

ready, the cook smothers the seafood in a blend of tomato, candlenut, chilli (not too much – they temper it for a foreign threshold), garlic, palm sugar, pepper, salt and oil. Take a seat at one of the tables on the beach (or on the beach itself) and while gorging you can watch the lights of Jimbaran's fishing fleet flicker on the horizon, the lights of landing planes and the lightning overhead. A meal here is very very expensive by Indonesian standards, but if you're going to splurge in Bali, this is a good splurge choice.

The hill town of Ubud has managed to maintain a more relaxed atmosphere than it's fiery cousin Kuta. Yes there are touts and traffic, but the cooler climate and verdant surrounds seem to placate the locals and visitors alike. Ubud is the perfect place to immerse yourself in Balinese dancing, painting, lan-

Sunset dining in Jimbaran, Bali

guage and food. You can partake in cooking courses at a number of restaurants where you learn to make Indonesian and Balinese dishes (cooking courses come and go, check with the Tourist Information office for details). Although the tourist restaurants outnumber the local eateries, there are a few places peppered around Ubud where you can sample the local cuisine.

Some restaurants cook up bebek betutu, but often you have to order a day in advance. Locals flock to the restaurant run by Ibu Oka, where Ibu Oka herself makes her popular **babi guling** (spit-roast pig; see the boxed text Ibu Oka in the Staples & Specialities chapter). There's also two eateries west of Ubud in Kedewatan that are famous for their memorably spicy **ayam goreng** (fried chicken). It'll take about an hour to walk there from central Ubud, but if you take back paths, a stroll to Kedewatan can be a rewarding luncheon outing, and check out the Ayung River after your meal.

Sumatra

Tumbling down the western side of the Malay Peninsula, the island of Sumatra holds enough room for cities as well as remote communities, and enough verdant terrain to satisfy the rich, often meat-heavy dishes of the region. Sumatra has always been home of a proud and independent people, and this is no more so than at the northern tip of the island, the homeland of the Acehnese, whose struggle for independence has produced both suffering within, and consolidation of, their community. The north of the island is home of the rich, coconut curries that have become popular across the country. Moving toward the south, coconut-based dishes give way to sharper cleaner stocks and fruitier flavours, as the locals make the most of river creatures and funky vegetation (welcome to durian central). Then there's West Sumatra, home of the hearty, hefty flavours of Padang cuisine.

Aceh & North Sumatra

The province of Aceh is the most traditionally Muslim area of Indonesia, helped by the fact that it was the stepping stone of Arab traders in the 13th century. The influence of Arab, Persian and Indian traders can be found in the food, however flavours have now been adapted and developed to the point that they hold little resemblance to those of their place of origin, apart from the name of some dishes. This is the case with the popular range of coconut curry dishes known as **kare** (or **gulai**). These rich, coconut-based dishes are traditionally made with buffalo, beef, goat, fish or poultry but have been adopted and made with tofu, vegetables and jackfruit in other regions. Here, however, curries remain predominantly meaty.

Although rice is as popular here as anywhere, there are a few doughy specialities worth sampling. The first is **roti jala** (literally, bread net), fried threads of batter that are eaten with curry. The second is **bika ambon**, a cake made with egg, sugar, tapioca flour, coconut milk and palm wine added both for flavour and to act as a rising agent. Aceh and North Sumatra also produce a wide range of cakes and pastries that go perfectly

DON'T MISS – Sumatra

- Hearty curries such as rendang (pictured)
- Padang cuisine – the national favourite
- The funky flavours of Palembang
- Crafty coffee concoctions
- Fish fresh from Lake Maninjau

Shopping in Pasar Bawah, Bukittinggi, Sumatra

with a cup of local coffee.
Speaking of which, you could
try the caffeine curiosity, **kopi
telur** (a raw egg and sugar
creamed together in a glass and
topped up with coffee).

The hill town of Brastagi is
famed for its fertile farms that
once supplied the Dutch with
carrots and other foods familiar
to Europe. These days the markets are still piled with euro
veggies, but are also a good
source for plump avocados,
tomatoes and the local fruity
flagship **markisa** (passionfruit)
that's made into cordial and
sold across the country. Of
course it's better eaten in its
natural state.

Moving into the centre of
the island you will find the
Batak people, a distinct cultural
enclave whose origins are said

The market gardens of Brastagi, Sumatra

to lie with the mountain tribes of Thailand and Myanmar. Forced out by
invading Mongolians and Siamese, the Batak travelled to Sumatra and set-
tled in the stunning yet hard-to-traverse mountainous region of Lake Toba,
where they lived separated from other communities for centuries. Despite
the impact of tourism, the result of isolation is still very apparent in their
religion (Bataks have adopted Christianity but traditional belief systems
remain strong) and food. The biggest difference between Bataks and most
other Sumatrans is their taste for pig and, to a lesser extent, dog (see the
boxed text Dog Food in the Staples & Specialities chapter). In fact there's
a suggestion that the name Batak was a name coined by Muslims meaning
'pig eater'. Pig or dog finds its way into the rich, meaty Batak dish,
sangsang. Pork also features in **babi panggang**, made by boiling pork in
vinegar and pig blood along with spices then roasting it. Another bloody
delicacy is **ayam namargota** (chicken cooked in spices and blood). Yes it's
all pretty ghoulish here in the Batak kitchen. And what's more they use a
local, mouth-numbing pepper called **lada rimba** (jungle pepper) in many
dishes. An acquired taste if ever there was one.

West Sumatra

About 600 years ago one of the Javanese kings ordered the people of West Sumatra to surrender their fertile, volcanic land. The locals, not wanting to give up so easily, challenged the Javanese to a buffalo fight. The Javanese pitted their strongest beast, but the West Sumatrans put their money on a weeny calf. When it came to the fight, the calf ran to the bull and nuzzled under its belly in search for milk. A moment later the Javanese bull groaned loudly and keeled over, its stomach dripping with blood. The Sumatran calf had had spikes attached to its horns and, hungry, had unwittingly speared the bull. Amazed, the onlookers cried "Minangkabau!" (the buffalo wins) inadvertently giving the local people a new name.

Ever since the buffalo knockout, buffaloes have played an important role in the proud and prevalent Minangkabau culture that, although Muslim, remains matriarchal. The roofs of traditional houses are shaped like buffalo horns, as are traditional headdresses worn on special occasions. Buffaloes are also of course valued for their ability to plough ricefields, as well as a source of milk and meat: the most famous Minangkabau dish being **rendang** (beef or buffalo coconut curry; see the recipe). In fact when Indonesians think of Sumatran cuisine they automatically think of the food that comes from the Minangkabau region: Padang cuisine (Padang is the capital of West Sumatra). This is Indonesia's own imperial cuisine, and in Indonesia a town isn't a town if there isn't a Padang restaurant to be

Grinding coffee in a river-powered pounder, Sumatra

REGIONAL VARIATIONS

Kapau cuisine at Bukittinggi's Pasar Atas, Sumatra

found – proof also of the Minangkabau people's business acumen. As well as rendang, there are hundreds of dishes to try in a Padang restaurant, most of them spicy, meaty and robust. Nowhere else in Indonesia is the cuisine so reflective of the people and place: West Sumatra is a fertile and less-populated region, so it's able to cater to the proud and hard-working Minangkabau's love of abundant fleshy dishes. Naturally enough there's a surfeit of Padang restaurants in the city of Padang itself, but good Padang food can be had absolutely anywhere across the archipelago (see the boxed text A Padang Selection and Padang Restaurants in the Where to Eat & Drink chapter).

Padang cuisine may be West Sumatra's culinary superstar, but there are plenty of other edible delights worth tracking down. The market in the hill town of Bukittinggi is a great place to sample **nasi Kapau** (cuisine originally from the village of Kapau). This culinary style is similar to Padang Food, however Nasi Kapau uses more vegetables and flavours dishes with shallot shoots and garlic. Everyday in Bukittinggi's Pasar Atas (Upper Market), Nasi Kapau sellers offer meals complete with **temusu** (cow-skin sausage with a filling of spiced egg), **ubi rendang** (diced sweet potato cooked in coconut milk and spices then deep fried; like rendang, it is cooked until dark), **sayur kapau** (cabbage, jackfruit and shallot shoots

Sunday morning at Bukittinggi's Pasar Bawah, Sumatra

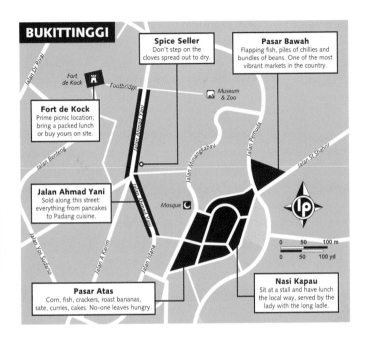

BUKITTINGGI

Spice Seller
Don't step on the cloves spread out to dry.

Pasar Bawah
Flapping fish, piles of chillies and bundles of beans. One of the most vibrant markets in the country.

Fort de Kock

Footbridge

Museum & Zoo

Fort de Kock
Prime picnic location; bring a packed lunch or buy yours on site.

Jalan Ahmad Yani
Sold along this street: everything from pancakes to Padang cuisine.

Mosque

0   50   100 m
0   50   100 yd

Pasar Atas
Corn, fish, crackers, roast bananas, sate, curries, cakes. No-one leaves hungry.

Nasi Kapau
Sit at a stall and have lunch the local way, served by the lady with the long ladle.

Jalan Dr Rival · Jalan Benteng · Jalan Yos Sudarso · Jalan A Karim · Jalan Istana · Jalan Ahmad Yani · Jalan Minangkabau · Jalan Pemuda · Jalan St Shahrir

---

cooked in coconut milk) and **pange** (fish stuffed with spiced egg). Ramadan is a fine time to be in Bukittinggi as at the end of each day's fast, big mamas set up Nasi Kapau stalls in the streets around the market and serve their fare to the ravenous.

Sate is also popular in West Sumatra, and here the skewered meat is served with pressed rice and a smooth peanut sauce. This type of sate is sold all over Indonesia as **sate Padang**.

Other regional specialities include two delicious sweet dishes that are perfect for a rainy Bukittinggi day (most days really). These are **ampiang dadiah** (buffalo yoghurt with palm sugar syrup, coconut flesh and rice) and **bubur kampiun** (mung-bean porridge with banana, rice yoghurt and a crème caramel-like custard).

For snacks you can't go past the exhaustive range of **kerupuk** (generic term for fried crackers) and you'll kick yourself if you don't sample the upper market's **pisang bakar** (grilled bananas).

Many travel agencies offer cultural tours of the Bukittinggi area that, although not solely focused on food, offer you a window on Minangkabau village life. As part of the tour you'll visit small-scale plantations, where farmers set out cinnamon and cloves to dry. You'll see lush rice terraces framed by banana palms, their bulbous red flowers stark against the green terrain. But the culinary highlight of this tour is the coffee mill at Batu Sangkar. Here the coffee beans are grown, roasted and ground all in the one place. Water is siphoned off from up the hill and irrigated into of aqueducts to power an old-fashioned water-wheel on the side of a hut. Inside is a line of wooden pounders that rise and fall like the pistons on a V8 engine. The hut is only really big enough for the grinder and two old women who sift and package the ground coffee. The women sit at the base of the grinder, risking their fingers each time they collect the powdered coffee from underneath the pounders. The whole hut rattles and clatters rhythmically as the coffee beans are ground down to a rich, dark powder, ready for market.

Not far from Bukittinggi and the coast at the gloriously blue Lake Maninjau, things get decidedly more fishy. The snack of choice here is **pengsi Maninjau** (cockles with a chilli sauce). And the fish here is as fresh as any: while dining on **ikan bakar** (grilled fish) you can peruse the bobbing boats that caught your fish moments before.

Lake Maninjau, Sumatra

South Sumatra

South Sumatra is a land of industry. Cash crops of pepper, palms and pineapples stretch for miles, and the capital of Palembang is an industrial hub complete with a port and pollution. The city is, however, home of the cuisine that's enjoyed across the region and beyond for its sour, spicy flavours. The most famous of Palembang's culinary offerings is **pempek** (deep-fried fish and sago dumpling; also called **empek-empek**). This is made by mixing the flesh of knife fish from the Musi River with sago flour. The resulting stodgy white mix is used in a multitude of pempek variations including **kapal selam** (pempek with a boiled egg inside) and is served swimming in **cuka** (literally, vinegar; sauce made with chillies, palm sugar, garlic, vinegar and soy sauce). Other specialities using the same mix include **tekwan** (small pempek dumplings and seaweed in a mildly sweet stock) and **lenggang** (chopped pempek combined in an omelette). Pempek is easy enough to find throughout Indonesia, but too often the dish on offer is chewy and bland, especially if they don't fry it in front of you.

South Sumatra is also home of fresh soup preparations known as **pindang** (spicy clear fish soup with water-based stock, soy and tamarind). Things get decidedly fruitier with **ikan brengkes** (fish in a spicy durian-based sauce), **tempoyak** (an accompaniment of shrimp paste, lime juice, chilli and fermented durian) and **sambal buah** (chilli sauce made with fruit such as pineapple or green mango). Sugar fiends will swoon over Palembang's favourite sweet snack, **srikaya** (green custard of sticky rice, sugar, coconut milk and egg). These sugar hits are served in weeny cups so, although rich, one is never enough.

Pindang, the South Sumatran speciality

Nusa Tenggara: Lombok, Sumbawa, Komodo & Rinca, Flores, Solor & Alor Archipelagos, Sumba, Roti & Sabu, West Timor

Eastward beyond the crowds of Bali stretch the string of islands known as Nusa Tenggara (literally, the South-East Islands). The terrain, people and cultures of this archipelago vary greatly both between and within the islands. In Flores alone there are five main language and cultural groups: Manggari, Ngada, Ende and Lio, Sikkanese and Lamaholot. The majority of people across Nusa Tenggara have adopted Islam or Christianity, however traditional belief systems remain strong and customs such as animal sacrifices continue (see the boxed text Death of the Party in the Celebrating chapter). This is also the region where the population's transition from Malay to Melanesian is most apparent. Add to this diversity the influence of cultures from other regions by way of invasion, trade and transmigration and you have a thoroughly mixed stock in the Nusa Tenggara pot. Consequently there are very few dishes that are distinct to any of the islands. The further east you travel in Nusa Tenggara the drier it gets, and as a result you'll eat less rice and more sago, corn, cassava and taro. Fish of course remains popular and in some areas subsistence whaling continues, such as on the Solor & Alor Archipelagos. One dish difficult to find elsewhere is Sumbawa's **sepat**, a tart-tasting dish of shredded fish in a sour sauce of coconut and young mango. Sumbawa is also renowned for its honey.

People come to the scraggly islands of Komodo and Rinca not to see what the locals eat, but what eats the locals. This is the domain of the **ora** (Komodo dragon), a massive monitor lizard with a taste for anything meaty, humans included. They can even down a water buffalo. Locals don't eat the dragons, preferring to steer clear and go after other wildlife on the island and fish in the surrounding seas.

The Sasak people of Lombok are predominantly Muslim, so the porky plethora found on Bali gives way to a diet of fish, chicken, vegetables and rice. In fact rice here is of the finest quality, yet the drier climate means that sometimes only one crop can be produced a year.

DON'T MISS – Nusa Tenggara

- Dining with a Komodo dragon
- Such spicy Sasak food as ayam Taliwang and pelecing
- Island hopping to Irian
- Azure waters teeming with fish

Collecting Kangkung in Lombok

Lombok's stocky **lumbung** (rice barns) are a symbol of prosperity on the island and you'll see them everywhere, although they're used less for rice storage and more as an architectural style for tourist accommodation.

The fact that **lombok** means 'chilli' in Indonesian makes sense as Sasaks like their food spicy, as with **ayam Taliwang** (whole split chicken roasted over coconut husks served with a peanut, tomato chilli and lime dip). This dish takes its name from the town of Taliwang on Sumbawa but it is a Lombok speciality.

The spicy sauce called **peleting**, made with chilli, shrimp paste and tomato is used liberally to make vegetable or chicken dishes. **Sares** is a dish made with chilli, coconut juice and banana palm pith; sometimes it's mixed with chicken or meat. Three non-meat dishes are **kelor** (hot soup with kangkung and/or other vegetables), **serebuk** (vegetables mixed with grated coconut) and **timun urap** (sliced cucumber with grated coconut, onion and garlic).

Ayam Taliwang, the Lombok speciality

Kalimantan

The Indonesian section of the island of Borneo, shared with Malaysia and Brunei, is fed and fuelled by an extensive system of waterways. On these rivers you'll see the transportation of timber, coal, pigs, locals heading to big towns looking for work and travellers heading from big towns looking for Kalimantan. There's a lot of money being made here from mining, logging and cash crops, and the wealth the region produces can easily be seen in cities such as Pontianak and Balikpapan. The image of Kalimantan being

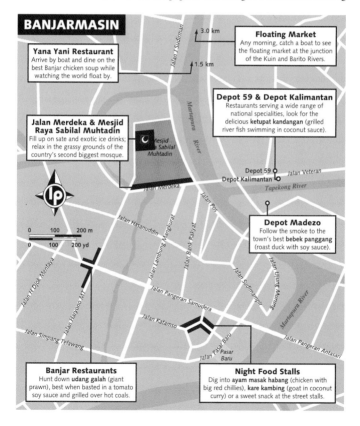

BANJARMASIN

Floating Market
Any morning, catch a boat to see the floating market at the junction of the Kuin and Barito Rivers.

Yana Yani Restaurant
Arrive by boat and dine on the best Banjar chicken soup while watching the world float by.

Depot 59 & Depot Kalimantan
Restaurants serving a wide range of national specialities, look for the delicious **ketupat kandangan** (grilled river fish swimming in coconut sauce).

Jalan Merdeka & Mesjid Raya Sabilal Muhtadin
Fill up on sate and exotic ice drinks; relax in the grassy grounds of the country's second biggest mosque.

Mesjid Raya Sabilal Muhtadin

Depot 59 — *Jalan Veteran*
Depot Kalimantan
Tapekong River

Depot Madezo
Follow the smoke to the town's best **bebek panggang** (roast duck with soy sauce).

Jalan I Sudirman
Marupura River
Jalan Merdeka
Jalan Hasanuddin
Jalan Lambung Mangkurat
Jalan Bank Rakyat
Jalan Pos
Jalan Sudirmanpir
Jalan Ujung Murung
Marupura River
Jalan H Djok Mentaya
Jalan Hasjiono MT
Jalan Simpang Telawang
Jalan Pangeran Samudera
Jalan Katamso
Jalan Pasar Baru
Pasar Baru
Jalan Pangeran Antasari

0   100   200 m
0   100   200 yd

Banjar Restaurants
Hunt down **udang galah** (giant prawn), best when basted in a tomato soy sauce and grilled over hot coals.

Night Food Stalls
Dig into **ayam masak habang** (chicken with big red chillies), **kare kambing** (goat in coconut curry) or a sweet snack at the street stalls.

3.0 km
1.5 km

REGIONAL VARIATIONS

rainforests and forest dwellers may still exist, but it's being destroyed at an alarming rate so as to feed, in the words of biologist Galdikas, "the spiritual vacuum concomitant with an increasingly global pop-culture endorsing instant gratification".

Kalimantan is home to a wide cross-section of people: Jakarta businessmen, mining expats and Javanese transmigrants have all made their home on the island. There is also a large Chinese-Indonesian community that has been here for a long time, as Kalimantan has been on trade routes since the time of Christ. With this steady influx has come a wide range of foods, from gado-gado to KFC, but for traditional Kalimantan cuisine we look to the kitchens of the indigenous Dayak and Banjar peoples.

The term 'Dayak' is not used by the people themselves, who prefer to use the specific name of each of the 20 different indigenous tribes such as Kenyah, Iban and Punan. It takes time, money and more time to visit traditional Dayak areas as villages are located deep in the interior, in hard to reach areas that are yet to be destroyed by loggers. As well as performing slash-and-burn agriculture, Dayak people have an incredible knowledge of forest vegetation, and it's from here that they obtain honey, fruit, vegetables and wildlife such as wild pig. Your opportunity to eat traditional Dayak food will probably occur within a traditional long house, as Dayak eateries are all but nonexistent. You may even have to insist on trying traditional

DON'T MISS – Kalimantan

- A thousand sweet treats to have with your tea including green pare-pare (pictured)

- Shopping at a floating market

- Trekking through rainforests (while they still exist)

- Cruising the rivers of Banjarmasin

- Brash Banjar flavours and massive prawns

foods since the locals will presume you want more familiar noodle or rice dishes. Of course Dayak food varies depending on the area each tribe lives in – you may sample **rembang**, a sour fruit that is made into a vegetable soup called **sayur asam rembang**. Bamboo roots are another source of sustenance, as are the top shoots of the rotan plant.

In the South Kalimantan capital of Banjarmasin, the local Banjar people live a moist existence. Their town is criss-crossed by a labyrinth of rivers and canals that not only have made the city a commercial centre, but act as a transport system, laundry, bathroom, playground, market and food source. Banjar houses line the waterways perched on stilts or float with the tides on bundles of logs, Banjar kiddies hurl themselves into the water for fun or are hurled in by their parents to keep clean, and the ingredients for Banjar cuisine are caught and sold from the traffic of bobbing boats. Luckily the Banjar love their freshwater fish and shellfish and you'll find many local restaurants grilling these creatures after basting them in a tomato soy sauce – this is one of the best ways to try **cumi-cumi** (squid) and massive **udang galah** (giant prawns). The local version of **pepes ikan** (spiced fish cooked in banana leaves; see the recipe) uses tamarind and lemongrass, all over and in the fish. The northern town of Kandangan has given the region **ketupat kandangan**, broiled river fish and pressed rice swimming in coconut sauce flavoured with lime. The fish used in this dish is **harawan** (snakehead; also called **gabus**) which has a very meaty, almost salami-like flavour. Indeed the Banjar love fleshy flavours and if they're not eating river life, some other animal has probably been put in the pot. The regional soup, **soto Banjar**, is a chicken broth made creamy by mashing and mixing boiled eggs into the stock. It's served with either rice or pressed rice, and extra flavour is added with soy, lime and chilli. Chicken also goes into **ayam masak habang**, cooked with large red chillies that impart a warm sweet flavour. Dishes such as **kare kambing** (goat in coconut curry) and **bebek panggang** (roast duck with soy sauce; also made with chicken) may be available elsewhere, but the Banjar versions are rightfully well known. And just to make you squirm, the locals enjoy eating **telur puyuh** (turtle eggs). They're the things that look – and taste like – ping pong balls.

Sugar freaks will have a field day in Banjarmasin trying the multitude of little local sweeties known as **ampar tatak** (literally, cut plate). These are moist treats that come in a range of shapes, colours and flavours, including **pare-pare** (green rice-flour sweet with a palm sugar filling), **srikaya nangka** (made with jackfruit) and **bingka kentang** (made with potato). Even beyond the ampar tatak selection there are sweet snacks such as **apam** (small palm sugar pancakes) and **pisang goreng** (fried bananas) sold from tea stalls everywhere, on land and water. (For more on Banjarmasin's river life see the Shopping & Markets chapter).

Sulawesi

Possibly the world's most stupidly shaped island, with tentacles of land reaching deep into the surrounding seas, Sulawesi was for many years thought to be a cluster of islands. But this Freudian doodle of a landmass is an island, and is home ofto a diverse range of people with equally diverse tastes. Southern Sulawesi is home of the Makassar, whose wide-reaching history and influence hinges on their skill as sailors. Similarly the Minahasans of North Sulawesi have had continuous contact with outside cultures, notably those of the nearby Philippines. In contrast the Torajans of the impenetrable mountainous interior preserved their culture well into the 20th century.

With so much coast and so many bubbling rivers, fish and other aquatic creatures are big on the menu throughout Sulawesi. Grouper, catfish, tuna and eel are just some of many species that could end up grilled, baked or swimming in your soup.

South Sulawesi

The Makassar empire extended throughout Indonesia and spread their influence as far as Australia, where their boats are even depicted in the Aboriginal rock paintings of Kakadu. The best known of their seafarers are the Bugis people, many of whom became pirates, and whose name is said to have entered the English language as the much feared 'Boogymen'. Even today the Makassar are renowned seafarers, and their high-boughed schooners can be seen in harbours across the country. While back on home

Coto Makassar

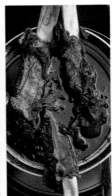

Sop konro

Es Pallubutun

turf the locals love nothing more than to feast on **ikan bakar** (grilled fish), pepes ikan and anything else the sea can dish up. Moving away from marine life the locals also indulge in **coto Makassar**, a warming soup made with beef offal, pepper, cumin and lemongrass that's usually served with pressed rice and lime. Similarly meaty is **sop konro** (beef-rib soup with kluwek). For the sugar junkies, South Sulawesi provides saccharine bliss in the form of **es pallubutun** (coconut custard and bananas swimming in a mixture of coconut milk and syrup).

The sprawling capital of Ujung Pandang has been a commercial sea port for centuries and is home of a huge harbour, impressive Dutch fort and one of Indonesia's finest eating districts, Pantai Losari. The food stalls of Pantai Losari stretch along the city's shoreline and serve up everything from octopus to avocado juice. It's when dining on seafood and watching the sun sink over the Makassar Strait that you understand why the local sailors always come home.

Central Sulawesi – Tana Toraja

There are two things that Tana Toraja is famous for, and one of them is death. Sound morbid? The funerals of Tana Toraja are some of the most vivid and lively ceremonies still practised in Indonesia. The second thing Tana Toraja is famous for? Buffaloes. From the moment you arrive in the region, you'll be bombarded with buffalo. They're relaxing in every field, chatting in the streets. Where buffalo can't go, they are represented artistically and even architecturally.

Getting to Tana Toraja takes some planning as it's located in the central highlands of Sulawesi. But whether you come as part of a tour group or by crossing the waters on the good ship Awu (named for the sound you make when the seas get rough), you'll appreciate how distance has preserved the local culture.

The Dutch only gained control of the region in 1905, whereas most of Indonesia had been under Dutch control since the 17th century. Although Torajan culture did diminish under the influence of the Dutch Christian Reformed Church, much of the traditional culture has remained. And that's what people come to see: the traditional houses, the ceremonial funerals, the cliff-graves, and the buffaloes.

Among the verdant hills that surround the central town of Rantepao, buffalo horns can be seen thrusting 40 feet into the air. No they aren't actually buffalo horns, but the buffalo horn-shaped roofs of **tongkonan** (Torajan houses). These imposing structures are constructed without nails, instead beams are slotted together and supported by large poles that are decorated with real buffalo horns. The more horns, the higher the household's status. In fact every facet of the tongkonan holds cultural significance, from

Traditional house in Tana Toraja, Sulawesi

which way the house faces right down to the colours used for decoration. The interior walls are covered with engravings of buffaloes: buffaloes fighting, relaxing, doing their thing. These decorations are created by skilled artisans who are paid for their work with the traditional mode of currency: buffaloes.

The fact that buffaloes represent wealth is why they're so prevalent. The more buffalo you have, the higher your status. But a buffalo isn't just a buffalo. The quality of each buffalo is based upon size, colour, and the shape of its horns. You won't get much return with a standard grey buffalo in your wallet; but if your packing a **tedong bonga** (spotted buffalo), you can go places. The Torajans hold on to a buffalo debt system between families that goes back for generations. For most of the time, these debts are not acted upon. However, when a death occurs in the family it's time to cough up big time as the expense and grandeur of a Torajan funeral ceremony can often bankrupt a family.

Torajan funerals are more a colourful and extravagant party than a solemn occasion, and the public nature of the ceremony makes it a big attraction. Since it's believed that the deceased should enter heaven in a manner reflecting their wealth, buffaloes are slaughtered, often by the truckload. The procedure is considerably gruesome, acted out with a cane-knife by the children of the deceased. They're motivated by the fact that the more buffaloes they slaughter, the larger the share of their parent's property they will receive. This is why before the funeral of an important family member, buffaloes can be seen lying in the rice-fields trying their hardest to look like ducks.

Much to the support of the buffalo population, there has been a move to reduce the number of buffaloes sacrificed at funerals over the years. During colonial times the Dutch put restrictions on how many buffaloes could be killed, and these days the government applies a tax for every head of buffalo sacrificed. Even so, killing buffaloes at funerals remains an intrinsic part of Torajan society.

Torajan funerals can last up to seven days and involve abundant food preparation. As well as serving buffalo meat, often in the form of **pamerasan** (buffalo meat in a black sauce), pigs are also killed and their meat stuffed into bamboo tubes along with vegetables and roasted over coals to produce the Torajan dish, **pa'piong**. This dish can also be made with chicken or fish. The food is distributed to all present, along with **balok** (palm wine; also called **tuak**) which can range in flavour (sweet to bitter) and colour (almost clear to red). Sticky-rice and rice-flour cakes are also distributed, including those made with the famous local brew, coffee (see Coffee Centres in the Drinks chapter).

Making pa'piong, a speciality of Central Sulawesi

As well as slaughtering animals, buffalo fights are staged, in which the normally placid creatures are revved up by having red chillies inserted up their backsides.

Once the funeral is over the remaining buffaloes can breathe a sigh of relief and get on with eating, ploughing and disassociating themselves from the elderly community. It can feel uncomfortable as an outsider to visit an area specifically to see the cultural aspects of death. But for the people of Tana Toraja death is a public aspect of life, and as long as outsiders treat it as a special occasion and not as a side show put on for their benefit, death can be a culturally enriching affair. No bull.

North Sulawesi

The northern tentacle of Sulawesi is home of some of the finest coastline in the country. Here the Minahasans use the land industriously for coconut, corn and cassava crops, and the healthy export market has made the region prosperous. The azure waters of North Sulawesi stretch toward the southern reaches of the Philippines and predictably enough fish is a dietary constant. A speciality here is **ikan panada**, a tuna pastry that was perhaps brought by Portuguese traders. But if you've had your fill of fish, the Minahasans have a few surprises for your taste buds. Are you up for some **kawaok** (fried forest rat) or **keluang** (fruit bat)? Or if you would prefer something more familiar ... woof! (see the boxed text Dog Food in the Staples & Specialities chapter).

If a dish has the name **rica-rica** it's prepared with a spicy paste of chilli, shallots, ginger and lime. Fish and chicken are popular versions. Things get extremely fishy with **bakasang**, a paste used for sambal and flavouring made by fermenting fish in a terracotta pot. It's used in **bubur tinotuan** (porridge made with corn, cassava, rice, pumpkin, fish paste and chilli). Minahasan cooking often uses a local herb called **daun gedi**, which gives the food a slimy texture. And to wash it all down there's **saguer**, a type of tuak made with sugar palm sap. It tastes like cider, but smells like sweet laundry powder.

Bubur tinotuan

Rica-rica

Maluku

Looking at these slow-paced, sun-drenched islands, it is hard to imagine that these are the islands which provoked European heavyweights to squabble, wage war and lose so much. The reason behind this is that these are the spice islands, the original home of cloves, nutmeg and mace (see the boxed text The Spice Race in the Culture chapter).

Now that the spices are found on dusty spice racks across the globe, the Maluku islands have more or less slipped into tropical obscurity, typified by the white, coconut fringed beaches. However, the main Maluku town of Ambon has tragically failed to avoid the unrest sparked by Indonesia's political upheaval.

The soil in this corner of Indonesia is nowhere near as fertile as verdant Bali or Java. Here coconuts, sago, taro, bananas, durian and cassava (used for both the leaves and the root) are the staple crops, along with leafy plants such as kangkung. The pith of the sago plant is used to make a wide variety of foods such as porridge, bread, and **mutiara** (moist sago tears; used in sweets and sweet drinks).

The food of Maluku is simple, and an easy meal of tuna and **dabu-dabu** (salad of raw vegetables such as beans and a chilli and fish paste sauce) is typical of the region. Sometimes fish is flavoured with **colo-colo** (sauce made with citrus fruit and chilli), or is made into **kohu-kohu** (fish salad with citrus fruit and chilli).

Neither cloves nor nutmeg feature much in Malukan cooking, but it's chewing cloves that keeps the local teeth so white, while clove cigarettes that makes their teeth yellow.

REGIONAL VARIATIONS

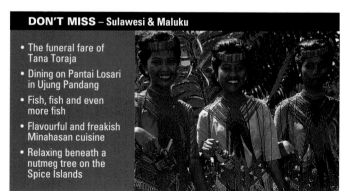

DON'T MISS – Sulawesi & Maluku

- The funeral fare of Tana Toraja
- Dining on Pantai Losari in Ujung Pandang
- Fish, fish and even more fish
- Flavourful and freakish Minahasan cuisine
- Relaxing beneath a nutmeg tree on the Spice Islands

Irian Jaya

The western part of New Guinea is a land of stunning mountainous terrain and enough cultural and sociolinguistic diversity to keep anthropologists scribbling notes for centuries. The coastal areas may have changed both culturally and culinarily with the influx of Indonesian migrants, but the interior highlands remain home to innumerable communities of Papuans, many of whom still wear traditional clothes such as grass skirts and penis gourds. The most well-known (and accessible) area is the Baliem Valley, home of a number of tribes collectively known as the Dani.

Nets to carry food, Baliem Valley, Irian Jaya

Here the sweet potato is king. The Dani grow around sixty varieties of this tuber, some of which can only be eaten by certain groups such as elders. Other plants such as sago palms are also cultivated in this rugged yet fertile region. As well as eating the pith, sago palms are sometimes left to rot so locals can collect and eat beetle grubs.

Chickens and pigs are also raised and on special occasions are cooked in earth ovens under hot rocks. In some areas the locals use pig fat to keep warm by smothering it on their bodies. Why they also put it in their hair is anyone's guess.

shopping

& markets

The **pasar** (market) is the nucleus of Indonesia. It's where every farmer's journey ends and where every meal begins. Yes, Indonesia's supermarkets and general stores stock many essentials, but for the serious shopper nothing can replace the fresh local produce and vibrant atmosphere of any market across the nation.

Markets

Many of Indonesia's markets are as you would have found them 100 years ago. Even central Jakarta's Pasar Senen food market, surrounded by modern shopping complexes and multi-lane highways, has an authentic air to it. This is mainly thanks to the fact that market laneways are so crammed with produce and people that cars and motorbikes cannot enter. And once you're in an aisle in the market, the roar of motors fade away, replaced with the more agreeable sounds of touting vendors and clucking chickens. Regulars may have their preferred sources – Bu Asti's yard-long beans are longer, the beef at Bu Didit's is freshly cut – but for us visitors, it's just a matter of roaming, smelling and surveying. Someone's bound to ask you where you're going, someone's bound to insist you buy a bag of chicken feet. Buy them if you want or just keep wandering, losing your way, tripping over beans and bumping into bag-laden grandmas. If overwhelmed, duck into a market warung for a coffee and a snack, then resume your market meandering.

And if the market is too far, it comes to you. Every morning vendors wheel their carts around residential streets selling a wide range of produce, from tomatoes to tempe. In the Kalimantan town of Banjarmasin the vendor does his round by boat, docking at riverside houses.

In larger towns markets are open every day (sometimes for 24 hours), but smaller places will have a specific market day. That's not to say the market isn't open other days, but with vendors coming in from faraway villages to sell their stock, market day really cranks.

Lively trade at Bukittinggi's Pasar Bawah, Sumatra

In Bekonang (near Solo), market day is still based on the Javanese calendar, occurring every six days. It's a small town but on market day the streets surrounding the market are thick with people and produce. The market itself spills out into the streets: fruit sold from the back of trucks, women roaming with bunches of garlic to sell, and just down the street the livestock market is in full swing.

Likewise, the Pasar Atas (Upper Market) in Bukittinggi is the town's life source. As its name suggests, the market sits at the highest point of the town, overlooking the spired roofs and surrounding mountains. From its vantage point, makeshift stalls and permanent shops trickle down laneways and steps into the surrounding suburbs. You can easily spend days in the labyrinthine market perusing the shoe stores, fabric shops and alarm clock stalls, but what will make you return again and again is the food on offer.

Kerupuk for sale in Mataram, Lombok

Bukittinggi market is a prime location for sampling Minangkabau specialities. There are lanes and lanes of stalls selling a wide range of **kerupuk** (generic term for fried crackers) that include **kerupuk jagung** (fried corn kernels), **kerupuk ubi** (sweet potato crisps) and **kerupuk kulit** (fried cow or buffalo skin; vegetarians beware as it looks deceptively like fried tofu). Tucked between fabric shops you'll be lured by the smoky aroma wafting from sate stalls. Probably less appealing are the shops selling **ikan asin** (salted fish) spread out on plastic sheets or piled up in baskets. A vendor may try to sell you a string of **belut asin** (dried baby eels) but a more immediately satisfying option is **jagung bakar**, a roasted cob of corn.

If you're after a full meal, head to the eastern side of the market where **Nasi Kapau** (Kapau village cuisine) stalls are in abundance (see West Sumatra in the Regional Variations chapter). Take a seat and watch as the woman perched above the food takes a selection of dishes and sauces from the surrounding pots with a long-handled spoon. Spare a thought for these women because, although they seem happy to sit up high talking with friends and passers-by, they would have been up since 3am preparing the day's dishes. Once you're full, grab a coffee from a nearby warung and watch as the afternoon rains roll in over the town.

After you've mustered enough energy, head back up through the market in search of **pisang bakar** (grilled bananas) the perfect after-dinner treat. Look for the old women grilling small bananas on chicken wire stretched over hot coals. Once cooked, the bananas are flattened in a wooden press then sprinkled with a palm sugar and coconut mixture. They're warm and sweet, but not too sweet. Even if you're full you'll find room for at least one, and once you've had one you'll want another. Best move on.

The eastern side of the market slopes down toward Jl Kemerdekaan (Independence St) and onto the Pasar Bawah (Lower Market). Take one of the many stairways down, but don't trip over the women selling bananas or dried fish on the steps. This market is where Bukittinggi buys its supplies. It is one of the most vivid, lively markets in Indonesia. Nearly all the produce is local, and the red chillies, bouquets of galangal, green beans, flapping fish and iridescently purple eggplants are a technicolour dream.

Even the meat market is worth lingering in. Normally the stench of butchered meat would be too oppressive, but here the flesh is cut daily and cooked by nightfall. Bukittinggi's market is open everyday until 6pm, but on Wednesday and Saturday, when out-of-towners come to sell their stuff, things really go ballistic.

In waterlogged Banjarmasin it makes sense to buy goods off the boat. It saves the farmers docking, unloading and restacking their goods. Better to choose a point on the river for people to converge and deal direct. This happens from

Kapau cuisine at Bukittinggi's Pasar Atas

SHOPPING & MARKETS

A floating soup seller, Banjarmasin

dawn every day at the junction of the Kuin and Barito Rivers, location of Banjarmasin's Pasar Terapung (Floating Market). Sellers travel for up to four hours to converge here and sell such goods as bananas, fish, yard-long beans, pumpkins and coconuts to anyone that paddles up. There's no real system, you just float around until you find what you're after. A lot of stuff here is bought in bulk to be sold on by grocers paddling along Banjarmasin's waterways from house to house.

When your shopping is done, look around for the floating soup seller or glide over to a **rombong** (floating warung). Here you'll find a selection of cakes and ready-to-go rice meals spread across the centre of the boat. The seller sits at the motor end with an urn between his legs, brewing up orders of coffee or tea. If you're hungry, look for the pole with a nail through its end, spike your snack of choice, then sit back with your breakfast and watch Banjarmasin's river life float by.

Delivering tomatoes, Sumatra

PASAR DEMANGAN, YOGYAKARTA

I first met Sum and Parin when I was 13 years old. They were housekeepers in the house we were renting. It was Sum who first introduced me to real Indonesian cooking: **gudeg** (jackfruit curry), **tempe kering** (sweet and crispy fried tempe) and other such memorable morsels. Her husband, Parin, also worked in the house, but the kitchen was Sum's domain. Sometimes we would go to the market with her and carry her bags while she picked over produce, squeezing avocados and complaining about the price. She would joke with the merchants about exchanging me for food. They would laugh, I would laugh, not knowing the joke was on me.

While visiting Sum and Parin, Sum decided to make a trip to the local market, Pasar Demangan, so we could make a lunch of **bacem** (tofu, tempe and/or chicken cooked in stock). Pasar Demangan is about 2km away, so we went by motorbike.

Although this is just a local market, one of many in Yogyakarta, the array of goods spilled out onto the surrounding footpaths. One step from where we parked the bike we could buy a ready-plucked chicken from a woman sitting on the ground next to a pile of poultry. Sum picked out a fresh clucker and the woman benignly chopped it up with a machete.

Next to the chicken lady was the tempe lady, and from her we bought six pieces wrapped in banana leaves. As we moved into the covered market, the sound of traffic on Jl Gejayan faded away, replaced by the hubbub of market commerce and tunes from roving musicians playing for loose change. In the centre of the aisles, people had set up stalls from which to sell young jackfruit, chillies, duck eggs and dried fish. Wherever there was space there was something to buy.

From one makeshift stall Sum lifted a piece of tofu and took a whiff. Still fresh, so she bagged half a kilo. We moved to the side of the market where, under a creaky shelter, sat a man surrounded by husked coconuts. We bought a bag of his shredded coconut flesh. Sum moved swiftly through the market, waving off beckoning sellers. I stumbled behind, chasing her to the chilli lady. While the chilli lady grabbed a handful of chillies, Sum picked through the tomatoes, grabbed two plump ones and chucked them in so she could make a sambal.

On the way back to the street, Sum stopped at a tarpaulin-covered stall and bought a chunk of palm sugar and a handful of shallots from an old lady wearing a **kain dan kabaya** (traditional blouse and sarong). I was now fully laden with market goodies and wondering how we were going to fare on the motorbike. Sum didn't seem so worried. Back at the bike she paid the parking attendant and attached our bags to the hooks under the handles. Shopping successfully completed, we headed home down the wrong side of the street through manic traffic to make our lunch of fresh **bacem** (see the recipe).

Patrick Witton

SHOPPING & MARKETS

Bacem (Tofu, Tempe and/or Chicken Cooked in Stock)
This recipe comes from the kitchen of Sum and Parin in Yogyakarta

Ingredients

1kg	fresh tofu, tempe and/or chicken pieces
2	bulbs shallots, sliced thick
5	cloves garlic, sliced thick
2cm	galangal, sliced thick
3 Tbs	palm sugar
2	salam leaves
1 tsp	salt
3 cups	coconut oil for deep-frying

Bacem can be made with tofu, tempe, chicken or a combination thereof. Cut whatever you are using into 5 sq cm pieces (use the wings, breast or drumsticks of a small chicken). Place them in a pot with all the other ingredients (except the oil) and fill the pot with water so the ingredients are just covered. Heat the pot on the stove until boiling then cover and reduce the heat. Let the liquid simmer until there's only about one inch of water left in the pot (about an hour). Take the pieces out of the pot and leave to drain. In a wok, heat the coconut oil to smoking. If you're cooking a combination, deep fry the tofu first, then the tempe, then the chicken. Once golden brown, drain the oil and let cool for at least 10 minutes before serving. Bacem keeps well and tastes even better after a day.

Serves four with rice and sambal or serve with other dishes as part of a banquet.

Deep-frying tofu at a market in Bandung, Java

Tofu and tempe bacem

General Stores & Supermarkets

At first glance Indonesia's supermarkets don't look like much of a cultural experience. The fluoro lights and Kenny G tunes seem more suburbia than South-East Asia. But look a little closer at what's on the shelves. Are you in need of some durian-flavoured sweets? Have you run out of coconut jam perhaps? Or are you just craving dried fish? It's all here, as well as more familiar products you may be missing such as cheese, chocolate and yoghurt. Many supermarkets also stock kitchenware, even stove burners and rice cookers. Despite the economic and political crisis of 1998, supermarkets continue to pop up all over Indonesia. Matahari and Hero are two major chains but there are plenty of others, including one that's called Tujuh-Sebelas ('7-11').

Modern shopping in Yogyakarta, Java

Not every town has a supermarket, but always a **toko umum** (general store). These stores carry a broad stock: eggs, biscuits, beer, rice, oil, bottled water. Some general stores sell vegetables, some sell car parts. As the name suggests, it's pretty general.

On the streets of Indonesia you'll also find specialist shops and stalls selling, for example, only fruit and vegetables, or perhaps just **kerupuk** (crackers). Most towns have a **toko roti** (bakery) and, although bread products aren't classically Indonesian, you will find local variations: a cheese and chocolate roll or durian-flavoured cream cakes.

Then there's the street-corner **kios** (kiosk) barely bigger than a phone booth yet stocking an incredible amount of necessities. Whether you need batteries, beer or biscuits, the kios will provide.

An Indonesian Picnic

There are some stunning landscapes in Indonesia, places perfect for a packed lunch. Generally speaking, though, Indonesians' behaviour in the great outdoors can be somewhat confusing. Yes they like to get out and about – often en masse with tupperware and music. And the litter! Still, Indonesia's natural wonders are worth visiting, and when you do it's good to eat. If a place is frequently visited by day-trippers you won't even have to bring any food; as there'll be eateries around, catering to the holiday crowds.

It's hard to 'get away from it all' in a country of 200 million people, but if you're willing to try and you want to take your lunch with you, the **bungkus** (packed meal) is the answer. Any eatery will happily provide you with a bungkus, and soup and drink sellers will happily pour your meal into a plastic bag. For the outdoors, a rice-based meal is a filling and tasty option; head to any restaurant with dishes displayed out the front and request "**minta nasi bungkus**" ("a packed meal please"); they will have a stash of greaseproof paper or banana leaves at the ready for a serve of rice. Add to this a few morsels from the selection, but perhaps not liquid-based dishes (just to be safe).

Good bungkus options include **ayam goreng** (fried chicken), **tempe kering** (sweet and crispy fried tempe), **telur dadar** (omelette), **kacang panjang** (yard-long beans), **ikan bakar** (grilled fish), **gulai tahu** (tofu in coconut curry) or any other **gulai** (coconut curry) dish, but go easy on the liquid. The good thing about such a meal is that it's meant to be eaten at room temperature and, to be really Indonesian, with your hands (see Etiquette in the Culture chapter).

SHOPPING & MARKETS

Picnic in the ricefields, Bali

Things to Take Home

Your country's quarantine laws may stop you from bringing back a duck, but many souvenirs of the culinary kind are worth stocking up on before heading home. Packaged foods shouldn't pose a problem at immigration, but steer clear of animal and dairy products. Look for things that you can't easily get at home, such as sambal, sachets of **jamu** (herbal medicine), local tea and coffee (and perhaps some tea lids to keep your brew warm), ready-to-fry kerupuk and strange-flavoured lollies (candy) such as durian or **asam** (tamarind). Balinese rice wine and grape wine can be purchased at the airport at Denpasar and at general stores. Markets,

Cooking utensils for sale, Yogyakarta

supermarkets and general stores stock some if not all of these, as well as cooking utensils – essential if you want to give your kitchen an Indonesian feel. If you can lift it, get a **cobek & ulek-ulek** (mortar & pestle) for making your own sambal. Coconut-shell ladles and handmade wire strainers are other good options. Although big, a rice pot with detachable colander is necessary if you're as serious about rice as Indonesians are.

where to
eat & drink

You're never far away from good food in Indonesia, especially in cities where there are eateries on almost every street. Even the streets devoid of food during the day can be enveloped in cooking aromas by nightfall, as makeshift kitchens are set up in car parks and on footpaths. And then there are the roving vendors beckoning from the street and bringing food to your doorstep. There's no escape.

Street Food

Indonesia may have had its fair share of corruption, but if an establishment's food isn't honestly good it won't survive the hunt for the dining dollar. There's a surfeit of eateries here and as most Indonesians can't afford to dine at the sort of restaurants where you pay more for service and surrounds, the most authentic food is found at street level. Even high rollers know this, so everyone from students to business executives dines at streetside stalls or buys their noodle fix from roving vendors. At night, car parks, footpaths and intersections are crammed with eateries, filling the evening air with the smells and sounds of stirfrying. Such eateries can stretch along roads for miles or wrap around markets, making designated dining areas such as a **pasar malam** (night market) look limited. There's always another food stall just around the corner.

Gianyar night market, Bali

To eat and drink in Indonesia is a never-ending adventure. Hungry or not you'll be tempted by strange foods, waylaid by exotic aromas and entranced by new flavours. And then there are the people, all 200 million of them, delighted to see you venturing beyond the world of bread and milk. "You can eat spicy food", they'll say surprised. "You like durian", they'll say amazed. "You're ordering another avocado juice", they'll say perplexed. As it is everywhere, food here is a conversation starter. Dining out on Indonesian streets is a social affair and you'll share bench space with families, soldiers, students and solicitors all bound in the hunt for good food.

Dining on Jimbaran beach, Bali

Bakul (Streetside Traders)

Let's start with the basics. There may be no place to sit, no kitchen in sight, yet a full meal appears in front of you like an epiphany. This scenario is played out every day across Indonesia as the nation's cooks take to the streets looking for stomachs to fill. In early morning Central Java you'll see old women in sarongs selling such regional dishes as **pecel** (peanut sauce with spinach and beansprouts) to office workers and becak drivers. Once beckoned she will spread out her bundled goods on a bamboo tray and put together a meal from her collection of small bags and baskets. Her food is cheap – she doesn't pay rent or wages – and is most often a taste of the region.

A streetside trader serves sate in Yogyakarta, Java

Pikulan (Stick Sellers)

Now here's where the stereotypes really come to life. You know the classic image of someone carrying goods in two bundles connected by a stick over their shoulders? Well, that's a pikulan and in Indonesia they're used to carry food to sell. The pikulan can be an impressive contraption with a gas stove and wok on one side and ready-to-fry ingredients on the other. Some sell **bakso** (meatball soup), with stock on the boil at one end, ingredients and bowls at the other. Do you want chilli sauce? He's probably got that stuffed away somewhere.

One of the many uses of a pikulan, Bali

Kaki-Lima (Roving Vendors)

Kaki-lima are an essential part of the Indonesian culinary landscape; roving vendors; their carts usually consist of a work bench, a portable stove and a glass display cabinet for ingredients and for advertising their speciality dish or drink. Kaki-lima means 'five legs', for the three wheels on the cart and the two legs on the vendor.

You'll find any and every type of dish, drink and snack sold from a kaki-lima, but two favourites are sate and bakso. Some kaki-lima have a permanent location that they set up at every day until their stocks are depleted. Others roam the streets, tempting the hungry from their homes or places of work. In this case the vendors will call out what they are selling, or advertise their provender with a signature tune or sound. You may be resting in your room, not even hungry, but when the *tock* of a wooden bakso bell is heard, your stomach will rumble. Sate sellers may just wail "saaateee!", but in some areas they sell sate from a boat-shaped cart with small bells attached that jingle as it's pushed along. At night the bells and shadow of the boat slinking through alleyways make for an appetisingly eerie scene.

Cruising past a kaki-lima in Yogyakarta, Java

Warung (Food Stalls)

Although restaurants call themselves warung (similar to restaurants in the west calling themselves 'the home-bake pantry cottage'), we define a warung as any eatery that offers a place to eat and shelter, but is disassembled after closure. As a result some of the best food will not be there when you want it, nevertheless a warung usually has a set time when it's open for business. The classic warung consists of a long table sheltered by a tarpaulin roof and a screen hung to separate the diners from the streetside cacophony. Written on the screen is what is sold within – often no more than one or two dishes, so a warung will become famous for a specific dish. Although there'll be a warung around at anytime of the day, they really come to life at night when more are set up along streets and in vacant lots to cater to the post-work hungry. What was by day an office car park can by night turn into a bustling food centre with warung after warung luring you with smells from the open kitchen. Indonesia's warung sell everything from regional dishes like Yogyakarta's **gudeg** (jackfruit curry) to national favourites such as **pecel lele** (fried catfish).

Hanging out at a warung kopi in Yogyakarta, Java

Evening warung favourites, especially for big groups, are the ones serving seafood dishes. You'll recognise these by the pictures of the sea critters on display along with the words 'seafood' or 'makanan laut'. Often the critters are kept alive in buckets until their time comes, morbid yet hygienic. The food is often Chinese style – oyster sauce, stirfried etc – and is a tad expensive by Indonesian standards, nevertheless a choice of dishes shared with friends makes for a great night out.

NGAMEN

Care for a little mood music? Maybe you don't. Well too bad 'cos you're gonna get some anyway. Indonesia's eateries are easy pickings for roaming musicians known as **ngamen**, who move from place to place playing for change. Ngamen can range from a traditional ensemble to one fella with a two-string ukulele, and the repertoire you'll hear can stretch from Top 40 hits to traditional Javanese tunes. Some ngamen are virtuosos, others are crap, all want your money. If you like the tunes let them finish and pay them with a smile, if their music sounds more like a dental extraction pay them sooner and they'll get the hint.

Ngamen in Ujung Pandang, Sulawesi

A simpler type of warung is the **warung kopi** (cafe stall), selling little more than fried snacks such as banana or tempe, and hot drinks like coffee and tea. At night warung kopi, lit by kerosene lamps, are where people go to hang out and where taxi drivers sip coffee between fares and keep warm by the coal stove. In some areas, especially Aceh and Kalimantan, the warung kopi is a morning institution, where people stop on their way to work (or just stop) for a sweet coffee and a snack. It's easy to lose half a day munching away at morsels.

Lesehan

Lesehan refers more to seating arrangements than food. If you're eating while sitting on a grass mat then you're eating at a lesehan. The most famous place for lesehan are in Yogyakarta, where they are set up along Jalan Malioboro to cater to evening crowds (some open all day). Some restaurants have lesehan-style areas set up with low tables and mats for you to sloth on after stuffing your face.

Rumah Makan (Restaurants)

Sometimes the only difference between street stall and restaurant is that one closes for business by locking the door and the other folds up the roof. Street stall offerings can be just as tasty and a tad cheaper but at restaurants you'll get more variety and a nicer dining environment – there won't be someone revving their scooter next to your table. Many restaurants specialise in one regional cuisine, others serve a range of fare too broad to be called anything more than 'Indonesian'.

The most common restaurant meal, often called **nasi campur** or **nasi rames** (both meaning 'mixed rice'), is the one you make with plain rice and a selection of other dishes. Where there is food set out for all to see, you can be certain you'll be choosing a selection yourself (see The Menu & Bill later in this chapter). This also gives you the chance to peruse the selection before committing yourself. The fact that the food is sitting out may send your hygiene warning system haywire, but this is how much restaurant and home-cooked Indonesian food is prepared, to be eaten on the same day at room temperature.

For truly authentic flavours, try to find restaurants that serve dishes from the region you are in. This will be easy in Padang, as Padang restaurants are everywhere, but you may only get a chance to try Banjar food in Banjarmasin. Nevertheless in bigger towns there will be a smattering of eateries serving food from other areas, so you won't have to go to Manado to try North Sulawesi cuisine.

Restaurants with menus and made-to-order meals are also popular, although usually more expensive. These include restaurants that sell sate and soup, Chinese cuisine, foreign cuisine and fresh seafood. Often these are not mutually exclusive, many Padang restaurants can also rustle up a nasi goreng.

Rumah Makan Padang (Padang Restaurants)

There's at least one Padang restaurant, serving West Sumatran cuisine in every town in Indonesia. You can easily spot these places because they're the ones with the food propped up in the front window and three or four fellas in matching shirts scurrying around inside whilst performing plate-balancing tricks.

For a first-timer, a meal at a Padang restaurant can be a confusing affair. Firstly, all that food left in the window can't be good for hygiene, and some of the dishes look like they were cooked with a blowtorch. Indeed Padang cuisine isn't very photogenic, but it's cooked to withstand a refrigeratorless environment. In fact some dishes, such as **rendang** (beef or buffalo coconut curry; see the recipe) are said to improve with age.

Serving up Padang cuisine in Bukittinggi, Sumatra

A PADANG SELECTION

Padang cuisine is loved across Indonesia for its fiery and filling reputation. The main players in this popular nosh are **santan** (coconut milk; used as the base of coconut curries) and **cabe hijau** (green chillies; the base for the wince-inducing Padang sambal). Padang food is meat heavy, but every restaurant will have at least a couple of fleshless dishes in their repertoire. Along with essential rice, here are but a few of the dishes that may be piled up in front of you when you sit down to a meal at one of a million Padang restaurants across Indonesia:

rendang	beef or buffalo coconut curry (see the recipe)
gulai ayam	chicken in coconut curry
gulai nangka	jackfruit in coconut curry
kangkung	water spinach
kacang panjang	yard-long beans
hati ayam	chicken liver
telur rebus	boiled egg
telur goreng	spiced fried egg
ikan belado	fried fish pieces covered in shallots and chilli
kalio	rendang that hasn't been fully reduced

A spread of Padang dishes in Bukittinggi, Sumatra

The next stumbling block for the Padang virgin will be the fact that there isn't a menu in sight. In a Padang restaurant they cut out the task of going through the ordering process – take a seat at any table and before you can say "I'll have a side order of hokey-pokey ice cream" one of the fellas will have scurried over and piled up your table with a selection of umpteen small dishes and rice. No need to shout "Waiter! I can't eat this much!" as here at a Padang restaurant you pay only for what you eat. If you don't touch the **ikan bakar** (grilled fish) you won't pay for it, it'll go back into the window display. Even if you just taste the sauce that the **gulai ayam** (chicken in coconut curry) is served in and decide that it's too spicy, it won't be on the bill.

So the food looks good, there's plenty of rice, but where's the cutlery? If you ask for a fork you'll probably get one, but like most Indonesian meals, Padang food is best eaten with your right hand. Put your left hand away and wash your right hand in the bowl of water provided (there's usually a basin nearby so you can do a thorough job).

Serve yourself some rice and select a few tasty morsels that take your fancy. Mix the sauce in with your fingers, break off some of the meat or other food and squeeze it together with the rice and pop it in your mouth. If you want some more rice, or another piece of rendang, one of the fellas will happily dish it up.

For drinks, the water in a jug on the table is both for pouring over your hand as well as for topping up your glass, and the fellas will certainly have the makings for tea and coffee (hot or iced) and maybe even juices and **es campur** (mixed ice).

So you're full, probably shouldn't have stuffed in that packet of **emping** (melinjo crackers) piled invitingly on the table. Tell one of the fellas you're finished and he'll head over with a piece of paper, look at the empty bowls and bones and tally up the bill – and don't forget to tell him how many emping you had. (See also West Sumatra in the Regional Variations chapter and the boxed text A Padang Selection).

Warteg

One exception to the warung permanency rule is the **warteg** (short for warung Tegal), which is a simple yet permanent restaurant that sells a wide range of dishes at cheap prices. Tegal is a town in Java and, although the owner will probably be from there, the food available isn't necessarily specific to the region (see Central Java in the Regional Variations chapter).

Warteg eateries are a good bet for vegetarians because meatless dishes, especially ones that are tofu or tempe based, are in abundance (see the boxed text Tips for the Vegan Traveller).

FEATHERWEIGHT FEAST

When I went to taste Mbok Sabar's famous **ayam goreng** (fried chicken), the whole restaurant seemed to be preoccupied with other activities. Surely in Yogyakarta, where the fight for the fried chicken dollar is so intense they would put more effort into service. But perhaps the food would speak for itself. Once I found myself a seat, I realised what was diverting everyone's attention: on the television mounted high above the cash register was a direct telecast of Barrera versus Hamed in the Featherweight Boxing Championship. It seemed I had come in at a pivotal point in the bout. Barrera was flying with punches but Hamed seemed to swerve like a snake. Nevertheless the restaurant was open and I was adamant that I would try Mbok Sabar's famous fried chicken.

Although many regions boast about the taste of their chicken dishes, in Yogyakarta the quest for ayam goreng supremacy has given the town an unheralded chicken image. Probably the most famous of all Yogyakarta's chicken purveyors is Mbok Berek (Mrs Berek) situated out near Prambanan on the road to Solo. Before frying her cluckers, Mbok Berek boils them in young coconut water, and the results are finger lickin'. (Right hand only, please.) A similar fate awaits chickens at Ayam Goreng Nyonya Suharti restaurants across the country. Here at Mbok Sabar on Jl Jagalan, the chooks are boiled in a sweet spice stock and then fried.

I wasn't sure of the ordering procedure so I just caught the eye of someone that looked like he might work there. He then mumbled something to the fella leaning against the wall who, reluctantly, pulled himself away from a very even round eight to tell the woman at the front of the shop that I wished to dine.

After about five minutes out came a bowl of steaming rice, another of raw cabbage, lettuce and cucumber, a serve of sambal, a bowl of water to clean my hand and a plate for the bones. Just as round 10 started a plate brimming with pieces of chicken was put before me. It must have been a whole chicken! Surely they weren't so preoccupied with the match that they forgot I was alone. I tried to share my surprise with the waiter, but Barrera seemed to be gaining control of the fight, the crowd at MGM hall was going ballistic. Too hungry, I separated some of the hot, tender flesh and scooped it up with some rice and sambal. The taste was strong and sweet, spicy but not overwhelming. Absolutely delicious. After each mouthful I took a bite of cucumber to cut through the grease. I didn't care that I may have to pay for a whole chicken when I ate only half. Plus the fight was reaching a climax, with Barrera working away at the run-down Englishman.

Once the winner was announced I asked to pay. The waiter grabbed his pad and came over to write up the bill. To work out what parts of the chicken I had eaten, he counted the bones left on my plate. What I didn't touch I didn't pay for. A fair price for a knockout meal.

Upmarket & Tourist Restaurants

In larger cities and in tourist areas a surfeit of restaurants serve foreign cuisine and cater to foreign tastebuds. Japanese, Korean, Indian, European, Tex-Mex, Thai can all be found in Jakarta, and to a lesser extent in other cities. Such establishments are expensive by Indonesian standards and offer more of a cultural escape than experience. In tourist areas you'll find many restaurants dishing up decent yet tame versions of Indonesian food to visiting stomachs. Favourites here include fried rice or noodles, chicken soup, waffles and the backpacker favourite, banana pancakes. Tourist restaurants can, however, be congenial places for having an ice-cold beer.

Gaja Biru Restaurant, Ubud, Bali

Chinese Restaurants

Although you'll find many Chinese-influenced dishes in other restaurants, there are plenty of restaurants that serve specifically Chinese cuisine. Here you'll no doubt get a decent nasi goreng, but you'll also get a multitude of stirfries, steamed dishes, seafood, pork, **cap cai** (mixed vegetables), dishes in **saus tiram** (oyster sauce), **asam manis** (sweet & sour dishes) and noodles by the wok-load. Some Chinese restaurants are simple affairs offering clean, fresh noodle soups such as **mie pangsit** (wonton noodle soup). Usually the noodles are made on location and the stock comes in a separate bowl for you to pour over the noodles or to slurp separately. As with Chinese restaurants anywhere, the menu can be as long as the Palembang telephone directory.

WHERE TO EAT & DRINK

COLONIAL REMNANTS

The days of pith helmets and robust moustaches may be over, but there are a few lingering reminders of how the Dutch dined during their dynasty, especially in the larger towns. Such establishments are recognised by a European menu (although other cuisine is often available), white tablecloths and genteel decor. There are a few of these dinosaurs around, including Toko Oen in the Javanese towns of Malang and Semarang.

Colonial charm in Cafe Batavia, Jakarta

The most famous restaurant of this kind is Jakarta's Cafe Batavia. The dining room is another world of starched linen, floorboards, wooden shutters, ferns, attentive waitstaff and well-stocked liquor cabinets. It has European, Indonesian and Chinese menus, so whether you want spatchcock or stirfry you'll be well catered to. If you don't want a full meal there's a cafe area where you can recline on plush leather couches, but a dessert here is well worth the splurge. Apart from filling your stomach, you'll feast your eyes on the eclectic decor comprising framed pictures that run the gamut between Dutch aristocracy to teenage bedroom circa 1985. Then there's the men's toilet, which offers something of a narcissistic experience.

Bar at the Domus in Jakarta

Food Courts & Fast Food

Indonesians love malls and shopping complexes. Not only do they provide access to consumer heaven, they are a place where friends can meet, peruse the stores and grab something for lunch. To cater to this, many fast-food chains have muscled in so you'll be hard pressed to find a shopping precinct without a McDonalds, Dunkin Donuts, KFC or Pizza Hut shining like a beacon. You will however find local twists in their preparations, as in the

McSatay and KFC's chicken & rice. Many shopping centres have a floor devoted to food stalls, which are a mix of local and international cuisines. Here you'll find local fast-food chains dishing up favourites such as bakso at Mr Bakso. The atmosphere in these food courts is air-con plastic fantastic and is often audibly bombarded by a nearby video game parlour.

Classic Kuta, Bali

Japanese fast food for sale on Jalan Veteran, Jakarta

The Menu & Bill

Menu? What menu? The name for it is **daftar makanan** and 'tidak ada' means 'there isn't one', which is what you'll hear when you ask for it. At a warung the one or two dishes available will be advertised boldly on the side screen and on the glass cabinet of a kaki-lima, so the choice is easy. Whatever the place, you'll glean a good idea of what's on offer in the name of the establishment, so a restaurant serving Padang cuisine will have 'Padang' as part of its signage. Sometimes the name of the restaurant *is* what is served, so **rumah makan bubur ketan hitam** (black rice porridge restaurant) serves a decent black rice porridge.

If the food is ready-made, there are a number of things that could happen. You may be asked to sit down and a selection of dishes will be placed on the table. In this case you'll pay for what you eat. Another possibility is that you'll be asked what dishes you want and the server will fill your plate accordingly. Another strategy is to give you a plate so you can help yourself (one piled spoonful of each dish, and you pay for meat by the piece). You can ask about the price, but rest assured it's low and that, of the nation's 14 million hospitality workers, probably only six of them are out to rip you off. Remember that meat, egg or fish will double the price of a meal and that it's easy to choose more than will fit in your stomach – the rice, meat, two veg and sambal rule works for us.

Once your selection is made you may be asked to pay for your meal first so they can see what's on your plate. More often, however, at the end of the meal you'll be asked what dishes you selected. They might tally a bill by looking at the empty plates, or they may well have worked out the bill total beforehand.

Restaurants are more likely to have menus, especially Chinese, tourist and upmarket establishments. If the menu doesn't include prices you can get a little suspicious and may want to ask prices, but most often the price is clear as are any surcharges.

If the staff give you a pen and paper with the menu, write down what you want and let them know when your order is ready. This do-it-yourself bill system avoids any confusion in the kitchen. The Indonesian menu is most often very honest: if you order fried chicken that's what you'll get, one piece of fried chicken. For this reason you may need to order a few things so as to create a full meal, such as white rice, a vegetable dish and the fried chicken.

Paying for your meal in a food court can sometimes be like a test in bureaucratic confusion: order your meal at stall K; receive a docket which you take to the third cashier; pay the required amount; take a seat and hope for the best.

Serving up fish on Jimbaran beach, Bali

WHERE TO EAT & DRINK

Road Food

If you're planning a long haul, fear not that hunger will be your travel companion. Whether by bus, boat or train there'll be an opportunity to dine well. At any transit point, sellers come aboard selling all sorts of snacks, drinks and full meals. Sometimes it's a wonder how they got on as the bus never seemed to slow down. If they're selling packaged snacks they may drop one onto each passenger's lap whilst extolling the virtues of their product. If you want it, hand over the money; otherwise return the package when they come back to you. Whatever their method they'll happily provision you for the journey. Both long-haul trains and larger boats have on-board diners as well as staff selling meals from cabin to cabin or car to car.

TIPS FOR THE VEGAN TRAVELLER

The foods that street eateries offer for the friendly vegan traveller can vary wildly but, thanks to internal ethnic dispersal (especially of Javanese and Chinese), the selection of street foods in any biggish town or city is pretty standard. Tempe and tofu products are in abundance, including chunky slabs of **tempe goreng** (fried tempe) with fresh sambal; sweet and crispy fried **tempe kering** (see the recipe); and the ever-so-moreish and succulent deep-fried stuffed **tahu isi**. Vegans are sure to be pleased.

Ironically though, finding a good variety of fresh veggies is likely to require more effort. Look for Chinese establishments; they reliably have super-hot woks at the ready to whip up **cap cai** (mixed vegetables).

A huge number of smaller establishments offer **nasi campur** (rice with a choice of side dishes). Here you can avoid animal products – as long as you can tell what is in the dishes on display. Be prepared for the odd tricky thing like the visual similarity between fried tempe and fried chicken feet.

The typical Padang eatery offers pre-cooked dishes that almost all include flesh. The rare exceptions are their **nangka** (jackfruit) dishes that, despite amazing flesh-like qualities, are not meat. If meat is in a dish it's usually obvious, however look out for the addition of **terasi** (fish paste) to **sambal** (chilli sauce). By no means are all sambals made with this but it seems the ones that locals recommend as delicious are fishy.

Be aware of the popularity of **susu kental** (condensed milk) following the huge marketing campaigns evident eeeeverywhere. Indonesians love to add it to juices, pancakes and to your coffee if you ask for milk.

Vendors with blenders can mix up some fine fruit concoctions. But even better and not to be forgotten is the fantastic variety of **buah-buahan** (fruit) available at the local market. Fresh simple tropical goodness.

Andrew Taylor likes Melbourne's swamps and vegan fried food

Children

One of the major culinary fears for people travelling with their children is that a hidden chilli is going to make their child explode. Most Indonesian children are also fearful of chilli attacks, so a proprietor will more often warn you that the dish you ordered is spicy. In any case you can always ask 'pedas tidak?' (is it spicy?) or 'makanan tidak pedas ada?' (are there non-spicy dishes?).

Children may well enjoy such dishes as **nasi goreng** (fried rice), **mie goreng** (fried noodles), **bakso** (meatball soup), **mie rebus** (noodle soup), **perkedel** (fritters), **pisang goreng** (banana fritters), **soto ayam** (chicken soup), sate, **bubur** (rice porridge) and of course the abundant fruit and fruit drinks. Indonesia's sugar-rich iced drinks are useful secret weapons for when energy levels are low and you're far from the hotel – both for you and your child. All of these are available at street stalls and restaurants. Not available, however, are highchairs and kiddy menus. That's not to say children aren't welcome in restaurants, in fact they're liable to get more attention than they can handle.

If your little fella yearns for a taste of home, supermarkets stock a wide range of western foods such as cereals, bread, milk and baby foods. Fast food is also becoming more and more available, if that's really what your child wants. Be warned that heat can hit your child hard, so always make sure they're getting enough liquid during the day.

The Mataram posse, Lombok

Where to Drink

All warung and restaurants will have drinking water or weak tea available at no cost, and most will also have a larger selection of drinks including hot or cold, sweet or plain tea and coffee, soft drinks and juices. Only upmarket and tourist restaurants serve alcohol.

There are in fact vendors whose speciality is drinks and only drinks, such as those selling **es campur** (mixed ice), **jus apokat** (avocado juice; see the recipe) or **es jeruk** (citrus juice) but to name a few. Whatever it is that they create, it'll clearly advertised on the side of the cart or at the front of the store. If you're dining at one stall and they don't have the drink you want, there's no problem with ordering it from next door. Tell the worker what you want and they'll know where to get it.

If a street stall consists of jars filled with multi-coloured jelly pieces swimming in syrup that would look more at home on a sci-fi film set, you've found yourself an **es campur** (mixed ice) proprietor. Next to the stand you'll see an industrial-sized ice shaver from which the vendor will collect a bowl of shaved ice. On top of this goes sugar syrup, the jelly pieces (made out of rice flour) and a blob of condensed milk. Bring on the sugar rush.

Drinks at Ubud market, Bali

Pubs & Clubs

If your only aim is to drink alcohol then your options depend on where you are. In small-town Sumatra for example you'll be lucky to find alcohol on sale at all (unless it's a tourist area in which case a tourist restaurant may provide). In other towns you may find beer on sale at a general store, but there won't be a pub as such. If there is, the concept of a 'cold one' may remain elusive: in one promising establishment the beer was served warm and frothy in a plastic jug. Cheers! Going out for a few drinks does become a real possibility in Indonesia's cities, and becomes a way of life in the larger metropoli, where club culture along with its vices has a firm grip on nocturnal happenings. As in many countries, discos, pubs and clubs can open, become trendy, get shut down and burn down overnight. Many places have reputations for being elitist, sleazy and/or a rip-off – often for good reason.

Gambling in Yogyakarta, Java

Going out at night in Indonesia will bear few cultural surprises. When you arrive there may be a cover charge (which may include a drink voucher), there may be a queue. Perhaps there'll be a live band playing – cover bands are very popular in Indonesia and a band that plays popular tunes well can gain a healthy following. The place might be packed with the fashionable set, it may be crowded with students from a local university, it may be peppered with expats, it could be scattered with single men and **kupu-kupu malam** ('night butterflies'; prostitutes).

Late-night snacks in Yogyakarta, Java

So you're thirsty? Beer and spirits are definites, followed by cocktails and wine. Although these places serve alcohol, you'll notice that many patrons stick to non-alcoholic beverages, whether for reason of religion, taste or finance. Most places have an army of waitstaff ready and willing to take your order, so in a busy club there's no need to wrestle your way to the front of the bar. Catch the attention of an employee, tell them your poison and they'll get it for you. If it's loud and dark, do what the locals do and hold your lighter in the air rock-concert style to catch the eye of a worker (ah the perks of being a smoker). Pay the waiter directly or if you've commandeered a table you could run up a tab. (See also the boxed text Dining under the Influence in the Drinks chapter.)

an indonesian
banquet

Preparing an Indonesian banquet is an exercise in simplicity. There are no courses to release in chronological order, no flambés to flame, no souffles to collapse, no fondues to fiddle with. All food is prepared before guests arrive, freeing you to relax and enjoy the meal along with your pals.

Your Indonesian banquet could be as much a cultural as a culinary experience for your guests; to do this you can go two ways. On the one hand, you could treat your friends in the manner that is the custom in many Indonesian homes: usher them into the living room, scurry off to leave them under the gaze of a thousand family portraits, find someone they've never met before to serve them tea, make sure all your neighbours' children are staring at them through the front window, dig up 37 photo albums for them to peruse, sit with them and ask questions of them like "are you married?", "do you have any children?" and "what is your salary?". When you've exhausted all similar avenues of conversation, lead them into the dining room, where the selection of dishes you have prepared is laid out. Ask them to help themselves and, when they've eaten half of what's on their plate, implore them to take more food. Do not take any yourself, just smile and let your guests ponder whether it is or isn't polite to use their hands to eat the chicken.

On the other hand you could take the more popular and less formal approach. As the host you have nothing to do except to make sure drinks are filled and that your guests have been introduced to each other. This will leave you to enjoy the night along with your guests.

Rempeyek (Peanuts Cooked in Rice-flour Crackers)

In Java, food that goes well with drinks is known as **tambul**, and rempeyek is a popular example.

Ingredients

250g	peanuts, shelled
300g	rice flour
1½ cups	coconut milk
2	candlenuts, ground
2cm	turmeric, finely chopped
3 cloves	garlic, crushed
2 tsp	salt
1-2 cups	coconut oil for deep-frying

Mix all the ingredients together (except the oil). Heat the oil in a wok. Cook the mixture in the oil a tablespoon at a time. One way to do this is to tilt the wok, spoon the mix onto the flat side then, once semi-cooked, let the mix slide into the centre of the wok. Either way, cook until golden then drain and cool on paper towels.

Makes 15-20 crackers

A temple ceremony in Ubud, Bali

INDONESIAN BANQUET

Either way, you prepare the entire dinner before people arrive – the dishes are meant to be eaten at room temperature. And, just to make things easier, there are no set courses: every dish is set out at once, perhaps covered with a cloth. All the recipes in this book can be used in the selection, even the chicken soup, from which diners take a little to spoon over plain rice. Speaking of which, it's the only thing you want to serve hot, so if you don't have a rice cooker prepare a batch just before people are set to arrive. That way it'll still be warm when it comes time to eat.

What to drink? Indonesians aren't big alcohol drinkers; they prefer water, juice or tea (hot or cold, sweet or plain, not milky). Nevertheless clean-tasting beers such as the locally brewed Bintang and Anker go well with spicy cuisine, especially when served ice cold.

But an Indonesian feast doesn't stop at the table. In fact the table isn't even a necessity as Indonesians often prefer to sit on a **tikar** (grass mat) rather than on chairs, making the post-meal transition from upright eating to sprawled-out relaxing an easy one. If you don't have a grass mat go for a wide blanket and some cushions. You could also decorate the room with some traditional sarongs you bought on your trip, such as tie-died and woven **ikat** from Nusa Tenggara, waxed and dyed **batik** from Java, and the silk and gold thread **songket** of North Sumatra.

Then there's music: you have a plenitude of styles to choose from, including the soporific **gamelan** of Java, the high-paced **gong sasak** of Lombok and the 'risqué' Sundanese **jaipongan**. For a more contemporary edge, choose from one of Indonesia's many successful rock or pop outfits.

A Sudanese spread, Bandung, Java

As anywhere, a band's popularity can flounder within days but bands such as Dewa (rock), Rif (hard rock), and Warna (schlock) were receiving a lot of airplay at the time of writing. Then there's the emotion-heavy **dangdut**, a mix of modern and traditional music. Any Indonesian music store will have a selection of traditional and modern Indonesian music for you to sample.

If Mother Nature isn't considerate enough to have put on a 30ºC day with 120% humidity, you can assist by turning up the heater. This is also important for another reason: Indonesian homes are shoes-off territory.

So the scene is set and friends are arriving. There's no need for you to be flapping about in the kitchen because all the dishes are ready. You're free to make sure drinks are full and that everyone has a comfy spot on the floor. While waiting for latecomers, get your guest's gastric juices flowing with a plate of **rempeyek** (peanuts cooked in rice-flour crackers; see the recipe). Once friends that live on **jam karet** ('rubber time') have arrived, it's time to dine. People should help themselves, but if they waver explain that they should take a spoonful of a few dishes rather than a serve of one.

Rempah-Rempah (Spicy Fish in Coconut Curry)

This recipe comes from Bungus Beach in West Sumatra. If you can get them, add a couple of kemangi leaves to the mix.

Ingredients

1kg	whole, gutted saltwater fish (each about 15cm long)
3 cups	coconut milk
1 stick	lemongrass
2cm	turmeric
2cm	ginger
2	tamarind seeds
2 tsp	salt
3-6	red chillies, seeded (depending on your threshold)
10	cloves shallots
3	cloves garlic

Heat the coconut milk in an uncovered wok over a very low flame. Add the lemongrass, turmeric, ginger, tamarind and kemangi leaves if you have them (don't cut these up). Crush the chillies, shallots and garlic to form a paste. For this you can use a food processor or a **cobek & ulek-ulek** (mortar & pestle; see the Home Cooking & Traditions chapter). Lightly fry this paste then add it and the salt to the coconut milk. Once the ingredients are heated through, add the fish and simmer for about 15 minutes, or until the fish is cooked through.

Serves 4 with rice or divide the fish and serve as part of a banquet.

Musicians in Ubud, Bali

And implore that they come back for more – if your guests are restraining themselves they obviously don't feel at ease, or worse they don't like your cooking. As guests they have a responsibility to stuff their faces.

Cutlery-wise, a fork and spoon is all people need. But if you really want to be authentic give each diner a small bowl filled with warm water and a piece of lemon. That way they can wash their right hand before digging in.

The fact that an Indonesian banquet is a serve-yourself, sit-anywhere affair means that it can stretch for hours and feel more like a prolonged get-together than a formal affair. People will eat big, keel over like beached whales, go back for second helpings, snooze, leaf through your holiday snaps, play music and ask about your decor. And since you've done all the work it's only fair that you kick back with them. You shouldn't be so rude as to ask guests to leave, however you can drop a hint by falling asleep.

PEPES IKAN

Living in another country is gastro-nomically exciting. The first few years I was in Australia I enjoyed exploring all the new foods. Inevitably, the time came when I started missing some of mum's recipes, so last time I returned to Indonesia with my wife, we took a notebook and recorded all our favourites. It was hard choosing one above the rest to include here, but when I discovered how simple my mum's version of pepes ikan is (it can be complicated), I knew this was the one to share. We usually use rockling, but this recipe works with any type of fish; fresh or ocean water. Try with your favourite fish, whether whole or in cutlets or fillets.

Pepes ikan and sambal

A couple of tips: if you don't have a bamboo steamer, try putting an enamel colander over the steaming pot. Make sure to fit a lid securely on top of the colander. Alternatively, use a pressure cooker. And if banana leaves are not available, use aluminium foil.

Kusnandar was born in Sumatra and grew up in Jakarta. He now lives in Melbourne and works as a designer and cartographer.

Other Recipes

- **Nasi Goreng** (Fried Rice) *see* the Staples & Specialities chapter
- **Rendang** (beef or buffalo coconut curry) *see* the Staples & Specialities chapter
- **Terong Belado** (eggplant with chilli sauce) *see* the Staples & Specialities chapter
- **Sambal Badjak** (dark chilli sauce) *see* the Staples & Specialities chapter
- **Bandrek** (ginger tea) *see* the Drinks chapter
- **Soto Ayam** (chicken soup) *see* the Home Cooking chapter
- **Bacem** (tofu, tempe and/or chicken cooked in stock) *see* the Shopping chapter

Pepes Ikan

Ingredients

1kg	rockling or other fish
4	leaves kemangi or Vietnamese mint
1	large tomato
1	salam leaf or bay leaf
4 Tbs	lemon juice

Spice Mix

2-3	red chillies, seeded
8	cloves shallots
2½cm	piece turmeric
2½cm	piece ginger
8	candlenuts
	salt and sugar to taste
4	stalks lemongrass
5cm	piece galangal

Marinate the fish in the lemon juice for 10 minutes then rinse. Pound the spice mix ingredients to a paste in a mortar & pestle or food processor. Apply paste all over the fish and marinate for 15-30 minutes. Put some thin tomato slices, some kemangi (or Vietnamese mint) and a salam leaf (or a bay leaf) on top. Wrap 4 cutlets of fish in 2 banana leaves – 35 x 25cm. Steam in a pressure cooker until the pressure whistle sings then reduce the heat and cook the fish for another 30 minutes. The same cooking time is required when using a traditional steamer.

Serves 4 with rice or divide the fish and serve as part of a banquet.

Karedok (Sudanese Salad)

The vegetables in this dish can be substituted with whatever is in season or in the fridge.

Salad

30cm	cucumber, peeled and diced
300g	green beans, yard-long beans or snowpeas, diced
300g	cabbage, diced
300g	bean sprouts

Sauce

6	cloves garlic
4-6	seeded red chillies
4cm	piece galangal (lesser galangal if you can get it)
2 tsp	shrimp paste
4 Tbs	lime juice
3 tsp	salt

Mix the vegetables together and place them in a serving bowl. Blend or crush the sauce ingredients (add water if it's too dry) and pour it over the vegetables.

This dish is best served with other food as part of a banquet.

Jus Apokat (Avocado Juice)

Don't knock it until you've tried it.

Ingredients

2	ripe avocados
¼ cup	sugar syrup
8	ice cubes
2 Tbs	chocolate syrup or condensed milk

Put the avocados, sugar syrup and ice cubes in a blender and blend until smooth. Pour into two large glasses and dribble the chocolate syrup or condensed milk over the top, to be mixed through by the drinker.

Makes 2 large drinks

Tempe Kering (Sweet & Crispy Fried Tempe)

Tempe can be bought in many Asian groceries, health-food stores and even some supermarkets.

Ingredients

600g	tempe
4	cloves shallots, finely chopped
4	cloves garlic, finely chopped
4-6	red chillies, seeded and sliced
2cm	galangal, finely chopped
½ cup	sweet soy sauce
5 Tbs	coconut oil

Chop the tempe into strips (3cm by ½cm). Heat 4 tablespoons of oil in a wok and stirfry the tempe strips until golden (you may need to do them in batches). Set the tempe aside to drain. Clean the wok and heat the remaining oil. Fry the shallots, garlic, chillies and galangal for one minute then add the sweet soy sauce followed by the tempe and stirfry until the sauce has reduced. Serves four with rice or serve with other dishes as part of a banquet.

Opor Ayam (Chicken in Pepper & Coconut Curry)

This Javanese dish is chilli-free, so is an excellent choice for your chilli-phobic friends.

Ingredients

1kg	chicken pieces, skin on
3	shallots, finely chopped
3	cloves garlic, finely chopped
2cm	ginger, finely chopped
1cm	galangal, finely chopped
1 Tbs	coriander seeds, crushed
½ tsp	white pepper
2 tsp	salt
5 cups	coconut milk
1	stalk lemongrass
2	salam leaves

In a blender or mortar & pestle, crush and mix the shallots, garlic, ginger, galangal, coriander, pepper and salt. Heat the coconut milk in a pot or wok and add the spice paste. Add the salam leaves as well as the lemongrass, but bend and press it so its juices come out. Add the chicken and simmer until tender (30-40 minutes).

Serves 4 with rice or cut the chicken to serve as part of a banquet.

Saus Kacang (Peanut Sauce)

This versatile sauce is the key ingredient in the favourite, **gado-gado**. This salad is made by blanching or steaming a selection of vegetables, typically includes beansprouts, thinly sliced spinach, carrots and green or yard-long beans. These ingredients are mixed together with deep-fried tofu chunks, thinly sliced cabbage and sliced hardboiled egg and the peanut sauce is dribbled over the top then sprinkled with prawn crackers. You can of course use any vegetables in the mix depending on location and season. Peanut sauce can also be used as a dip with raw carrot or celery sticks. You could crush your own peanuts for the recipe, however it's easier to cheat and use peanut butter.

Ingredients

3	cloves shallots, finely chopped
3	cloves garlic, finely chopped
3-6	red chillies (depending on your threshold), seeded and finely chopped
2cm	kencur (lesser galangal), minced
1 tsp	shrimp paste
2 tsp	palm sugar
2	lime leaves
3 cups	coconut milk
3 Tbs	peanut butter or 200g crushed peanuts
1 Tbs	lime juice
2 Tbs	soy sauce
2 Tbs	coconut oil

Heat the oil in a wok and fry the shallots, garlic, chillies, kencur, shrimp paste, palm sugar and lime leaves. Once these are lightly browned, add the coconut milk, peanuts, lime juice and soy sauce and lower the heat so the sauce is slowly bubbling away. Let the sauce reduce to a thick consistency. Taste the sauce and if it needs more peanuts, lime or soy, add accordingly.

Makes enough sauce for 4 serves of gado-gado or for a bowl of dip.

fit & healthy

There's no denying that by eating in Indonesia you're running risks and risking runs. But no matter where you are, a change of diet can cause the stomach to miss a step and most of the time problems will 'pass' soon enough. By following a few rules of common sense, and listening to your body, you can lower the chances of Bali belly and heighten the enjoyment of your culinary adventure.

If you are going to eat (and eat well) in Indonesia you'll have to forget a couple of rules. First is the don't-eat-from-street-vendors rule; it sees you missing out on the best food and most atmospheric dining. And the don't-eat-what-you-don't-see-cooked rule means you won't eat at a multitude of places (including homes) that make their dishes fresh every morning to be eaten at room temperature throughout the day. In Indonesia you should worry more about wayward motorcycle drivers than hidden bacteria.

Take it easy at first. Don't try to push your chilli threshold and don't eat meat in huge amounts. Do as the locals do and eat a lot of rice with your tasty morsels. Rice is highly nutritious, easily digestible and carries flavour well. Environment is also important, so eat where you can relax and take time over a meal. Don't rush. Chew your food.

Chickens for sale, Denpasar Market

MSG (Monosodium Glutamate)

In 2000 a scare rippled across Indonesia when it was alleged that a major producer of MSG was adding a pork by-product to its goods. Indonesians are generally enthusiastic users of the simple, non-synthetic compound of glutamate, water and sodium, but it looked like MSG was leaving the Indonesian kitchen. MSG-phobes breathed a collective sigh of relief.

The company in question has since amended its recipe and given the green light for Muslims to use MSG again without fear of consuming pork. MSG remains a popular additive across the country.

Other names for MSG are: **vetsin** and Aji-No-Moto (brand name).

Hygiene

Health regulations may be more lax in Indonesia than in some other countries, but proprietors tend to keep their shops clean and their food bug free – it's good for business. Eat at places that look popular but also check that surfaces and utensils are clean and that your waiter or cook isn't covered in welts. Indonesian food can look and taste strange, but a strange flavour or aroma is different to a suspect one, so if you think a dish is dubious, leave it.

But hygiene is also your responsibility. Be sure to wash your hands before eating, especially if you're eating with your right hand. Most restaurants will provide a basin for this reason, as well as a bowl of water for each person at the table. And when it comes to self catering, don't eat uncooked food that you can't peel and/or clean with a safe water source. Follow this advice and you'll be able to enjoy Indonesia's delicious fruit and vegetables with very little risk.

Spa products, Bali

FIT & HEALTHY

Hot springs of Banjar, Bali

Fluids

Tap water is not safe to drink in Indonesia. The locals don't drink it. If you're offered a drink in a home or restaurant you can be sure it has been purified by boiling (usually it's still warm). Bottled water is widely available and cheap – make sure the seal isn't broken. Instead of buying a new bottle whenever you're thirsty, boil your own water with an electric immersion coil, available in department stores and supermarkets. Water can also be sterilised by iodine or chlorine tablets, and by water filters. Many hotels provide their guests with purified water, so refill your bottle at home base.

Water for sale in Denpasar, Bali

The main thing to remember is to drink. Indonesia is a hot place to be wandering so you'll have to put back what you'll sweat out. Keep a water bottle in your bag and take time out at stalls where soft drinks and juices are sold. Remember tea and coffee don't replenish your liquid levels as they are diuretics. Nothing beats plain water.

Ice is a bit dicey in Indonesia. It is made with purified water but businesses often keep a brick of ice out in the open and chip off pieces as they need them so, although minimal, there is a risk of bug action. Ice that comes in readymade cubes (which is more the norm) will have come from the ice factory in a sealed bag. We've had no problems with iced drinks, but that's not to say they're 100% safe.

Nyomen with flowers, Bali

JAMU (Herbal Medicine)

If you're looking for alternative medicine don't go past the **toko jamu** (herbal remedy shop). There's a toko jamu in every town, identifiable by its bright yellow decor and walls festooned with medicinal sachets. Choose your sachet according to the descriptive cheesy graphic or ask the **ahli jamu** (herbalist) at the counter for assistance. There is a jamu remedy for everything from **bau badan** (body odour) to **ketidakmampuan** (impotence). For the full jamu experience ask the ahli jamu to whip up a remedy on the spot, complete with a raw egg yolk. It's enough to make you well.

Mixing together jamu, Yogyakarta, Java

Eating For Health

Eating well is all about making sure you get enough of the right nutrients to enable you to function at your best, mentally and physically. It also makes you less vulnerable to illness. The best way to ensure you get enough water, carbohydrates, protein, fat, vitamins and minerals is to eat a varied diet. This shouldn't be difficult in Indonesia, where the diet consists of carbohydrates (rice, noodles, tubers), protein (fish, meat, tempe, tofu) and a wide range of fruit and vegetables. Fatty and sugary foods also have a place in a balanced diet, but don't overindulge.

Fading Away

It's easy to lose weight in hot, humid Indonesia. This may sound appealing to the love-handled, but if your baggage falls off too quickly you'll become more susceptible to fatigue and illness. Be sure not to miss meals and keep your liquid intake flowing. If you're not eating meat you'll have to eat more plant foods, but also make the most of Indonesia's tofu and tempe dishes to get your protein. A multivitamin supplement is a good thing to pack along with your toothbrush.

Diarrhoea

Diarrhoea can be caused by unclean foods, but just getting used to new foods and climate can also result in a case of the runs. Nevertheless a few rushed toilet trips with no other symptoms is not indicative of a major health emergency.

The main worry with diarrhoea is dehydration so it's vital you replace as much fluid as you're losing. Check your urine to assess how much liquid replenishment you need: small amounts of dark urine means you should increase your intake by drinking small amounts regularly. Good sources of fluid are water (duh) and carbonated drinks left to go flat and mixed with an equal amount of clean water. If diarrhoea is hefty you may need extra help with replacing minerals and salts. There are a range of oral rehydration salts (ORS) available, and although they are available from pharmacies in Indonesia – ask for **bubuk glukosa elektrolit** (glucose electrolyte powder) – pack some so you're not caught without. For DIY rehydration, take one litre of water and mix into it half a teaspoon of salt and six teaspoons of sugar.

> **Food on the Runs**
>
> **Eat** plain rice, plain bread, plain noodles, dry biscuits (salty or not too sweet) and bananas
>
> **Avoid** fruit & vegetables (except bananas), spicy foods, dairy products (including yoghurt) and greasy foods

HEALTHY LAND

These days there are doctors and chemists in every town, but traditional medicine remains popular across Indonesia. Made Ria from Munduk in Bali is showing me around his district, where coffee, rice and cloves are grown. Of course there are many other plants growing in the area, and every so often Made will stop and let me in on a few medicinal secrets.

"This is the **tempunyak** plant, similar to lantana. Crush its leaves and mix with water and it cures any stomach problems. This, the **sembung gantung** plant relieves a headache, but it's really bitter. And this is the **dap dap tis** (coral tree), very important for small children. If your child has a fever, crush its leaves and place them on their forehead. If your child isn't digesting well, put the leaves on their stomach. Got a sprained ankle? Pick some **gumitir** plant leaves, crush them along with fennel and shallots then place them on the sprain. And cassava leaves? Boil and mix them with soy sauce and lemongrass. It won't cure anything but it tastes bloody good!"

If you don't feel like eating, don't force yourself but don't try to do anything else. Stay in and recover. If you feel like eating, take it easy and stick to small amounts of food at regular intervals. Keep to a diet of plain rice, **lontong** (rice steamed in banana leaves), plain noodles, dry biscuits and bananas. Avoid fruit (except bananas), vegetables, spicy and greasy foods as you recover. And rest.

Be aware that anti-diarrhoeal drugs don't actually cure the problem, they just slow the plumbing down so you don't have to visit the loo so often. These drugs, however, can be helpful if you're ill and have to make a long journey, otherwise let things run their course.

If diarrhoea is only one symptom and, for example, you're also suffering a high fever or passing blood, consult a doctor immediately.

eat your words
language guide

- Pronunciation Guide 216
- Useful Phrases 217
- English – Indonesian Glossary 225
- Indonesian Culinary Dictionary 241

Pronunciation

Bahasa Indonesia is the lingua franca of the archipelago. Almost identical to Malay, it's usually learned second to an Indonesian's own regional language and is pretty easy to understand, thanks to a basic structure and the inclusion of many foreign words. With your attempts to speak their language, Indonesians are often quick to commend and reluctant to correct. A good way to learn pronunciation and to clear up mistakes before they become habitual is to ask an Indonesian to run through a few words with you.

Transliterations only give an approximate guide to correct pronunciation; so we include this guide for those who want to try their hand at pronouncing Bahasa Indonesia more like a native speaker. Transliterations are to the far right.

Consonants

Consonants are pronounced as they are in English, with the following exceptions:

b	at the end of a word, as the ´p´ in ´up´ elsewhere, as the ´b´ in ´better
k	at the end of a word, a glottal stop (the sound made between the words ´uh-oh´) elsewhere, as the ´k´ in ´king´
g	as the ´g´ in ´goat´, never as the ´g´ in ´gentle´
´	glottal stop; the sound made between the words ´uh-oh´
h	stressed a little more strongly than in English, as if you were sighing – particularly for words in which the ´h´ appears between two identical vowels
c	as the ´ch´ in ´chair´, never as the ´c´ in ´cable´ or the ´c´ in ´cedar´
j	as the ´j´ in ´joke´
ng	as the ´ng´ in ´sing´ (but when followed by another ´g´, ´as the ng´ in ´anger´)
ny	as the ´ny´ in ´canyon´
r	always trilled clearly and distinctly
sy	as the sound ´sh´

Vowels

a	as the ´a´ in *The Sound of Music's* ´do-re-me-*fa*´ (the ´a´ as in ´bat´ is not found in Bahasa Indonesia)
e	when stressed, as the ´e´ in ´bet´ when not stressed, as the ´a´ in ´about´
i	as the ´i´ in ´unique´
o	at the end of a syllable, as the ´o´ in ´hot´ elsewhere, as the the ´o´ in ´for´
u	as the ´oo´ in ´book´

Diphthongs

Bahasa Indonesia has three vowel combinations:

ai	as the 'y' in 'fly', but longer
au	as the 'ow' in 'cow', but longer
ua	as the 'oo' in 'too' + the 'a' in 'father', with a slight 'w' in between

Stress

Stress falls on the second-last syllable of a word. Therefore the first syllable is stressed in two-syllable words.

Enak!   en-ahk!   Delicious!

Useful Phrases

Do you speak English?
  ah-pah-kah ahn-dah berr-bah-hass-ah ing-griss?
  Apakah Anda berbahasa Inggris?
Are you hungry?
  ah-pah-kah ahn-dah lah-pahrr?
  Apakah Anda lapar?

I'm hungry.	sai-yah lah-pahrr	*Saya lapar.*
Have you eaten yet?	suh-dah mah-kahn bluhm?	*Sudah makan, belum?*
I've already eaten.	sai-yah mau mah-kahn	*Saya sudah makan.*

Eating Out — Makan di Luar Rumah

Where's a ... ?	... dih mah-nah	... di mana?
cheap restaurant	ruh-mah mah-kahn muh-rrah	rumah makan murah
food stall	wah-rruhng	warung
night market	pah-sahrr mah-lahm	pasar malam
restaurant	ruh-mah mah-kahn	rumah makan
roving vendor	kah-kih lih-mah	kaki-lima
Padang restaurant	ruh-mah mah-kahn pah-dahng	rumah makan Padang

Table for ... please.
  min-tah meh-jah uhn-tuhk ... orr-ahng
  Minta meja untuk ... orang.
Do you accept credit cards?
  bih-sah bah-yahrr deng-ahn karr-tuh krreh-diht?
  Bisa bayar dengan kartu kredit?
Can I smoke here?
  boh-leh meh-rroh-kohk dih sih-nih?
  Boleh merokok di sini?

Just Try It! — Coba Saja!

What's that?
  ah-pah ih-tuh?
  Apa itu?
What's the speciality of this region?
  mah-sah-kahn kahs dai-rrah ih-nih ah-pah?
  Masakan khas daerah ini apa?
What's the speciality here?
  mah-sah-kahn kahs dih sih-nih ah-pah?
  Masakan khas di sini apa?

What do you recommend?
ahn-dah meng-uh-suhl-kahn
mah-sah-kahn ah-pah?

*Anda mengusulkan
masakan apa?*

What are they eating?
meh-reh-kah mah-kahn ah-pah?

Mereka makan apa?

I'll try what they're having.
sai-yah mau mah-sah-kahn seh-perr-tih
yahng meh-reh-kah peh-sahn

*Saya mau masakan seperti
yang mereka pesan.*

The Menu

Daftar Makanan

Can I see the menu, please?
min-tah dahf-tarr mah-kah-nahn?

Minta daftar makanan?

Do you have a menu in English?
ah-pah-kah ah-dah dahf-tarr mah-kah-nahn
dah-lahm bah-hass-ah ing-grriss?

*Apakah ada daftar makanan
dalam bahasa Inggeris?*

I'd like ...   sai-yah mau mah-kahn ...
What does it include?   terr-mass-uhk ah-pah?
What do you have?   ah-dah ah-pah?

*Saya mau makan ...
Termasuk apa?
Ada apa?*

Is service included in the bill?
ah-pah-kah bon terr-mass-uhk
ong-koss serr-viss?

*Apakah bon termasuk
ongkos servis?*

Can I get it to takeaway?
bih-sah buhng-kuhss?

Bisa bungkus?

Throughout the Meal

What's in this dish?
mah-sah-kahn ih-nih terr-mass-uhk ah-pah?

Masakan ini termasuk apa?

Do you have sauce?   ada keh-chahp?
Not too spicy, please. kuh-rrahng peh-dass

*Ada kecap?
Kurang pedas.*

Is that dish spicy?
ah-pah-kah mah-sah-kahn ih-tuh peh-dass?

Apakah masakan itu pedas?

I like it hot and spicy.
sai-yah suh-kah mah-sah-kahn peh-dass

Saya suka masakan pedas.

It's not hot. (spicy)
mah-sah-kahn ih-nih kuh-rrang peh-dahss

Masakan ini kurang pedas.

It's not hot. (temperature)
mah-kah-nahn ih-nih tih-dahk pah-nass

Makanan ini tidak panas.

I didn't order this.
sai-yah tih-dahk meh-meh-sahn
mah-sah-kahn ih-nih

*Saya tidak memesan
masakan ini.*

I'd like something to drink.
sai-yah mau mih-nuhm

Saya mau minum.

It's taking a long time. Please hurry up.
suh-dah lah-mah. toh-long leh-bih
cheh-paht

Sudah lama. Tolong lebih cepat.

Thank you, that was delicious.
eh-nahk skah-lih, trrih-mah kah-sih

Enak sekali, terima kasih.

The bill, please.   min-tah bon

Minta bon.

Can you please bring me (some/more) ...?	bih-sah min-tah ... (lah-gih)?	*Bisa minta ... (lagi)?*
an ashtray	ahs-bahk	asbak
chilli sauce/relish	sahm-bahl	sambal
beer	bihrr	bir
a cup	chahng-kihr	cangkir
a fork	gahrr-puh	garpu
a glass	glahss	gelas
a knife	pih-sau	pisau
a napkin	tih-suh	tisu
a plate	pih-rring	piring
rice	nah-sih	nasi
salt	gah-rram	garam
soy sauce	keh-chahp	kecap
a spoon	sen-dohk	sendok
tea (with sugar)	teh mah-niss	teh manis
tea (without sugar)	teh pah-yiht	teh pahit
water	airr mih-nuhm	air minum

This food is (too) ...	mah-kah-nahn ih-nih (terr-lah-luh)	*Makanan ini (terlalu) ...*
bitter	pah-yiht	pahit
brilliant/delicious	en-ahk	enak
burnt	goh-song	gosong
cold	ding-in	dingin
hot	pah-nahss	panas
spoiled	buh-suhk	busuk
undercooked	men-tah	mentah

Children

Anak-Anak

Are children allowed?
ah-pah-kah ahn-ahk-ahn-ahk
bih-sah mah-suhk?

Apakah anak-anak bisa masuk?

Do you have a highchair for the baby?
ah-dah kurr-sih uhn-tuhk bai-yih?

Ada kursi untuk bayi?

You May Hear

Do you want anything to drink?
mau mih-nuhm ah-pah?

minum apa?

Anything else?	ah-dah lah-gih?	*Ada lagi?*
We have no	... tih-dahk ah-dah	*... tidak ada.*
Enjoy your meal!	slah-maht mah-kahn!	*Selamat makan!*

Family Meals

Can I bring anything?
  bih-sah sai-yah bah-wah ses-suah-tuh?

Let me help you.
  sai-yah bih-sah meh-noh-long

Can I watch you make this?
  ah-pah-kah sai-yah bih-sah meh-lih-aht
  proh-sess mah-sahk?

You're a great cook!
  ahn-dah peh-mah-sahk yahng baik!

This is brilliant!   eh-nahk!

Do you have the recipe for this?
  ah-pah-kah ahn-dah ah-dah reh-sep
  uhn-tuhk mah-sah-kahn ih-nih?

Is this a family recipe?
  ah-pah-kah ih-nih reh-sep mah-sah-kahn
  keh-luarr-gah?

Are the ingredients local?
  ah-pah-kah bah-hahn-nyah dah-rihh
  dai-rrah ih-nih?

I've never had a meal/eaten food like this before.
  sai-yah bluhm perr-nah mah-kahn
  mah-sah-kahn ih-nih

Is this a vegetable?   ah-pah-kah ih-nih sah-yuhrr?
Is this a fruit?   ah-pah-kah ih-nih buh-ah?

If you ever come to (Australia) I'll cook you a local dish.
  kah-lauh ahn-dah ke (au-trrah-lih-yah)
  sai-yah mah-sahk mah-sah-kahn
  (au-trrah-lih-yah)

Could you pass the (salt), please?
  min-tah (gah-rrahm)

One is enough, thank you.
  sah-tuh chuh-kuhp trrih-mah kah-sih

Do you use ... in this?
  ah-pah-kah ah-dah ... dah-lahm
  mah-sah-kahn ih-nih ?

No thank you. I'm full.
  trrih-mah kah-sih. suh-dah keh-nyahng

Thanks very much for the meal.
  trrih-mah kah-sih bahn-yahk ah-tahs
  mah-kah-nahn

I really appreciate it.
  sai-yah sahng-aht meng-harr-gai

Brilliant/delicious   en-ahk

Masakan Keluarga

Bisa saya bawa sesuatu?

Saya bisa menolong.

Apakah saya bisa melihat
  proses masak?

Anda pemasak yang baik!

Enak!

Apakah Anda ada resep
  untuk masakan ini?

Apakah ini resep masakan
  keluarga?

Apakah bahannya dari
  daerah ini?

Saya belum pernah makan
  masakan ini.

Apakah ini sayur?
Apakah ini buah?

Kalau Anda ke (Australia)
  saya masak masakan
  (Australia).

Minta (garam).

Satu cukup, terima kasih.

Apakah ada ... dalam
  masakan ini?

Terima kasih. Sudah kenyang.

Terima kasih banyak atas
  makanan.

Saya sangat menghargai.

enak

Vegetarian & Special Meals

Makanan Nabati & Makanan Istimewa

I'm a vegetarian
  sai-yah hah-nyah mah-kahn sah-yuhrr-ahn *Saya hanya makan sayuran.*

I'm a vegan, I don't eat meat or dairy products.
  sai-yah tih-dahk mah-kahn dah-ging *Saya tidak makan daging*
  dahn suh-suh *dan susu.*

I don't want any meat at all.
  sai-yah tih-dahk mau dah-ging *Saya tidak mau daging.*

Don't add egg.
  jahng-ahn pah-kai teh-luhr *Jangan pakai telur.*

I don't eat ...	sai-yah tih-dahk suh-kah/ tah-hahn mah-kahn ...	*Saya tidak suka/* *tahan makan ...*
chicken	ai-yahm	*ayam*
eggs	teh-luhr	*telur*
fish	ih-kahn	*ikan*
meat	dah-ging	*daging*
milk and cheese	suh-suh dahn keh-juh	*susu dan keju*
pork	dah-ging bah-bih	*daging babi*
poultry	ai-yahm	*ayam*
seafood	mah-kah-nahn laut	*makanan laut*

Do you have any vegetarian dishes?
  ah-dah mah-kah-nahn nah-bah-tih? *Apakah ada makanan nabati?*

Can you recommend a vegetarian dish?
  dah-paht-kah ahn-dah meng-uh-suhl-kahn *Dapatkah Anda mengusulkan*
  suh-ah-tuh mah-sah-kahn *suatu masakan nabati apa?*
  nah-bah-tih ah-pah?

Does this dish have meat?
  ah-pah-kah mah-sah-kahn ih-nih ah-dah *Apakah masakan ini ada*
  dah-ging-nyah? *dagingnya?*

Can I get this without the meat?
  bih-sah min-tah mah-sah-kahn ih-nih *Bisa minta masakan ini*
  tahn-pah dah-ging? *tanpa daging?*

Is the sauce meat-based?
  ah-pah-kah saus ih-nih dah-rrih dah-ging *Apakah saus ini dari daging?*

Does it contain eggs/dairy products?
  ah-pah-kah ih-nih mehn-gahn-dung *Apakah ini mengandung*
  teh-luhr/suh-suh? *telur/susu?*

I'm allergic to (peanuts).
  sai-yah tih-dahk tah-han mah-kahn *Saya tidak tahan makan*
  (kah-chahng). *(kacang).*

I'd like a halal meal.
  sai-yah mau mah-kah-nahn hah-lahl? *Saya mau makanan halal.*

Is this halal?
  Ah-pah-kah ih-nih hah-lahl? *Apakah ini halal?*

At the Market/Self Catering

Di Pasar/Masakan Sendiri

Where's the nearest (market)?
   Dih mah-nah (pah-sahrr) terr-deh-kaht?

Di mana (pasar) terdekat?

Where can I find (sugar)?
   (guh-lah) dih mah-nah?

(Gula) di mana?

When does this shop open?
   toh-koh ih-nih buh-kah jahm brrah-pah

Toko ini buka jam berapa?

Can I have a ...	min-tah	*Minta ...*
bottle	boh-totl	*botol*
can	kah-leng	*kaleng*
packet	pah-ket	*paket*
tin of ...	se-kah-leng	*sekaleng ...*

How much? (cost)
   brrah-pah harr-gah?

Berapa harga?

How much is (a kilo of mangoes)?
   brrah-pah harr-gah (se-kih-loh mahng-gah)?

Berapa harga (sekilo mangga)?

Do you have anything cheaper?
   ah-pah-kah ah-dah yahng leh-bih muh-rrah?

Apakah ada yang lebih murah?

Can you give me a discount?
   bih-sah dah-paht diss-kon?

Bisa dapat diskon?

Give me (half) a kilo, please.
   min-tah (se-teng-ah) kih-loh

Minta (setengah) kilo.

I'd like (six) bananas.
   sai-yah mau (eh-nahm) pih-sahng

Saya mau (enam) pisang.

How much (for) ... ?	brrah-pah harr-gah (uhn-tuhk) ... ?	*Berapa harga (untuk) ... ?*
both	keh-dua-nyah	*keduanya*
per fruit	sah-tuh bua	*satu buah*
per piece	sah-tuh porr-sih	*satu porsi*
this	ih-nih	*ini*

I'm just looking.
   sai-yah lih-haht lih-haht sah-jah

Saya lihat lihat saja.

This is a present for someone.
   kah-doh ih-nih uhn-tuhk seh-seh-orr-ahng

Kado ini untuk seseorang.

No!	tih-dahk	*Tidak!*
Best before ...	mah-kahn se-bluhm	*Makan sebelum ...*
Can I taste it?	boh-leh chih-chip?	*Boleh cicip?*
I am looking for ...	sai-yah men-cha-rri ...	*Saya mencari ...*

Is this the best you have?
   ah-pah-kah ih-nih yahng terr-baik?

Apakah ini yang terbaik?

What's the local speciality?
   mah-sah-kahn kahs dai-rrah ih-nih ah-pah?

Masakan khas daerah ini apa?

Where can I buy ...?
   sai-yah bih-sah mem-beh-lih dih mah-nah?

Saya bisa membeli di mana?

I'd like to buy ...	sai-yah mau mem-beh-lih ...	*Saya mau membeli ...*
chilli sauce/relish	sahm-bahl	*sambal*
chillies	chah-beh	*cabe*
eggs	teh-luhrr	*telur*
fish	ih-kahn	*ikan*
fruit and vegetables	bua-han dan sah-yuhrr-ahn	*buahan dan sayuran*
jam	seh-lai	*selai*
meat	dah-ging	*daging*
milk	suh-suh	*susu*
noodles	mih	*mie*
oil	mih-nyahk	*minyak*
rice (uncooked)	brahss	*beras*
salt	gah-rrahm	*garam*
soy sauce	keh-chahp	*kecap*
sugar	guh-lah	*gula*

At the Bar

Di Bar

Shall we go for a drink?
  ai-yoh ke barr?

Ayo ke bar?

I'll buy you a drink.
  sai-yah mem-beh-lih ahn-dah
  mih-nuh-mahn

Saya membelikan Anda minuman.

Thanks, but I don't feel like it.
  trrih-mah kah-sih tih-dahk

Terima kasih, tidak.

I don't drink (alcohol).
  sai-yah tih-dahk mih-nuhm
  (mih-nuh-mahn krrahs)

Saya tidak minum (minuman keras).

What would you like?
  ahn-dah mau mih-nuhm ah-pah?

Anda mau minum apa?

You can get the next one.
  ahn-dah boh-leh bah-yahrr yahng
  berr-ih-kuht

Anda boleh bayar yang berikut.

It's on me.
  sai-yah bah-yahrr

Saya bayar.

It's my round.
  sai-yah bah-yahrr kah-lih ih-nih

Saya bayar kali ini.

Okay.
  baik

Baik.

Can I buy you a coffee?
  sai-yah mem-beh-lih koh-pih uhn-tuhk
  ahn-dah yah?

Saya membeli kopi untuk Anda ya?

I don't drink (coffee).
  sai-yah tih-dahk mih-nuhm (koh-pih)

Saya tidak minum (kopi).

I'm next.
sai-yah yahng berr-ih-kuht

Saya yang berikut.

Excuse me.
  perr-mih-sih

Permisi.

I was here before this person.
    sai-yah men-uhng-guh leh-bih duh-luh
    dah-rrih-pah-dah dih-yah

Saya menunggu lebih dulu daripada dia.

I would like (a) ...   sai-yah mau ..

Saya mau ...

Please give me (a) ...   min-tah ...

minta ...

rice wine	ah-rahk	arak
beer	birr	bir
wine	ahng-gurr	anggur
vodka	vod-kah	vodka
vodka and lemonade	vod-kah dahn lim-on-ahde	vodka dan limonade.

Cheers!   slahm-aht!   *Selamat!*
No ice.   tahn-pah ess   *Tanpah es.*
Can I have ice, please? min-tah ess   *Minta es.*

Same again, thanks.
    Yahng sah-mah trrih-mah kah-sih

Yang sama, terima kasih.

Is food available here?
    ah-pah-kah ah-dah mah-kah-nahn
    dih sih-nih?

Apakah ada makanan di sini?

This is hitting the spot.
    ih-nih en-ahk

Ini enak.

Where's the toilet?
    weh-seh dih mah-nah?

WC di mana?

I'm a bit tired. I'd better get home.
    sai-yah chah-peh. puh-lahng duh-luh

Saya cape. Pulang dulu.

I've drunk too much.
    sai-yah mih-nuhm terr-lah-luh bah-nyahk

Saya minum terlalu banyak.

One more and I'll be under the table.
    seh-dih-kit lah-gih sai-yah pass-tih sah-kit

Sedikit lagi saya pasti sakit.

So, do you come here often?
    ah-pah-kah ahn-dah srring ke sih-nih?

Apakah Anda sering ke sini?

I really, really love you.
    sai-yah behn-arr behn-arr chin-tah ka-muh

Saya benar-benar cinta kamu.

What did I do last night?
    sai-yah buat ah-pah tah-dih mah-lahm?

Saya buat apa tadi malam?

I'm never, ever, drinking again.
    sai-yah tahk perr-nah
    mih-nuhm lah-gih

Saya tak akan pernah minum lagi.

I'm feeling drunk.	sai-yah mah-buhk	*Saya mabuk.*
I'm pissed.	sai-yah mah-buhk skah-lih	*Saya mabuk sekali.*
I feel ill.	sai-yah mual	*Saya mual.*
I want to throw up.	sai-yah mau muhn-tah	*Saya mau muntah.*
S/he's passed out.	dih-yah ping-sahn	*Dia pingsan.*
I'm hung over.	sai-yah sah-kit keh-pah-la	*Saya sakit kepala.*

English – Indonesian Glossary

Plurals are made in Indonesian by repeating the item: anak (child) anak-anak (children). Often you won't need to repeat the noun, as context will indicate whether you're talking about one or more items. For example, if you're buying six bananas, you'd ask for enam pisang ('six banana').

A

abalone	*keh-rrahng laut*	kerang laut
alcohol	*mih-nuh-mahn krrahs*	minuman keras
allergic	*al-err-gee*	alergi
anchovy	*ih-kahn bih-liss/teh-rih*	ikan bilis/teri
appetiser	*mah-kah-nahn keh-chill*	makanan kecil
apple	*ah-pel*	apel
apricot	*ah-prih-kot*	aprikot
aroma	*harr-uhm/wahng-ih*	harum/wangi
ashtray	*ahs-bahk*	asbak
asparagus	*ahs-pah-rrah-goos*	asparagus
aubergine	*trrohng*	terong
avocado	*ah-poh-kaht/al-pu-kaht*	apokat/alpukat

B

to bake	*pahng-gahng*	panggang
bakery	*toh-koh rroh-tih*	toko roti
bamboo	*buh-luh/bahm-buh*	bulu/bambu
–shoot	*reh-buhng*	rebung
banana	*pih-sahng*	pisang
–leaf	*daun pih-sahng*	daun pisang
barley	*gerrst*	gerst
basil, lemon	*keh-mahng-ih*	kemangi
bass	*ih-kahn gah-rruh-pah*	ikan garupa
batter	*ah-doh-nahn*	adonan
bean	*kah-chahng*	kacang
–curd (tofu)	*tah-hu*	tahu
green	*kah-chahng buhn-chiss*	kacang buncis
kidney	*kah-chahng meh-rrah*	kacang merah
lima	*kah-chahng jah-wah*	kacang jawa
mung	*kah-chahng hih-jau*	kacang hijau
–sprout	*tau-geh*	tauge
string	*buhn-chiss*	buncis
yard-long	*kah-chahng pahn-jahng*	kacang panjang
beef	*dah-ging sah-pih*	daging sapi
beer	*bihrr*	bir
stout	*bihrr hih-tahm*	bir hitam
berries	*beh-rrih*	berry
betel nut	*sih-rrih*	sirih
bill	*bon*	bon

biscuit	*bih-skit*	biskit
bitter	*pah-yiht*	pahit
boar, wild	*bah-bih lih-ahrr/huh-tahn*	babi liar/hutan
to boil	*reh-buhs*	rebus
bottle	*boh-tohl*	botol
−opener	*pem-buh-kah boh-tohl*	pembuka botol
bowl	*mahng-kuhk*	mangkuk
brains	*oh-tahk*	otak
bran	*kuh-liht pah-dih*	kulit padi
brandy	*brren-dih*	brendi
bread	*roh-tih*	roti
bun, steamed	*bahk-pao*	bakpao
breakfast	*mah-kahn pah-gih*	makan pagi
breast/brisket	*dah-dah*	dada
broccoli	*brroh-koh-lih/koh-biss*	brokoli/kobis
broth	*buh-lih-yon*	bulyon
Brussel sprouts	*kohl mih-nih*	kol mini
bubble	*glem-buhng*	gelembung
buckwheat	*soh-bah*	soba
buffalo	*kerr-bau*	kerbau
burn	*bah-kahrr*	bakar
butter	*men-teh-gah*	mentega

C

cabbage	*kohl*	kol
cake	*kuh-way*	kue
can	*kah-leng*	kaleng
−opener	*pem-buh-kah kah-leng*	pembuka kaleng
candlenut	*kmih-rrih*	kemiri
candy	*perr-men*	permen
cantaloupe	*meh-lohn*	melon
capon	*ah-yahm ke-bih-rrih*	ayam kebiri
capsicum (pepper)	*chah-beh beh-sarr*	cabe besar
green	*chah-beh hih-jau beh-sarr*	cabe hijau besar
red	*chah-beh meh-rrah beh-sarr*	cabe merah besar
caraway seed	*bih-jih je-muh-juh*	biji jemuju
cardamom	*kah-puhl*	kapul
carp	*ih-kahn mahss*	ikan mas
carrot	*wohrr-tell*	wortel
cashew	*jahm-buh meh-teh*	jambu mete
cashier	*kah-sah*	kassa
cassava	*sing-kong*	singkong
−root	*uh-bih kai-yuh*	ubi kayu
catfish	*ih-kahn leh-leh/leh-leh*	lele
cauliflower	*kohl kem-bahng*	kol kembang
celery	*seh-leh-deh-rrih*	selederi
champagne	*sahm-pah-nyeh*	sampanye

English	Pronunciation	Indonesian
cheap	*muh-rrah*	murah
cheese	*keh-juh*	keju
chef	*juh-ruh mah-sahk*	juru masak
cherry	*cherr-ih*	ceri
chestnut	*brrahng-ahn*	berangan
chicken	*ah-yahm*	ayam
–claw	*chah-kahrr ah-yahm*	cakar ayam
free-range	*ah-yahm kahm-pung*	ayam kampung
fried	*ah-yahm gorr-eng*	ayam goreng
grilled	*ah-yahm bah-kahrr*	ayam bakar
–liver	*hah-tih ah-yahm*	hati ayam
sate	*sah-teh ah-yahm*	sate ayam
chilli	*chah-beh*	cabe
bird's eye	*chah-beh rah-wit*	cabe rawit
green	*chah-beh hih-jau*	cabe hijau
red	*chah-beh meh-rrah*	cabe merah
–sauce/relish	*sahm-bahl*	sambal
chives	*kuh-chai/loh-kih-oh*	kucai/lokio
chocolate	*choh-klaht*	coklat
cigarettes, clove	*kre-tek*	kretek
cilantro	*keh-tuhm-barr*	ketumbar
cinnamon	*kai-yuh mah-niss*	kayu manis
citrus	*bua jerr-uhk*	buah jeruk
–juice	*ess jerr-uhk*	es jeruk
clam	*keh-rrahng*	kerang
to clean/clean	*berr-sih*	bersih
clear (of liquids)	*beh-ning*	bening
closed	*tuh-tuhp*	tutup
cloves	*cheng-keh*	cengkeh
cockles	*peng-sih*	pengsi
cocoa	*bih-jih choh-klaht*	biji coklat
coconut	*keh-lah-pah*	kelapa
–water	*airr kel-ah-pah*	air kelapa
–milk	*sahn-than*	santan
–flesh, dried & shredded	*choh-prah*	copra
coffee	*koh-pih*	kopi
black, with sugar	*koh-pih tuh-brruhk*	kopi tubruk
–with egg and sugar	*koh-pih teh-luhrr*	kopi telur
–spiced, with coconut	*bah-jih-guhrr*	bajigur
–with milk	*koh-pih suh-suh*	kopi susu
–without sugar	*koh-pih pah-yiht*	kopi pahit
–with sugar	*koh-pih deng-ahn guh-lah*	kopi dengan gula
cold	*ding-in*	dingin
condiment	*buhm-buh*	bumbu
congee (porridge)	*bu-buhrr*	bubur
conserve	*ah-wet-tahn*	awetan

English	Pronunciation	Indonesian
consomme	*kahl-duh*	kaldu
to cook	*mah-sahk*	masak
cooked	*mah-tahng*	matang
cookie	*bih-skit/bih-skuit*	biskit/biskuit
cordial	*sih-rrop*	sirop
coriander	*keh-tuhm-barr*	ketumbar
corn	*jah-guhng*	jagung
–fritters	*perr-keh-del jah-guhng*	perkedel jagung
grilled	*jah-guhng bah-kahrr*	jagung bakar
–meal	*teh-puhng jah-guhng*	tepung jagung
cost (of item)	*harr-gah*	harga
cost (of service)	*ong-koss*	ongkos
courgette	*trruhng hih-jau*	terung hijau
cow	*sah-pih*	sapi
crab	*keh-pih-ting*	kepiting
crackers	*krruh-puhk*	kerupuk
melinjo nut	*em-ping*	emping
rice	*in-tip*	intip
shrimp	*krruh-puhk uh-dahng*	kerupuk udang
crayfish	*uh-dahng kah-rrahng*	udang karang
cream	*krrim*	krim
cress	*kahng-kuhng*	kangkung
crispy	*gah-rring*	garing
croquette	*perr-keh-del*	perkedel
cucumber	*keh-tih-muhn*	ketimun
cuisine	*mah-sah-kahn*	masakan
cumin	*jin-ten*	jinten
cup	*chahng-kihrr*	cangkir
curd	*dah-dih*	dadih
currant	*kiss-miss*	kismis
curry	*kah-rreh/guh-lai*	kare/gulai
–paste/powder	*buhm-buh kah-rrih*	bumbu kari
custard apple	*srrih-kah-yah*	srikaya
to cut	*poh-tong*	potong
cutlery	*sen-dohk garr-puh*	sendok garpu
cutlet	*sah-yah-tahn*	sayatan

D

English	Pronunciation	Indonesian
dates	*kuhrr-mah*	kurma
to deep-fry	*gorr-eng*	goreng
delicious	*en-ahk*	enak
dessert	*pen-chuh-chih muh-luht*	pencuci mulut
to dice	*dih-poh-tong*	dipotong
dinner	*mah-kahn mah-lahm*	makan malam
dirty	*koh-torr*	kotor
dish	*mah-sah-kahn*	masakan

dog	*ahn-jing/beh sah-tuh/err-weh*	anjing/B1/RW
dried	*krring*	kering
drink	*mih-nuh-mahn*	minuman
to drink	*mih-nuhm*	minum
cold	*mih-nuh-mahn ding-in*	minuman dingin
hot	*mih-nuh-mahn pah-nahs*	minuman panas
ice	*mih-nuh-mahn ess*	minuman es
duck	*beh-behk/ih-tihk*	bebek/itik
dumpling	*pahng-sit*	pangsit
durian	*duh-rrih-ahn*	durian

E

to eat	*mah-kahn*	makan
eel	*bluht*	belut
egg	*teh-luhrr*	telur
boiled	*teh-luhrr rreh-buhs*	telur rebus
fried	*teh-luhrr gorr-eng*	telur goreng
poached	*teh-luhrr ceh-plok*	telur ceplok
eggplant	*trrohng*	terong
endive	*ahn-deh-wee*	andewi
entrails	*jerr-oh-wahn*	jeroan
entree	*mah-kah-nahn keh-chill*	makanan kecil

F

to fast (not eat)	*pwahss-ah*	puasa
fennel	*ah-dahs*	adas
–seed	*bih-jih ah-dahs*	biji adas
fernshoot	*pah-kiss*	pakis
fig	*ah-rrah*	ara
to fill	*ih-sih*	isi
to fillet	*poh-tong tih-piss*	potong tipis
fish	*ih-kahn*	ikan
anchovy	*ih-kahn bih-liss/teh-rih*	ikan bilis/teri
bass	*ih-kahn gah-rruh-pah*	ikan garupa
carp	*ih-kahn mahss*	ikan mas
catfish	*ih-kahn leh-leh/leh-leh*	lele
flat	*ih-kahn se-bla*	ikan sebelah
garfish	*ih-kahn jah-luhng jah-luhng*	ikan julung-julung
goldfish	*ih-kahn mahss*	ikan mas
grouper	*ih-kahn gah-rruh-pah*	ikan garupa
mackerel	*ih-kahn tong-kohl/teng-gih-rrih*	ikan tongkol/tenggiri
pampel	*bah-wahl*	bawal
perch	*keh-rrah-puh; ih-kahn kah-kahp*	kerapu; ikan kakap
pomfret	*ih-kahn bah-wal*	ikan bawal
ray	*ih-kahn pah-rrih*	ikan pari

GLOSSARY

–roe	*teh-luhrr ih-kahn*	telur ikan
salmon	*ih-kahn sah-lem*	ikan salem
sardine	*ih-kahn leh-muh-rru/sarr-den*	ikan lemuru/sarden
shark	*ih-kahn hih-yuh*	ikan hiu
sole	*ih-kahn lih-dah*	ikan lidah
snakehead	*gah-buhs/hah-rrah-wahn*	gabus/harawan
trout	*ih-kahn airr tah-wahr*	ikan air tawar
tuna	*tong-kohl*	tongkol
whitebait	*ih-kahn teh-rrih*	ikan teri
flavour	*rah-sah*	rasa
flour	*teh-puhng*	tepung
food	*mah-kah-nahn*	makanan
food stall	*wah-ruhng*	warung
fork	*garr-puh*	garpu
free (of cost)	*grrah-tiss*	gratis
fresh	*seh-garr*	segar
fritter	*perr-keh-del*	perkedel
frog	*koh-dohk*	kodok
fruit	*bua bua-hahn*	buah-buahan
dried	*bua bua-hahn krring*	buah-buahan kering
to fry	*gorr-eng*	goreng
full (content)	*ken-yahng*	kenyang

G

galangal	*lah-ohs*	laos
lesser	*ken-churr*	kencur
garfish	*ih-kahn jah-luhng jah-luhng*	ikan julung-julung
garlic	*bah-wahng puh-tih*	bawang putih
general store	*toh-koh uh-mum*	toko umum
giblets	*jerr-oh-wahn*	jeroan
ginger	*jah-heh*	jahe
glass	*glahss*	gelas
goat	*kahm-bing*	kambing
goldfish	*ih-kahn mahss*	ikan mas
goose	*ahng-sah*	angsa
grape	*ahng-guhrr*	anggur
grapefruit	*jerr-uhk kerr-ih-puht*	jeruk keriput
grapes	*bua ahng-guhrr*	buah anggur
to grate	*meh-mah-rruht*	memarut
grater	*pah-ruh-tahn*	parutan
gravy	*kuh-wah*	kuah
grease	*leh-mahk*	lemak
to grill	*peh-mahng-gahng*	pemanggang
grilled	*bah-kahrr*	bakar
grouper	*ih-kahn gah-rruh-pah*	ikan garupa
guava	*jahm-buh*	jambu

H

halal	*hah-lal*	halal
ham	*dah-ging bah-bih*	daging babi
–burger	*hum-burr-gurr*	hamburger
hare	*terr-weh-luh*	terwelu
heart	*jahn-tuhng*	jantung
hearty	*guh-rrih*	gurih
herbal medicine	*jah-muh*	jamu
honey	*mah-duh*	madu
hot (spicy)	*peh-dahs*	pedas
hot (temperature)	*pah-nahs*	panas
hungry	*lah-pahr*	lapar

I

ice	*ess*	es
–cream	*ess krrim*	es krim
indigenous	*khas*	khas
Indonesian laurel	*daun sah-lahm*	daun salam
ingredient	*bah-hahn*	bahan

J

jackfruit	*nahng-kah*	nangka
jam	*seh-lai*	selai
jicama	*beng-kuang*	bengkuang
juice	*juhs*	jus

K

kaffir lime	*jerr-uhk prruht*	jeruk perut
–leaf	*daun jerr-uhk prruht*	daun jeruk perut
ketchup	*saus toh-maht*	saus tomat
kettle	*keh-tell/cherr-et*	ketel/ceret
kidney	*gin-jahl*	ginjal
kitchen	*dah-puhrr*	dapur
kiwi fruit	*kih-wih*	kiwi
knife	*pih-sau*	pisau
knuckle	*buh-kuh jah-rrih*	buku jari

L

ladle	*sen-dohk beh-sarr*	sendok besar
lamb	*ah-nahk dom-bah*	anak domba
langsat	*duh-kuh*	duku
lard	*bah-bih*	lemak babi
leaf	*daun*	daun
leek	*bah-wahng peh-rrai*	bawang perai
leg	*kah-kih*	kaki

231

legumes	*kah-chahng*	kacang
lemon	*lih-mon*	limon
lemongrass	*seh-rreh*	sereh
lentils	*mih-juh mih-juh*	miju-miju
lettuce	*seh-lah-dah*	selada
lime		
green	*jerr-uhk lih-mau*	jeruk limau
yellow	*jerr-uhk nih-piss*	jeruk nipis
little (amount)	*seh-dih-kit*	sedikit
liver	*hah-tih*	hati
lobster	*uh-dahng kah-rrahng*	udang karang
loin	*ping-gahng*	pinggang
lollies	*perr-men*	permen
longan	*leng-keng*	lengkeng
lunch	*mah-kahn sih-yahng*	makan siang
lychee	*leh-chih*	leci

M

mace	*buhng-ah pah-lah*	bunga pala
mackerel	*ih-kahn tong-kohl/teng-gih-rrih*	ikan tongkol/tenggiri
main course	*mah-sah-kahn oo-tah-mah*	masakan utama
maize	*teh-puhng jah-guhng*	tepung jagung
mandarin	*jerr-uhk mahn-dahrr-in*	jeruk mandarin
mango	*mahng-gah*	mangga
mangosteen	*mahng-giss*	manggis
manioc	*sing-kong*	singkong
margarine	*men-teh-gah*	mentega
marinade	*ah-sin-nahn*	asinan
to marinate	*meng-ah-sin-kahn*	mengasinkan
market	*pah-sahrr*	pasar
night	*pah-sahrr mah-lahm*	pasar malam
marmalade	*seh-lai jerr-uhk*	selai jeruk
marrow	*suhm-suhm*	sumsum
meal	*mah-kah-nahn*	makanan
–to go	*buhng-kuhs*	bungkus
meat	*dah-ging*	daging
–less/free	*tahn-pah dah-ging*	tanpa daging
medium (cooked)	*se-teng-ah mah-tahng*	setengah matang
melon	*meh-lohn*	melon
menu	*dahf-tahrr mah-kah-nahn*	daftar makanan
merchant	*tuh-kahng/pen-jual*	tukang/penjual
milk	*suh-suh*	susu
condensed	*suh-suh ken-tahl*	susu kental
soy	*suh-suh keh-deh-lai*	susu kedelai
to mince	*chin-chahng*	cincang
mineral water	*airr mih-nerr-ahl*	air mineral
to mix	*chum-puhrr*	campur

molasses	*guh-lah teh-tess*	gula tetes
money	*uh-wahng*	uang
mortar & pestle	*choh-bek dahn uh-lek-uh-lek*	cobek dan ulek-ulek
monosodium glutamate	*vet-sin*	vetsin
muscle	*oh-tot*	otot
mushrooms	*jah-muhr*	jamur
mussel	*keh-rrahng*	kerang
mutton	*dah-ging dom-bah*	daging domba

N

napkin	*serr-bet*	serbet
neck	*leh-hehrr*	leher
noodles	*mih*	mie
bean-flour vermicelli	*soh-huhn*	sohun
cellophane	*mih-huhn*	mihun
egg	*bah-mih*	bami
flat rice	*kuay-tau*	kuaytau
fried	*mih gorr-eng*	mie goreng
mung-bean	*soh-huhn*	sohun
rice-flour	*bahk-mih*	bakmi
–soup	*mih reh-buhs*	mie rebus
nut	*kah-chahng*	kacang
nutmeg	*pah-lah*	pala
nutritious	*berr-gih-zih*	bergizi

O

octopus	*guh-rrih-ta*	gurita
offal	*jerr-oh-wahn*	jeroan
oil	*mih-nyahk*	minyak
coconut	*mih-nyahk keh-lah-pah*	minyak kelapa
corn	*mih-nyahk jah-gung*	minyak jagung
palm	*mih-nyahk sah-wit*	minyak sawit
peanut	*mih-nyahk kah-chahng*	minyak kacang
sesame	*mih-nyahk bih-jahn*	minyak bijan
vegetable	*mih-nyahk tuhm-buh-hahn*	minyak tumbuhan
okra	*ohk-rra*	okra
old	*tuh-wah*	tua
omelette	*teh-luhrr dah-darr*	telur dadar
onion	*bah-wahng bom-bay*	bawang bombay
pickled	*bah-wahng ah-chahrr*	bawang acar
open	*buh-kah*	buka
orange (citrus fruit)	*jerr-uhk mah-niss*	jeruk manis
organic	*orr-gah-nik*	organik
oven	*tah-nurr*	tanur
oyster	*tih-rrahm*	tiram
–sauce	*saus tih-rrahm*	saus tiram

P

palm (tree)	*jah-kah*	jaka
–fruit	*bluh-luht*	belulut
–wine	*tuh-wahk*	tuak
pampel fish	*bah-wahl*	bawal
pandanus (screwpine) leaf	*daun pahn-dahn*	daun pandan
papaya	*pah-pai-yah*	papaya
paprika	*pah-prih-kah*	paprika
parsley	*peh-terr-seh-lih*	peterseli
passionfruit	*marr-kih-sah*	markisa
pasta	*pah-stah*	pasta
pastry	*kuh-way krring*	kue kering
pawpaw	*pah-pai-yah*	papaya
pea (green)	*kah-chahng bel-ihm-bing*	kacang belimbing
peach	*perr-sihk*	persik
peanut	*kah-chahng tah-nah*	kacang tanah
salted	*kah-chahng ah-sin*	kacang asin
–sauce	*saus kah-chahng*	saus kacang
pear	*perr*	per
peel (outer layer)	*kuh-liht*	kulit
pepper (black)	*meh-rrih-chah/lah-dah*	merica/lada
pepper (capsicum)	*chah-beh beh-sarr*	cabe besar
perch	*keh-rrah-puh; ih-kahn kah-kahp*	kerapu; ikan kakap
persimmon	*keh-seh-mahk*	kesemak
pheasant	*peh-gahrr*	pegar
to pickle	*meng-ah-sin-kahn*	mengasinkan
pickles	*ah-chahrr*	acar
picnic	*pik-nik*	piknik
pig	*bah-bih*	babi
spit-roast	*bah-bih guh-ling*	babi guling
pigeon	*buh-rrung dah-rrah*	burung dara
pineapple	*nah-nahs*	nanas
plate	*pih-rring*	piring
plum	*prrem*	prem
Java	*jahm-blahng*	jamblang
to poach	*meh-rreh-buhs*	merebus
pomegranate	*deh-lih-mah*	delima
pomelo	*jerr-uhk muhn-tiss*	jeruk muntis
pomfret	*ih-kahn bah-wal*	ikan bawal
popcorn	*jah-guhng meh-leh-tuhs*	jagung meletus
poppy	*bnih ah-pih-oon*	benih apiun
pork	*dah-ging bah-bih*	daging babi
porridge (congee)	*bu-buhrr*	bubur
port	*porrt*	port
pot	*pahn-chih*	panci

potato	*ken-tahng*	kentang
–chips/crisps	*ken-tahng keh-rrip-ihk*	kentang keripik
fried	*ken-tahng gorr-eng*	kentang goreng
roasted	*ken-tahng pahng-gahng*	kentang panggang
poultry	*uhng-gahs*	unggas
prawn	*uh-dahng*	udang
price (of item/meal)	*harr-gah*	harga
price (of service)	*ong-koss*	ongkos
prune	*prrem krring*	prem kering
pulses (legumes)	*kah-chahng*	kacang
pumpkin	*lah-bu*	labu

Q

quail	*puh-yuh*	puyuh

R

rabbit	*keh-lin-chih*	kelinci
radish	*loh-bahk*	lobak
raisin	*kiss-miss*	kismis
raspberry	*frrum-boss*	frambos
rare (cooked)	*se-teng-ah men-tah*	setengah mentah
raw	*men-tah*	mentah
receipt	*bon*	bon
red	*meh-rrah*	merah
regional cuisines	*mah-sah-kahn kass dai-rrah*	masakan khas daerah
reservation	*peh-sah-nahn*	pesanan
restaurant	*rest-or-ahm/ruh-mah mah-kahn*	restoran/rumah makan
rhubarb	*kel-em-bahk*	kelembak
ribs	*tuh-lahng rruh-suhk*	tulang rusuk
rice		
black	*keh-tahn hih-tahm*	ketan hitam
brown	*brrahs meh-rrah*	beras merah
cooked	*nah-sih*	nasi
–crackers	*keh-rrahk/in-tip*	kerak/intip
–field, dry	*lah-dahng*	ladang
–flour	*teh-puhng brrahs*	tepung beras
–flour noodles	*bahk-mih*	bakmi
fried	*nah-sih gorr-eng*	nasi goreng
glutinous	*keh-tahn*	ketan
–noodles	*bih-hun*	bihun
plain white	*nah-sih pu-tih*	nasi putih
plant, growing; unhusked	*pah-dih*	padi
post-harvest, uncooked	*brrahs*	beras
post-harvest, un-husked/pre-milled	*gah-bah*	gabah

–pudding (black-rice)	*buh-buhrr keh-tahn hih-tahm*	bubur ketan hitam
–pudding (plain white)	*buh-buhrr leh-muh*	bubur lemu
steamed in banana leaves	*lon-tong*	lontong
steamed in coconut palm packages	*keh-tuh-paht*	ketupat
wild	*pah-dih lih-yarr*	padi liar
rich (of food)	*guh-rrih*	gurih
ripe	*mah-tahng*	matang
to roast	*pahng-gahng*	panggang
roving vendors	*kah-kih lih-mah*	kaki-lima
rump	*pahn-taht*	pantat

S

sago	*sah-guh*	sagu
salad	*seh-lah-dah*	selada
salam leaf	*daun sah-lahm*	daun salam
salmon	*ih-kahn sah-lem*	ikan salem
salt	*gah-rrahm*	garam
salty	*ah-sin*	asin
sapodilla	*sah-woh mah-nih-lah*	sawo manila
sardine	*ih-kahn leh-muh-rru/sarr-den*	ikan lemuru/sarden
satay	*sah-teh*	sate
satisfied	*pwahss*	puas
sauce	*kwah/saus*	kuah/saus
peanut	*saus kah-chahng*	saus kacang
soy	*keh-chahp*	kecap
saucepan	*pahn-chih berr-gah-gahng*	panci bergagang
sausage	*oh-rret/soh-siss*	oret/sosis
scales	*tim-bahng-ahn*	timbangan
scallop	*reh-miss*	remis
scissors	*guhn-ting*	gunting
screwpine/	*daun pahn-dahn*	daun pandan
seafood	*mah-kah-nahn laut*	makanan laut
seaweed	*ruhm-puht laut*	rumput laut
seller	*tuh-kahng/pen-jual*	tukang/penjual
servant	*pem-bahn-tuh*	pembantu
server	*peh-lai-yahn*	pelayan
service	*peh-lai-yah-nahn*	pelayanan
sesame seed	*bih-jih bih-jahn*	biji bijan
shallot	*bah-wahng meh-rrah*	bawang merah
shank	*tuh-lahng krring*	tulang kering
shark	*ih-kahn hih-yuh*	ikan hiu
shellfish	*keh-rrahng keh-rrahng-an*	kerang-kerangan
shin	*gah-rrahs*	garas

English	Pronunciation	Indonesian
to shop/shopping	*blahn-jah*	belanja
shoulder	*bah-hoo*	bahu
shrimp	*uh-dahng*	udang
dried	*eh-bih*	ebi
–paste	*trrah-sih*	terasi
to sieve/sift	*ah-yah-kahn*	ayakan
sifter	*ah-yah-kahn*	ayakan
to simmer	*dih-dih*	didih
sirloin	*dah-ging ping-gahng*	daging pinggang
skewer	*tuh-suhk*	tusuk
skin	*kuh-liht*	kulit
slice	*ih-riss*	iris
to slice	*meng-ih-rris*	mengiris
to smell (also to kiss)	*men-chium*	mencium
smell (aroma)	*bau*	bau
to smoke	*meng-ah-sahp*	mengasap
smoked	*ah-sahp*	asap
snack	*jah-jah-nahn;*	jajanan; makanan kecil
	mah-kah-nahn keh-chill	
snake	*uh-lahrr*	ular
snakehead fish	*gah-buhs/hah-rrah-wahn*	gabus/harawan
snapper	*kah-kahp*	kakap
snow pea	*kah-prih*	kapri
sole	*ih-kahn lih-dah*	ikan lidah
soup	*soh-toh/sop*	soto/sop
chowder	*sop ken-tahl*	sop kental
consomme	*kahl-duh*	kaldu
meatball	*bahk-soh*	bakso
noodle	*mih reh-buhs*	mie rebus
oxtail	*sop buhn-tuht*	sop buntut
wonton	*mih pang-sit*	mie pangsit
sour	*ah-sahm*	asam
soursop	*sirr-sahk*	sirsak
soybeans	*keh-deh-lai*	kedelai
fermented (tempe)	*tem-peh*	tempe
fermented (tempe), fried	*tem-peh gorr-eng*	tempe goreng
soy sauce	*keh-chahp*	kecap
salty	*keh-chahp ah-sin*	kecap asin
sweet	*keh-chahp mah-niss*	kecap manis
spare rib	*tuh-lahng ih-gah*	tulang iga
spatula	*suh-dip*	sudip
spice mixture/paste	*buhm-buh*	bumbu
spinach	*bai-yahm*	bayam
water	*kahng-kuhng*	kangkung

English	Pronunciation	Indonesian
spirits	*mih-nuh-mahn krrahs*	minuman keras
Balinese rice	*brrem*	brem
distilled from palm sap or rice	*ah-rrahk*	arak
distilled from sugarcane	*chih-yuh*	ciu
spit-roast	*guh-ling*	guling
spoiled/stale	*buh-suhk*	busuk
spoon	*sen-dohk*	sendok
spring onion (scallion)	*daun bah-wahng*	daun bawang
squash	*lah-bu*	labu
squid	*chuh-mih chuh-mih*	cumi-cumi
star anise	*ah-dahs chih-na*	adas cina
starfruit	*blim-bing*	belimbing
steak	*bih-stek/bih-stik*	bistek/bistik
to steam	*meng-uh-wah-pih*	menguapi
steamer	*kuh-kuh-sahn*	kukusan
stew	*reh-buhs-ahn*	rebusan
stock	*kahl-duh*	kaldu
beef	*kahl-duh sah-pih*	kaldu sapi
chicken	*kahl-duh ah-yahm*	kaldu ayam
fish	*kahl-duh ih-kahn*	kaldu ikan
vegetable	*kahl-duh tuhm-bu-hahn*	kaldu tumbuhan
store	*toh-koh*	toko
stove burner	*kom-pohr*	kompor
strawberry	*ahrr-bay*	arbei
street	*jah-lahn*	jalan
stuffing	*ih-sih*	isi
sugar	*guh-lah*	gula
aren palm	*guh-lah ah-ren*	gula aren
icing	*lah-pih-sahn guh-lah*	lapisan gula
palm	*guh-lah meh-rrah/jah-wah*	gula merah/jawa
supermarket	*pah-sahrr swah-lai-yahn*	pasar swalayan
sweet	*mah-niss*	manis
sweet & sour	*ah-sahm mah-niss*	asam manis
sweetcorn	*jah-guhng*	jagung
sweet potato	*uh-bih/eh-rom*	ubi/erom
sweets	*perr-men*	permen

T

English	Pronunciation	Indonesian
table	*meh-jah*	meja
tablecloth	*tah-peh-lahk/tah-plahk*	tapelak/taplak
tail (of an animal)	*buhn-tuht*	buntut
takeaway/takeout	*buhng-kuhs*	bungkus
tamarind	*ah-sahm*	asam
tangerine	*jerr-uhk gah-rrut*	jeruk garut

taro	*tah-lahs/keh-lah-dih*	talas/keladi
tea	*teh*	teh
ginger	*teh*	teh jahe
green	*teh hih-jau*	teh hijau
iced	*ess teh*	es teh
lemon	*teh*	teh limon
rose	*teh mah-warr*	teh mawar
sweet	*teh mah-niss*	teh manis
–with milk	*teh suh-suh*	teh susu
–without sugar	*teh pah-yiht*	teh pahit
–with sugar	*teh guh-lah*	teh gula
teaspoon	*sen-dohk keh-chill*	sendok kecil
thigh	*pah-hah*	paha
tip	*tip*	tip
toast	*roh-tih bah-kahrr*	roti bakar
toaster	*peh-mahng-gahng roh-tih*	pemanggang roti
tofu	*tah-hu*	tahu
fried	*tah-hu gorr-eng*	tahu goreng
tomato	*toh-maht*	tomat
–sauce	*saus toh-maht*	saus tomat
tongs	*tahng/jeh-pih-tahn*	tang/jepitan
tongue	*lih-dah*	lidah
toothpick	*tuh-suhk gih-gih*	tusuk gigi
topping	*lah-pih-sahn ah-tahs*	lapisan atas
tradition	*ah-daht*	adat
tripe	*bah-baht*	babat
trout	*ih-kahn airr tah-wahr*	ikan air tawar
tuna	*ih-kahn chah-kah-lahn/tong-kohl*	ikan cakalan/tongkol
turkey	*kahl-kuhn*	kalkun
turmeric	*kuh-nyiht*	kunyit
turnip	*loh-bahk chih-na*	lobak cina
turtle	*pehn-yuh/kuh-rrah-kuh-rrah*	penyu/kura-kura

U

uncooked	*men-tah*	mentah
unripe	*men-tah*	mentah
to use	*pah-kai*	pakai

V

vanilla	*pah-nih-lih*	panili
veal	*dah-ging ah-nahk lem-buh*	daging anak lembu
vegetable	*sah-yuhrr*	sayur
vegetables	*sah-yuhrr-ahn*	sayuran
vegetarian	*nah-bah-tih/veh-geh-tah-rriahn*	nabati/vegetarian
venison	*dah-ging men-jahng-ahn*	daging menjangan
vinegar	*chuh-kah*	cuka
vodka	*vod-kah*	vodka

W

waiter	*peh-lai-yahn*	pelayan
to wash	*chuh-chih*	cuci
water	*airr*	air
boiled	*airr rreh-buhs/mah-tahng*	air rebus/matang
bottled drinking	*airr boh-tohl*	air botol
drinking	*airr mih-nuhm*	air minum
mineral	*airr mih-nerr-ahl*	air mineral
pure/boiled drinking	*airr pu-tih*	air putih
soda	*airr soh-dah*	air soda
tap	*airr leh-ding*	air leding
tonic	*airr ton-ih-kuhm*	air tonikum
water apple	*jahm-buh airr*	jambu air
water chestnut	*suh-nek*	sunek
watermelon	*seh-mahng-kah*	semangka
well done (cooked)	*mah-tahng mah-tahng*	matang-matang
whale	*ih-kahn paus*	ikan paus
wheat	*gahn-duhm*	gandum
–flour	*teh-puhng trrih-guh*	tepung terigu
–germ	*bnih gahn-duhm*	benih gandum
whisky	*wiss-kih*	wiski
whitebait	*ih-kahn teh-rrih*	ikan teri
wide	*leh-bahr*	lebar
wild	*lih-yarr*	liar
wine	*ung-guhrr*	anggur
red	*ung-guhrr meh-rrah*	anggur merah
white	*ung-guhrr pu-tih*	anggur putih
with	*deng-ahn/pah-kai*	dengan/pakai
wok	*kuh-wah-lih/wah-jahn*	kuali/wajan
wonton	*pahng-sit*	pangsit

Y

yam bean	*beng-kuang/jih-kah-mah*	bengkuang/jicama
yeast mould	*rah-gih*	ragi
yellow	*kuh-ning*	kuning
yoghurt	*suh-suh mah-sahm ken-tahl*	susu masam kental
young	*muh-dah*	muda

Z

| zucchini | *trruhng hih-jau* | terung hijau |

Indonesian Culinary Dictionary

In Indonesian stress falls on the second-last syllable of a word. Therefore the first syllable is stressed in two-syllable words. Cross references are marked in bold, and regional information is in brackets after the definition eg, (West Java).

A

abon *ah-bon* spiced and shredded meat used as filling or with to rice dishes

acar *ah-chahrr* pickles; vegetables in salt, vinegar, sugar and water

adas *ah-dahs* fennel

–**cina** *ah-dahs chih-na* star anise, often used in dishes of Chinese origin

adat *ah-daht* custom/tradition

adonan *ah-doh-nahn* batter

agar-agar *ah-garr-ah-garr* gelatine-like substance obtained from seaweed

air *airr* water

–**botol** *boh-tohl* bottled water

–**jeruk** *airr jerr-uhk* citrus fruit juice

–**kapur** *airr kah-puhrr* limewater, added to sticky rice to make it more chewy

–**kelapa** *airr kel-ah-pah* coconut water

–**kelapa muda** *airr kel-ah-pah mu-dah* coconut water served in the coconut

–**leding** *airr leh-ding* tap water

–**matang** *airr mah-tung* boiled water

–**minum** *airr mih-nuhm* potable water

–**putih** *airr pu-tih* 'white water' – boiled, potable water

–**rebus** *airr rreh-buhs* boiled water

–**soda** *airr soh-dah* soda water

Aji-No-Moto *ah-jee noh moh-toh* MSG (monosodium glutamate) brand name

alam *ah-lahm* **daun pandan** and rice-flour pudding cooked in a banana leaf cylinder (Bali)

alat *ah-laht* utensil/instrument

–**cincang** *ah-laht chin-chung* mincer

–**pengupas** *ah-laht peng-oop-ahs* peeler

alergi *al-err-gee* allergic

alpukat *al-pu-kaht* avocado; also **apokat**

amandel *ah-mahn-del* almond

ambu-ambu *ahm-buh-ahm-buh* tuna

ampar tatak *ahm-pahrr tah-tahk* 'cut plate', moist sweets in various shapes, colours and flavours (Kalimantan)

ampiang dadiah *ahm-piahng dah-diah* buffalo-milk yoghurt with palm syrup, coconut and rice (West Sumatra)

anak domba *ah-nahk dom-bah* lamb

andewi *ahn-deh-wee* endive

anggur *ahng-guhrr* grape/wine

–**merah** *ahng-guhrr meh-rrah* red wine

–**putih** *ahng-guhrr pu-tih* white wine

angsa *ahng-sah* goose

anjing *ahn-jing* dog

Anker *ahn-kerr* brand of local beer

anyaman *ahn-yah-manh* female-only collectives that make **banten** (Bali)

apam *ah-pahm* palm-sugar pancakes

apel *ah-pel*

apem *ah-pehm* palm-sugar pancakes

apokat *ah-poh-kaht* avocado

aprikot *ah-prih-kot* apricot

Aqua *ah-quah* brand of bottled water

arak *ah-rrahk* spirits distilled from palm sap or rice

–**attack** *ah-rrahk attack* arak mixed with lemonade or orange juice

arbei *ahrr-bay* strawberry

arem-arem *ah-rrem ah-rrem* mixture of pressed rice, tempe, sprouts, soy sauce, coconut and peanuts (East Java)

asam *ah-sahm* tamarind, sold in compressed blocks; adds a sour flavour to cooking; also sour; also to pickle

–**manis** *ah-sahm mah-niss* 'sour sweet'; served in a sweet & sour sauce; eg **ikan asam manis** (sweet & sour fish)

asap *ah-sahp* smoked

asbak *ahs-bahk* ashtray

asin *ah-sin* salty

asinan *ah-sin-nahn* marinade; salad of salted vegetables and/or young fruit

asparagus *ahs-pah-rrah-goos* asparagus

awetan *ah-wet-tahn* conserves

ayakan *ah-yah-kahn* sieve/sifter

aya kurik *ai-yah kuh-rrihk* tuna (Pacific)

ayam *ah-yahm* chicken

–bakar *ah-yahm bah-kahrr* grilled chicken

–belanda *ah-yahm blahn-da* 'Dutch chicken', turkey

–goreng *ah-yahm gorr-eng* fried chicken

–kampung *ah-yahm kahm-pung* 'village chicken', free-range chicken

–kebiri *ah-yahm ke-bih-rrih* capon

–masak habang *ah-yahm mah-sahk hah-bahng* chicken cooked with large red chillies (Kalimantan)

–namargota *ah-yahm nah-mah-goh-tah* chicken cooked in spices and blood (Batak, North Sumatra)

–rica rica *ah-yahm rrih-chah rrih-chah* chicken with a paste of chilli, shallots, ginger and lime (North Sulawesi)

–Taliwang *ah-yahm tah-li-wahng* whole split chicken roasted over coconut husks served with a peanut, tomato chilli, lime dip (Lombok)

B

B1 *beh sah-tuh* dog

B2 *beh du-ah* pig

ba'mi *bah-mih* rice-flour noodles

ba'so *bah-soh* noodle and meatball soup; also called **bakso**

babat *bah-baht* tripe

babi *bah-bih* pork

–guling *bah-bih guh-ling* spit-roast pig stuffed with chilli, turmeric, garlic and ginger, smothered in turmeric (Bali)

–hutan *bah-bih huh-tahn* wild boar

–panggang *bah-bih pahng-gahng* pork boiled in vinegar and pig blood with spices then roasted (Batak)

bacem *bah-chem* tempe, tofu or chicken cooked in stock (*see* the recipe)

bahan *bah-hahn* ingredient

bahu *bah-hoo* shoulder

bajigur *bah-jih-guhrr* spiced coffee with coconut milk (West Java)

bak pia patuk *bahk piah pah-tuhk* mung bean cake (Central Java)

bakar *bah-kahrr* grilled; burn

bakasang *bah-kah-sahng* paste made by fermenting fish in a terracotta pot (North Sulawesi)

bakmi *bahk-mih* rice-flour noodles, fried to make **bakmi goreng** or used in soup

–goreng *bahk-mih gorr-eng* fried rice-flour noodles

bakpao *bahk-pao* steamed bun with filling, often meat or bean paste

bakso *bahk-soh* noodle and meatball soup with; also called **ba'so**

–ayam *bahk-soh ah-yahm* chicken soup with noodles and meatballs

bakul *bahk-uhl* streetside food sellers

bakwan *bahk-wahn* vegetable fritter (Central Java); also called **bala-bala**

–malang *bahk-wahn mah-lahng* soup with noodles, meatballs and fried wontons (East Java)

bala-bala *bah-lah bah-lah see* **bakwan**

bami *bah-mih* egg noodles

bandrek *bahn-drrek* ginger tea with coconut (West Java; *see* the recipe)

banten *bahn-ten* Hindu offerings (Bali)

bapak *bah-pahk* father; also polite form of address to an older man

batagor *bah-tah-gor* fried fish/meat dumplings with peanut sauce

bau *bau* smell/odour

bawal *bah-wahl* pampel fish

bawang *bah-wahng*

–bakung *bah-wahng bah-kung* leek

–bombay *bah-wahng bom-bay* onion

–cina *bah-wahng chih-na* spring onion

–goreng *bah-wahng gorr-eng* crispy fried shallots – used as a garnish

–merah *bah-wahng meh-rrah* shallot

–perai *bah-wahng peh-rrai* leek

–putih *bah-wahng puh-tih* garlic

bayam *bai-yahm* spinach

bebek *beh-behk* duck

–betutu *beh-behk beh-tuh-tuh* duck stuffed with spices, wrapped in banana leaves and coconut husks and cooked in a pit of embers (Bali)

–panggang *beh-behk pahng-gahng* roast duck or chicken with soy sauce

belacan *blah-chahn see* **terasi**
belanja *blahn-jah* to shop, shopping
belimbing *blim-bing* starfruit – fruit shaped like a star when viewed end-on
–wuluh *blim-bing wuh-luh* small fruit related to **belimbing**, used in cooking for its sour flavour
belulut *bluh-luht* palm tree fruit
belut *blut* eel
–asin *blut ah-sin* dried baby eels
bengkuang *beng-kuang* jicama
benih apiun *bnih ah-pih-oon* poppy
bening *beh-ning* clear, as in a clear soup
berangan *brrahng-ahm* chestnut
beras *brrahs* harvested raw rice
–belanda *brrahs blahn-dah* pearl barley
–coklat *brrahs choh-klaht* brown rice
–merah *brrahs meh-rrah* red rice
bergizi *berr-gih-zih* nutritious
bersih *berr-sih* to clean; clean
besaran *beh-sarr-ahm* mulberry
bihun *bih-hun* small rice noodles; also called cellophane noodles, or **mihun**
biji *bih-jih* seed
–adas *bih-jih ah-dahs* fennel seed
–bijan *bih-jih bih-jahn* sesame seed
–cemara *bih-jih che-mah-rrah* pine nut
–coklat *bih-jih choh-klaht* cocoa
–jemuju *bih-jih je-muh-juh* caraway seed
bika ambon *bih-kah ahm-bon* cake made with egg, sugar, tapioca flour, coconut milk and palm wine added both for flavour and to act as a rising agent (Aceh & North Sumatra)
bingka kentang *bihng-kah ken-tahng* sweet made with potato (Kalimantan)
Bintang *bin-tahng* brand of local beer
bir *bihrr* beer
–hitam *bihrr hih-tahm* stout
biskit *bih-skit* biscuits/cookies
bistek/bistik *bih-stek/bih-stik* steak
bon *bon* bill/receipt
bongko *bong-koh* kidney beans, coconut and spices cooked in a banana leaf
botol *boh-tohl* bottle
brem *brrem* type of **arak**, distilled from white and black rice (Bali)

brendi *brren-dih* brandy
brokoli *brroh-koh-lih* broccoli
brongkos *brrong-kohs* beef and bean stew with **kluwek** (Central Java)
buah *bua* fruit/piece
–anggur *bua ahng-guhrr* grapes
–jeruk *bua jerr-uhk* citrus fruit
–buahan *bua bua-hahn* fruit
–buahan kering *bua bua-hahn krring* dried fruit
buat *buat* to use; to contain; to make
bubur *bu-buhrr* rice porridge/congee, can be sweet or savoury and is made with rice, grains or pulses
–ayam *bu-buhrr ah-yahm* rice porridge with chicken
–campur *bu-buhrr chahm-puhrr see* **bubur ketan hitam kacang hijau**
–jagung *bu-buhrr jah-guhng* hominy
–kacang hijau *buh-buhrr kah-chahng hih-jau* mung bean porridge with coconut milk
–kampiun *bu-buhrr kahm-piun* mung bean porridge with banana, rice, yoghurt and custard (West Sumatra)
–ketan hitam *buh-buhrr keh-tahn hih-tahm* black rice porridge with coconut milk
–ketan hitam kacang hijau *buh-buhrr keh-tahn hih-tahm kah-chahng hih-jau* black rice and mung bean porridge; also called **bubur campur**
–lemu *buh-buhrr leh-muh* rice pudding
–tinotuan *bu-buhrr tih-noh-tuan* rice porridge with corn, cassava, pumpkin, fish paste and chilli (North Sulawesi)
buka *buh-kah* open
buku jari *buh-kuh jah-rrih* knuckle
bulu *buh-luh* bamboo
bulyon *buh-lih-yon* broth
bumbu *buhm-buh* spice mix/paste/sauce
–kari *buhm-buh kah-rrih* curry paste
buncis *buhn-chis* beans; string beans
bunga kol *buhng-ah kohl* cauliflower
bunga lawang *buhng-ah lah-wahng* star anise, used in dishes of Chinese origin
bunga pala *buhng-ah pah-lah* mace

bungkus *buhng-kuhs* packed meal; meal to go; takeaway

buntut *buhn-tuht* tail as in **soto buntut**

burung *buh-rrung* bird

–dara *buh-rrung dah-rrah* pigeon

busuk *buh-suhk* spoiled/stale

C

cabai *chah-bai* chilli

cabe *chah-beh* chilli

–besar *chah-beh beh-sarr* capsicum (pepper)

–hijau *chah-beh hih-jau* green chilli

–merah *chah-beh meh-rrah* red chilli

–rawit *chah-beh rah-wit* bird's eye chilli (small and hot)

cakalang *chah-kah-lang* tuna

cakar ayam *chah-kahrr ah-yahm* chicken claw (the tastiest part)

campur *chum-puhrr* to mix

cangkir *chahng-kihrr* cup

cap cai *chahp-chai* stirfried vegetables

cempedak *chem-pe-dahk* fruit similar to a jackfruit but sweeter, more tender

cengkeh *cheng-keh* clove, not eaten but made into **kretek** (Maluku)

ceplok *cheh-plok* fried egg

ceret *cherr-et* kettle

ceri *cherr-ih* cherry

cincang *chin-chahng* mince

ciu *chih-yuh* sugarcane spirit

cobek & ulek-ulek *choh-bek dahn uh-lek-uh-lek* similar to a mortar & pestle. The ulek-ulek is shaped like a big fat cigar and is used to push ingredients along the cobek, a shallow circular grinding stone. Both are made from heavy volcanic rock. Used to make **bumbu** and **sambal**; it grinds the ingredients well, but leaves some texture.

coklat *choh-klaht* chocolate

colenak roasted cassava with sweet coconut sauce (West Java)

colo-colo *choh-loh choh-loh* sauce made with citrus fruit and chilli (Maluku)

coto Makassar *cho-toh mah-kah-sahrr* soup of beef offal, pepper, cumin and lemongrass, usually served with pressed rice and lime (South Sulawesi)

cuci *chuh-chih* to wash

cuka *chuh-kah* vinegar; sauce made with chillies, palm sugar, garlic, vinegar and soy sauce and served with **pempek** (South Sumatra)

–jawa *chuh-kah jah-wah* palm blossom vinegar

cumi-cumi *chuh-mih chuh-mih* squid

D

dabu-dabu raw vegetables (especially green beans) in a chilli and fish paste sauce (Maluku)

dada *dah-dah* breast/brisket

dadar *dah-dahrr* omelette

dadih *dah-dih* buttermilk/curd

daftar makanan *dahf-tahrr mah-kah-nahn* menu

daging *dah-ging* meat

–babi *dah-ging bah-bih* ham/pork

–kambing *dah-ging kahm-bing* goat/mutton

–menjangan *dah-ging men-jahng-ahn* venison

–pinggang *dah-ging ping-gahng* sirloin

–sapi *dah-ging sah-pih* beef

dapur *dah-puhrr* kitchen

daun *daun* leaf

–bawang *daun bah-wahng* spring onion; scallion

–gedi *daun geh-dih* herb that gives food a slimy texture (North Sulawesi)

–jeruk perut *daun jerr-uhk prruht* kaffir lime leaf

–pandan *daun pahn-dahn* pandanus leaf/screwpine – used for colour and flavour in sweet dishes

–pisang *daun pih-sahng* banana leaf

–salam *daun sah-lahm* salam leaf; also called Indonesian laurel

delima *deh-lih-mah* pomegranate

didih *dih-dih* simmer

dingin *ding-in* cold

dipotong *dih-poh-tong* diced

dodol *doh-doll* chewy, toffeed sweet made of rice, coconut milk and palm sugar (West Java)

domba *dom-bah* mutton

duku *duh-kuh* small, yellow-coloured fruit. Peeled to reveal a jelly-like flesh with a sweet yet sharp taste.

durian *duh-rrih-ahn* large green/yellow-coloured fruit with a spiky exterior and a 'pungent' aroma

E

ebat five dish feast. At an **odalan**, men prepare the ebat; it may feature such specialties as **lawar** (Bali).

ebi *eh-bih* shrimp, dried; often found lurking in **nasi goreng** and **kangkung**

empal genton *em-pahl gen-tohn* beef and turmeric soup (West Java)

emping *em-ping* crackers made from dried **melinjo** nuts

enak *en-ahk* delicious

erom *eh-rom* sweet potato (Irian Jaya)

es *ess* ice; also iced drink

–apokat *ess ah-poh-kaht* avocado mixed with ice, sugar and condensed milk or chocolate syrup

–buah *ess buah* variety of **es campur** in which a few different fruits are featured

–campur *ess chum-puhrr* sweet drink of coconut milk, fruit, jelly and shaved ice, often served in a bowl

–cendol *ess chen-doll* dessert-drink of green rice-flour jelly droplets, coconut milk and palm-sugar syrup

–cincau *ess chin-chau* dessert-drink of black **cincau**, sugar syrup and ice

–dawet *ess dah-wet* dessert-drink of green rice-flour jelly droplets, coconut milk and palm-sugar syrup

–durian *ess duh-rrih-ahn* durian with ice and sugar syrup

–jeruk *ess jerr-uhk* citrus juice with ice and sugar syrup

–ketimun *ess keh-tih-muhn* shredded cucumber with ice and sugar syrup

–krim *ess krrim* ice cream (try durian flavour)

–mangga *ess mahng-gah* mango shake

–nangka *ess nahng-kah* jackfruit with ice and sugar syrup

–pallubutun *ess pah-luh-buh-tuhn* coconut custard and bananas swimming in coconut milk and sugar syrup (South Sulawesi)

–teh *ess teh* iced tea

–teler *ess teh-lehr* 'drunk ice'; coconut milk with fruit and ice

F

frambos *frrum-boss* raspberry

fu yung hai *fuh yahng hai* sort of sweet & sour omelette

G

gabah *gah-bah* rice that has been harvested, but not yet husked and milled

gabus *gah-buhs* snakehead fish, has a very meaty, almost salami-like flavour (Kalimantan); also called **harawan**

gado-gado *gah-doh-gah-doh* vegetables with peanut sauce (Jakarta)

gandum *gahn-duhm* wheat

garam *gah-rrahm* salt

garang asam *gah-rrahng ah-sahm* chicken innards, spices, starfruit and coconut milk cooked in a clay pot (Tegal, Central Java)

garas *gah-rrahs* shin

garing *gah-rring* crispy

garpu *garr-puh* fork

gelas *glahss* glass

gelembung *glem-buhng* bubble

gempol pleret *gem-pohl pleh-rret* discs of spiced rice flour made with coconut milk (Central Java)

gendong *gen-dohng* street vendors of **jamu**; means carry on your back or side

geplak *geh-plahk* sticky rice sweet with palm sugar and coconut (Central Java) gepuk *geh-puhk* flattened and fried spiced beef (West Java)

gerst *gerrst* barley

ginjal *gin-jahl* kidney

goreng *gorr-eng* deep-fry, fry, to fry

gorengan *gorr-eng-ahn* fried snacks, eg **pisang goreng** and **tempe goreng**

gowok *goh-wohk* small purple-coloured fruit; it grows in bunches and can be eaten with the peel but not the seed

gratis *grrah-tiss* free (of cost)

Green Sands soft drink not from sand, but from malt, apple and lime juice

gudeg *guh-deg* jackfruit curry – young jackfruit and spices slowly cooked in coconut milk and served with chicken, egg and/or buffalo skin cooked the same way (Central Java)

gula *guh-lah* sugar

–gula *guh-lah guh-lah* lollies/candy

–halus *guh-lah, ha-luhs* caster sugar

–jawa *guh-lah jah-wah* palm sugar – sold compressed in 'cakes'

–kelapa *guh-lah kel-ah-pah* coconut palm sugar

–merah *guh-lah meh-rrah* palm sugar

–tetes *guh-lah teh-tess* molasses

gulai *guh-lai* coconut curry; also called **gule**, **kare**

–ayam *guh-lai ah-yahm* chicken coconut curry

–itik *guh-lai ih-tihk* duck coconut curry

–kambing *guh-lai kahm-bing* goat coconut curry

–nangka *guh-lai nang-kah* jackfruit coconut curry

–tahu *guh-lai tah-hu* tofu coconut curry

gule *guh-leh see* **gulai**

gurami *guh-rrah-mih* large freshwater fish

gurih *guh-rrih* rich/hearty (food)

gurita *guh-rrih-ta* octopus

H

halal *hah-lal* halal

hamburger *hahm-burr-gurr* hamburger

harawan *hah-rrah-wahn see* **gabus**

harga *harr-gah* price/cost

haring *hah-ring* herring

harum *harr-uhm* aroma

hati *hah-tih* liver. Indonesians consider it the cradle of one's emotions, just as westerners regard the heart.

–ayam *hah-tih ah-yahm* chicken liver

I

ibu *ih-buh* mother; also polite form of address to an older woman

ikan *ih-kahn* fish

–air tawar *ih-kahn airr tah-wahr* trout

–asam manis *ih-kahn ah-sahm mah-niss* sweet & sour fish

–asin *ih-kahn ah-sin* salted fish, popular due to its shelf life

–bakar *ih-kahn bah-kahrr* grilled fish

–basah *ih-kahn bah-sah* fresh fish

–bawal *ih-kahn bah-wal* pomfret

–belado *ih-kahn beh-lah-doh* fried fish covered in spring onions and chilli

–belida *ih-kahn beh-lih-dah* large river fish

–bilis *ih-kahn bih-liss/ih-kahn trr-ih* anchovy; also called **ikan teri**

–bilis goreng kacang *ih-kahn bih-liss goh-rreng kah-chahng* fried peanuts and anchovies

–brengkes *ih-kahn brreng-kess* fish cooked in a spicy durian-based sauce (South Sumatra)

–cakalang *ih-kahn chah-kah-lahng* tuna

–danau *ih-kahn dah-nau* freshwater fish

–garupa *ih-kahn gah-rruh-pah* grouper

–hiu *ih-kahn hih-yuh* shark

–julung-julung *ih-kahn jah-luhng jah-luhng* garfish

–kakap *ih-kahn kah-kahp* perch

–laut *ih-kahn laut* saltwater fish

–lawang *ih-kahn lah-wahng* flying fish

–lele *ih-kahn leh-leh* catfish

–lemuru *ih-kahn leh-muh-rru* sardine

–lidah *ih-kahn lih-dah* sole

–mas *ih-kahn mahss* carp/goldfish

–panada *ih-kahn pah-nah-dah* tuna pastry (North Sulawesi)

–pari *ih-kahn pah-rrih* ray
–paus *ih-kahn paus* whale
–rica-rica *ih-kahn rrih-chah-rrih-chah* fish prepared with paste of shallots, chilli, ginger and lime (North Sulawesi)
–salem *ih-kahn sah-lem* salmon
–sarden *ih-kahn sarr-den* sardine
–sebelah *ih-kahn se-bla* flatfish
–segar *ih-kahn seh-garr* fresh fish
–tambak *ih-kahn tahm-bahk* freshwater fish
–teri *ih-kahn teh-rrih* anchovy/whitebait
–tongkol *ih-kahn tong-kohl* mackerel/tuna
intip *in-tip* rice crackers
iris *ih-riss* slice
isi *ih-sih* to fill, stuffing, filling
itik *ih-tihk* duck

J

jagung *jah-guhng* corn/sweetcorn
–bakar *jah-guhng bah-kahrr* grilled corn
–brondong/meletus *jah-guhng brron-dohng/meh-leh-tuhs* popcorn
jahe *jah-heh* ginger
jajan pasar *jah-jahn pah-sahrr* snacks
jajanan *jah-jah-nahn* snacks
jaje *jah-jeh* rice and tapioca cakes
jaka *jah-kah* palm tree
jalan *jah-lahn* road/street
jamblang *jahm-blahng* Java plum – small, purple fruit with a sweet flesh similar to a ripe grape
jambu *jahm-buh* guava
–air *jahm-buh airr* water apple, glossy white or pink bell-shaped fruit
–biji *jahm-buh bih-jih* guava
–klutuk *jahm-buh kluh-tuhk* guava
–mete *jahm-buh meh-teh* cashew
jamu *jah-muh* herbal medicine
jamur *jah-muhr* mushrooms
jantung *jahn-tuhng* heart
jenewer *jen-eh-wehr* gin
jengkol *jeng-kohl* a starchy fruit that's used in savoury dishes
jeroan *jerr-oh-wahn* giblets/offal/entrails
jeruk *jerr-uhk* orange; citrus fruit

–bali *jerr-uhk bah-lih* pomelo
–baras *jerr-uhk bah-rras* small tangerine-like oranges
–garut *jerr-uhk gah-rrut* tangerine
–keriput *jerr-uhk kerr-ih-puht* grapefruit
–limau *jerr-uhk lih-mau* green lime
–mandarin *jerr-uhk mahn-dahrr-in* mandarin
–manis *jerr-uhk mah-niss* oranges
–muntis *jerr-uhk muhn-tiss* pomelo
–nipis *jerr-uhk nih-piss* lemon/lime
–purut *jerr-uhk prruht* kaffir lime
jerunga *jerr-uhng-gah* pomelo
jicama *jih-kah-mah* yam bean
jinten *jin-ten* cumin
–manis *mah-niss* fennel
juru masak *juh-ruh mah-sahk* chef
jus *juhs* fresh juice
–apokat *juhs ah-poh-kaht* avocado juice with sugar syrup and ice *(see the recipe)*

K

kacang *kah-chahng* bean/nut/pulse
–asin *kah-chahng ah-sin* salted peanuts
–belimbing *kah-chahng bel-ihm-bing* pea
–buncis *kah-chahng buhn-chiss* green bean
–hijau *kah-chahng hih-jau* mung bean
–jawa *kah-chahng jah-wah* lima bean
–mente *kah-chahng men-teh* cashew
–merah *kah-chahng meh-rrah* red kidney bean
–panjang *kah-chahng pahn-jahng* yard-long bean
–putih *kah-chahng puh-tih* peanut
–tanah *kah-chahng tah-nah* peanut
kakap *kah-kahp* snapper
kaki *kah-kih* leg
kaki-lima *kah-kih lih-mah* roving food vendor. Carts usually consist of bench top, a stove and a glass display cabinet for ingredients and for advertising. Literary, 'five legs' for the three wheels of the cart and the two of the vendor.
kaldu *kahl-duh* consomme/stock
–ayam *kahl-duh ah-yahm* chicken stock
–ikan *kahl-duh ih-kahn* fish sauce/stock

–sapi *kahl-duh sah-pih* beef stock

–tumbuhan *kahl-duh tuhm-bu-hahn* vegetable stock

kaleng *kah-leng* can

kalio *kah-lih-oh* **rendang** that hasn't been fully reduced

kalkun *kahl-kuhn* turkey

kambing *kahm-bing* goat

kangkung *kahng-kuhng* cress; water spinach

kantan *kahm-tahn* ginger bud

kapal selam *kah-pahl seh-lahm* **pempek** with a boiled egg inside (Sumatra)

kapri *kah-prih* snow pea

kapul *kah-puhl* cardamom

kapulaga *kah-puhl-ah-gah* cardamom

karak *kah-rrahk* rice crackers

karamel *kah-rrah-mell* caramel

kare *kah-rreh* coconut curry *(see also* **gulai**)

karedok *kah-rreh-dohk* Sundanese salad with yard-long beans, beansprouts and cucumber with a spicy sauce (West Java; *see* the recipe)

kassa *kah-sah* cashier

kawaok *kah-wah-ok* fried forest rat (North Sulawesi)

kayu manis *kai-yuh mah-niss* 'sweet wood', cinnamon

kayu pemotong *kai-yuh peh-moh-tong* chopping board

kecap *keh-chahp* sauce; soy sauce

–asin *keh-chahp ah-sin* salty soy sauce

–manis *keh-chahp mah-niss* sweet soy sauce

Kedaso *Keh-dah-soh* tenth full-moon festival. Purification festival when sacred images are cleaned and pigs sacrificed to the gods. (Bali)

kedelai *keh-deh-lai* soybean

keju *keh-juh* cheese

kelapa *keh-lah-pah* coconut

–kopyor *keh-lah-pah koh-pyorr* coconut with loose flesh that grows on ordinary palms and is made into great ice cream

kelapa muda *keh-lah-pah* 'young coconut'; it makes a refreshing drink

kelembak *kel-em-bahk* rhubarb

kelepon *keh-lep-on* rice-flour dumpling coloured green with **daun pandan**, rolled in shredded coconut with a palm-sugar centre (Central Java)

kelinci *keh-lin-chih* rabbit

kelor *keh-lorr* hot soup with kangkung and/or other vegetables (Lombok)

keluang *keh-luang* fruit bat (North Sulawesi)

kemangi *keh-mahng-ih* lemon basil

kembang kol *kem-bahng kohl* cauliflower

kemiri *kmih-rrih* candlenut, crushed and used to thicken and add a nutty flavour to sauces; must be cooked as it is toxic when raw

kencur *ken-churr* ginger-like rhinzome often called lesser galangal

kentang *ken-tahng* potato

–goreng *ken-tahng gorr-eng* fried potatoes

–keripik *ken-tahng keh-rrip-ihk* potato chips/crisps

–panggang *ken-tahng pahng-gahng* roasted potatoes

kenyang *ken-yahng* full/content

kepiting *keh-pih-ting* crab

kerang *keh-rrahng* mussels/clam

–laut *keh-rrahng laut* abalone

–kerangan *keh-rrahng keh-rrahng-an* shellfish

kerapu *keh-rrah-puh* perch

kerbau *kerr-bau* buffalo

kering *krring* dried

kerupuk *krruh-puhk* crackers – brittle and opaque before cooking, they puff up when deep-fried

–jagung *krruh-puhk jah-guhng* fried corn kernels

–kulit *krruh-puhk kuh-lit* fried cow or buffalo skin

–ubi *krruh-puhk uh-bih* sweet potato crisps

–udang *krruh-puhk uh-dahng* shrimp crackers

kesemak *keh-seh-mahk* persimmon

ketan *keh-tahm* glutinous rice

–hitam *keh-tahm hih-tahm* black rice

ketel *keh-tell* kettle

ketimun *keh-tih-muhn* cucumber

ketoprak *keh-toh-prrak* tofu, noodles and beansprouts with soy and peanut sauce (Jakarta)

ketumbar *keh-tuhm-barr* coriander (cilantro) used for the seeds

ketupat *keh-tuh-paht* rice steamed in boxes made from fancily woven coconut palms. Ketupat packets are a symbol of Ramadan.

–kandangan *keh-tuh-paht kahn-dahng-ahn* broiled river fish and pressed rice swimming in coconut sauce flavoured with lime (Kalimantan)

–tahu *keh-tuh-paht tah-hu* pressed rice, beansprouts and tofu with soy and peanut sauce (West Java)

khas *khas* indigenous

kijing *kih-jing* clam

kios *kih-oss* kiosk; freestanding stalls, found on many street corners, are barely bigger than a phone booth yet stock a vast amount of comestibles

kismis *kiss-miss* currant/raisin

kluwek *kluh-wek* seed that adds an earthy flavour to dishes and darkens their colour

kobis *koh-biss* broccoli

kodok *koh-dohk* frog

kohu-kohu *koh-huh-koh-huh* fish salad with citrus fruit and chilli (Maluku)

kol *kohl* cabbage

–merah *meh-rrah* red cabbage

–mini *kohl mih-nih* Brussel sprouts

–putih *kohl pu-tih* white cabbage

kolak *koh-lahk* fruit in coconut milk

kompor *kom-pohr* stove burner

kopi *koh-pih* coffee

–dengan gula *koh-pih deng-ahn guh-lah* coffee with sugar

–dengan susu *koh-pih deng-ahn suh-suh* coffee with milk, usually condensed

–jahe *koh-pih jah-heh* coffee mixed with ginger when brewing

–pahit *koh-pih pah-yiht* 'bitter coffee', coffee without sugar

–susu *koh-pih suh-suh* coffee with milk, often condensed or non-dairy creamer

–telur *koh-pih teh-luhrr* raw egg and sugar creamed together and topped up with coffee (Aceh & North Sumatra)

–tubruk *koh-pih tuh-brruhk* freshly ground coffee straight into the glass with sugar and boiling water

kopra *khoh-prah* dried, shredded coconut flesh

kotor *koh-torr* dirty

krecek *kreh-chek* beef or buffalo skin, often served with **gudeg**

kretek *kre-tek* clove cigarettes

krim *krrim* cream

kroket *krroh-ket* mashed potato cake with minced meat filling

kuah *kuh-wah* gravy; sauce

kuali *kuh-wah-lih* wok; also called **wajan**

kuaytau *kuay-tau* flat rice noodles

kubis *kuh-biss* broccoli

kucai *kuh-chai* chives

kue *kuh-way* cake

–buah-buahan *kuh-way bua bua-han* fruit cake

–kering *kuh-way krring* pastry

–lapis *kuh-way lah-piss* layer cake

–sus *kuh-way suhs* custard-filled pastry

kukusan *kuh-kuh-sahn* steamer

kulit *kuh-liht* peel/skin

–jeruk *kuh-liht jerr-uhk* zest

–padi *kuh-liht pah-dih* bran

kumut *kuh-muht* solids from cooking coconut milk

kuning *kuh-ning* yellow

kunyit *kuh-nyiht* turmeric, used to flavour and colour soups, curries and rice dishes, such as **nasi tumpeng**

kurma *kuhrr-mah* dates

L

labu *lah-bu* pumpkin/squash

–siam *lah-buh sih-ahm* kind of pumpkin

lada *lah-dah* pepper

–merah *lah-dah meh-rrah* cayenne

–rimba *lah-dah rrim-bah* local, mouth-numbing pepper (Batak)

ladang *lah-dahng* dry rice field

lak lak *lahk lahk* small pancake with palm sugar and coconut (Bali)

laksa *lahk-sah* spicy noodle soup with coconut milk

lalap *lah-lahp* raw vegetable salad served with **sambal**

lalapan *lah-lah-pahn* raw vegetable salad

laos *lah-ohs* galangal; rhinzome with the same shape as ginger but bright orange and with a more bitter taste

lapar *lah-pahr* hungry

lawar *lah-wahrr* salad of chopped coconut, garlic and chilli with pork (or chicken) meat and blood (Bali)

leci *leh-chih* lychee

leher *leh-hehrr* neck

lele *leh-leh* catfish

lemak *leh-mahk* grease

–babi *bah-bih* lard

lemper *lem-pehrr* sticky rice with a filling of spiced and shredded meat steamed in a banana leaf

lenggang *leng-gahng* chopped **pempek** mixed in an omelette (South Sumatra)

lengkeng *leng-keng* longan

lesehan *leh-seh-hahn* night time streetside eatery where patrons sit on grass mats, sometimes with low tables

leunca *luhn-chah* bitter-tasting fruit that looks like a green pea

liar *lih-yarr* wild

lidah *lih-dah* tongue

limon *lih-mon* lemon

lobak *loh-bahk* radish

–cina *loh-bahk chih-na* turnip

lokio *loh-kih-oh* chive

lombok *lom-bok* chilli (*see* also **cabe**)

lontong *lon-tong* rice steamed in banana leaves and sliced into cubes

lotek *loh-tek* peanut sauce with vegetable and pressed rice (Central Java)

lumpia *luhm-pih-yah* spring rolls filled with shrimp and beansprouts and fried (Semarang speciality)

M

madu *mah-duh* honey

makan *mah-kahn* the verb 'to eat'

–malam *mah-kahn mah-lahm* dinner

–pagi *mah-kahn pah-gih* breakfast

–siang *mah-kahn sih-yahng* lunch

makanan *mah-kah-nahn* food/meal

–kecil *mah-kah-nahn keh-chill* snacks

–laut *mah-kah-nahn laut* seafood

–pembuka *mah-kah-nahn pem-buhk-ah* appetiser/entree

mangga *mahng-gah* mango

manggis *mahng-giss* mangosteen, a fruit with purple skin and sweet white flesh

mangkuk *mahng-kuhk* bowl

manis *mah-niss* sweet

manisan pala *mah-nis-ahn pah-lah* preserve made with the fruit of the nutmeg

markisa *marr-kih-sah* passionfruit

martabak *marr-tah-bahk* crispy-skin omelette fried in a shallow wok with cucumber, garlic, shallots and meat; also a sweet, chunky pancake served hot with toppings like banana, chocolate sauce, condensed milk and nuts.

masak *mah-sahk* ripe (fruit); to cook, cooked

–habang *mah-sahk hah-bahg* variety of dishes cooked with large red chillies (Kalimantan)

masakan *mah-sah-kahn* dish/cuisine

–khas daerah *mah-sah-kahn kass dairrah* regional cuisines

–utama *mah-sah-kahn* main course

matang *mah-tahng* ripe/cooked

–matang *mah-tahng mah-tahng* well done (cooked)

meja *meh-jah* table

melinjo *meh-lihn-joh* nut from the gne-tum tree, used to make **emping**

melon *meh-lohn* melon/cantaloupe

memarut *meh-mah-rruht* to grate

memotong persegi empat *meh-moh-tong perr-seh-gih em-paht* to dice

mencium *men-chium* to smell; to kiss

mengasinkan *meng-ah-sin-kahn* to pickle/marinate

mengawetkan *meng-ah-wet-kahn* to cure

mengiris *meng-ih-rris* to slice

menguapi *meng-uh-wah-pih* to steam

mentah *men-tah* uncooked/unripe

mentega *men-teh-gah* butter/margarine

merah *meh-rrah* red

merebus *meh-rreh-buhs* to poach

merica *meh-rrih-chah* pepper

mi/mie *mih* noodles

–goreng *mih gorr-eng* fried noodles with vegetables and sometimes meat

–kocok *mih koh-chohk* beef and egg noodle soup (West Java)

–kuah *mih kuh-wah* noodle soup

–pangsit *mih pang-sit* wonton and noodle soup

–rebus *mih reh-buhs* noodle soup

–toprak *mih toh-prahk* beef noodle soup with tempe, peanuts and spinach

mihun *mih-huhn* small rice noodles; also called cellophane noodles or **bihun**

miju *mih-juh mih-juh* lentil

minum *mih-nuhm* to drink

minuman *mih-nuh-mahn* drink (n)

–dingin *mih-nuh-mahn ding-in* cold drink

–es *mih-nuh-mahn ess* ice drink

–keras *mih-nuh-mahn krrahs* alcohol/spirits

–panas *mih-nuh-mahn pah-nahs* hot drink

minyak *mih-nyahk* cooking oil

–bijan *mih-nyahk bih-jahn* sesame oil

–jagung *mih-nyahk jah-gung* corn oil

–kacang *mih-nyahk kah-chahng* peanut oil

–kelapa *mih-nyahk keh-lah-pah* coconut oil

–sawit *mih-nyahk sah-wit* palm oil

–tumbuh-tumbuhan *mih-nyahk tuhm-buh-tuhm-buh-hahn* vegetable oil

mudah *muh-dah* young

mulut *muh-luht* mouth

murah *muh-rrah* cheap

mutiara *muh-tih-ah-rrah* sago droplets; used in sweets and drinks (Maluku)

N

nabati *nah-bah-tih* vegetarian

nanas *nah-nahs* pineapple

nangka *nahng-kah* jackfruit

nasi *nah-sih* cooked rice

–campur *nah-sih chum-puhrr* rice with a selection of meat and vegetable dishes on one plate

–gabah *nah-sih gah-bah* brown rice

–goreng *nah-sih gorr-eng* fried rice *(see the recipe)*

–goreng istimewa/spesial *nah-sih gorr-eng ih-stih-meh-wah/spesh-ahl* **nasi goreng** crowned with a fried egg

–gudeg *nah-sih guh-deg* unripe jackfruit cooked in coconut milk and served up with rice, pieces of chicken and spices

–gurih *nah-sih guh-rrih* rice cooked in coconut milk

–jenggo *nah-sih jeng-goh* white rice with spicy sauce served in a banana leaf

–krismon *nah-sih kriss-mon* 'monetary crisis meal', a filling meal made with any cheap ingredients

–kuning *nah-sih kuh-ning* rice cooked in turmeric

–lengko *nah-sih len-koh* rice with tofu, tempe, beansprouts, cucumber and peanut sauce (West Java)

–liwet *nah-sih lih-wet* rice cooked with coconut milk, **labu siam**, garlic, shallots and **kumut**, served with chicken or egg (Central Java)

–pecel *nah-sih peh-chel* salad similar to **gado-gado**, with boiled papaya leaves, tapioca, beansprouts, string beans, **tempe**, cucumber, coconut shavings and peanut sauce

–putih *nah-sih pu-tih* plain white rice

–rames *nah-sih rah-mess* rice with a selection of meat and vegetable dishes on one plate

–rawon *nah-sih rah-wohn* rice with spicy hot beef soup, fried onions and spicy sauce

–tambanan *nah-sih tahm-bahn-nahn* brown rice (Tambanan)

–timbel *nah-sih tim-bel* rice cooked in banana leaves served with sambal, chicken, tofu, salted fish and/or tempe (West Java)

–uduk *nah-sih uh-duhk* rice cooked in coconut milk served with meat, tofu and/or vegetables (Jakarta)

nata de coco *nah-tah de choh-choh* jelly-like sweet made by mixing coconut water with sugar, an acid bacteria and leaving it to solidify

ngamen *ngah-men* roving musician that plays for money; busker

nyale *nyah-leh* variety of fish; worm-like in appearance

nyepi *nyeh-pih* major annual festival in the Hindu calendar, a day of complete stillness after a night of chasing evil spirits (Bali)

O

odalan *oh-dah-lan* birthday of Hindu temple (Bali)

oncom *on-chom* fermented peanut residue created once the oil is extracted from the nuts

onde-onde *on-deh on-deh* sesame balls with a sweet mung bean filling

ongkos *ong-koss* price/cost (of service)

opor ayam *op-or ah-yahm* chicken in pepper and coconut curry (Central Java; *see* the recipe)

ora *orr-ah* Komodo dragon

orak-arik *oh-rrahk-ah-rrik* vegetables fried with pepper; beaten egg is added at the end (Central Java)

oret *oh-rret* sausage

oseng-oseng *oh-seng-oh-seng* fried **kangkung**, yard-long beans and soy sauce (Central Java)

–ayam *oh-seng-oh-seng ah-yahm* **oseng-oseng** with chicken (Central Java)

–jamur *oh-seng-oh-seng jah-muhrr* **oseng-oseng** with dog (Central Java)

otak *oh-tahk* brains

otot *oh-tot* muscle

P

pa'piong *pah pyong* pork stuffed into bamboo tubes with vegetables and roasted over coals (Central Sulawesi)

padi *pah-dih* growing rice plant; rice pre-harvest & unhusked

–berat *pah-dih ber-aht* slow-growing rice

–cere *pah-dih cheh-rreh* quick-growing rice

–gadu *pah-dih gah-duh* wet-field rice

–gogo *pah-dih goh-goh* dry-field rice

–liar *pah-dih lih-yarr* wild rice

–radin *pah-dih rah-din* swamp rice

–padian *pah-dih pah-dih-ahn* millet

paha *pah-hah* upper leg; thigh

pahit *pah-yiht* 'bitter' – word meaning 'no sugar' in tea or coffee

pais *pais see* **pepes**

pakai *pah-kai* with; to use

pakis *pah-kiss* fernshoots, commonly used in sambals and fish dishes

pala *pah-lah* nutmeg

palai *pah-lai see* **pepes**

pamerasan *pah-meh-rrah-sahn* buffalo meat in black sauce (Central Sulawesi)

panas *pah-nahs* hot (temperature)

panci *pahn-chih* pot

–bergagang *pahn-chih berr-gah-gahng* saucepan

pandan *pahn-dahn see* **daun pandan**

pange *pahng-eh* fish stuffed with spiced egg (West Sumatra)

panggang *pahng-gahng* to bake/roast, usually over hot coals

pangsit *pahng-sit* soup with meat dumplings; wonton

panili *pah-nih-lih* vanilla

pantat *pahm-taht* rump

papaya *pah-pai-yah* papaya/pawpaw

paprika *pah-prih-kah* paprika

pare-pare *pah-rreh pah-rreh* green rice-flour sweet with a palm-sugar filling (Kalimantan)

parutan *pah-ruh-tahn* grater

pasar *pah-sahrr* market

–ikan *pah-sahrr ih-kahn* fish market

–malam *pah-sahrr mah-lahm* night market

–swalayan *pah-sahrr swah-lai-yahn* supermarket

pasta *pah-stah* pasta

pecel *peh-chell* peanut sauce with spinach and beansprouts Java; also a spicy sauce made from chilli, peanuts and/or tomato

–lele *peh-chell leh-leh* deep-fried catfish served with rice and pecel

pedas *peh-dahs* hot (spicy)

pegar *peh-gahrr* pheasant

pelayan *peh-lai-yahn* waiter/waitress

pelayanan *peh-lai-yah-nahn* service

pelecing *peh-leh-ching* sauce of chilli, shrimp paste and tomato used to make vegetable or chicken dishes (Lombok)

pemanggang *peh-mahng-gahng* grill

pembantu *pem-bahn-tuh* live-in house-keeper; servant

pembuka *pem-buh-kah* opener

pempek *pem-pek* deep-fried fish and sago dumpling; also called **empek-empek** (South Sumatra)

pencuci mulut *pen-chuh-chih muh-luht* 'mouth cleaner' – dessert

pengsi *peng-sih* cockles

–maninjau *peng-sih mah-nin-jau* cockles with a chilli sauce (West Sumatra)

pepes *peh-pes* steamed or roasted in banana leaves; also called **pais, palai**

–ayam *peh-pes ah-yahm* spiced chicken steamed in banana leaves

–ikan *peh-pes ih-kahn* spiced fish cooked in banana leaves *(see* the recipe)

per *perr* pear

perangsang selera *perr-ahng-sahng seh-leh-rrah* entree/appetiser

perkedel *perr-keh-del* croquette/fritter; often made with corn or potato

–jagung *perr-keh-del jah-guhng* corn fritters

permen *perr-men* lollies/sweets/candy

persik *perr-sihk* peach

pesanan *peh-sah-nahn* reservation

pete *peh-teh* large odorous bean that grows in a massive pod

peterseli *peh-terr-seh-lih* parsley

petis ikan *ih-kahn* fish paste

piknik *pik-nik* picnic

pikulan *pih-kuh-lahn* sellers that carry goods in two bundles connected by a stick that goes over their shoulders

pindang *pin-dahng* spicy clear fish soup with water-based stock, soy and tamarind (South Sumatra)

pinggang *ping-gahng* loin

piring *pih-rring* plate

pisang *pih-sahng* banana

–bakar *pih-sahng bah-kahrr* bananas grilled over hot coals, flattened in a wooden press then sprinkled with a palm sugar and coconut mixture

–goreng *pih-sahng gorr-eng* fried banana fritters; a popular street-side snack

–kepok *pih-sahng keh-pohk* banana used in cooking, similar to plantain

–molen *pih-sahng moh-len* banana wrapped in pastry and fried

pisau *pih-sau* knife

polong *poh-long* legumes

pondok *pon-dohk* open-sided, grass-roofed shelter

port *porrt* port

potong *poh-tong* cut; to cut

–tipis *poh-tong tih-piss* to fillet

potongan babi *poh-tong-ahn bah-bih* pork chops

prem *prrem* plum

–kering *prrem krring* prune

puas *pwahss* satisfied

puasa *pwahss-ah* fasting/abstaining

pukis *puh-kiss* crescent-shaped cake

pulut *puh-luht* glutinous rice

putu *puh-tuh* steamed coconut cylinder with a palm-sugar centre

puyuh *puh-yuh* quail

R

ragi *rah-gih* yeast mould

raja *rah-jah* lord/prince

Ramadan *rah-mah-dahn* Muslim month of fasting

rambutan *rahm-buht-tahn* bright red fruit covered in soft, hairy spines. Break it open to reveal a delicious white fruit that tastes like lychee.

rasa *rah-sah* flavour

rawon *rah-won* hearty beef stew with **kluwek** (Java)

rebung *reh-buhng* bamboo shoot

rebus *reh-buhs* boil

rebusan *reh-buhs-ahn* stew

rekening *reh-keh-ning* bill

rembang *rem-bahng* sour fruit

remis *reh-miss* scallop

rempeyek *rem-peh-yehk* peanuts cooked within rice-flour crackers (*see* the recipe)

rempah-rempah gulai ikan *rem-pah-rem-pah guh-lai ih-kahn* spicy fish in coconut curry (*see* the recipe)

rendang *ren-dahng* beef or buffalo coconut curry (West Sumatra; *see* the recipe)

restoran *rest-or-ahn* restaurant

rica rica *rih-chah rih-chah* dish prepared with a spicy paste of chilli, shallots, ginger and lime (North Sulawesi)

rijsttafel *riss-tah-fell* 'rice table', Dutch adaptation of an Indonesian banquet encompassing a wide variety of dishes

rombong *rom*-bong floating warung

roti *roh-tih* bread/pastry

–**bakar** *roh-tih bah-kahrr* toast; bread with a filling of jam, chocolate and/or cheese fried on a hot plate

–**jala** *roh-tih jah-lah* 'bread net', fried threads of batter eaten with curry (Aceh & North Sumatra)

rujak *ruh-jahk* fruit served with a sour, spicy sauce of peanuts, sugar and chilli

–**cingur** *ruh-jahk cing-uhrr* peanut sauce with cow skin and lips (Central Java)

rumah makan *ruh-mah mah-kahn* 'eating place', restaurant

–**Padang** *ruh-mah mah-kahn Pah-dahng* restaurant serving Padang cuisine

rumput laut *ruhm-puht laut* seaweed

RW *err-weh* dog

sago *sah-goh* starchy, low protein food extracted from a variety of palm tree; staple diet in many parts of Indonesia

saguer *sah-guehrr* palm sap **tuak**

salak *sah-lahk* brown snake-skin fruit of the zalacca palm

salam *daun sah-lahm* see **daun salam**

sambal *sahm-bahl* chilli sauce or paste served as an accompaniment; contains chillies, garlic or shallots and salt

–**badjak** *sahm-bahl bah-jahk* chilli sauce made with shallots, sugar, tamarind, galangal and shrimp paste. Fried to a caramel consistency (*see* the recipe).

–**brandal** *sahm-bahl brrahn-dahl* chilli sauce made with shallots and shrimp paste

–**buah** *sahm-bahl buah* chilli sauce made with fruit such as pineapple or green mango (South Sumatra)

–**jeruk** *sahm-bahl jerr-uhk* chilli sauce made with lime juice, lime peel, salt and vinegar

–**leunca** *sahm-bahl luhn-chah* chilli sauce made with **leunca** (West Java)

–**terasi** *sahm-bahl trrah-sih* chilli sauce with lime and roasted shrimp paste

–**ulek** *sahm-bahl uh-lehk* chilli sauce made with vinegar and lots of chillies.

sampanye *sahm-pah-nyeh* champagne

sangsang *sahng-sahng* rich, meaty dish made with pig or dog (Batak)

santan *sahn-tahn* coconut milk; liquid obtained by soaking grated coconut in hot water and squeezing it out

sapi *sah-pih* cow; beef

sarapan *sah-rrah-pahn* breakfast

sares *sah-rres* dish made with chilli, coconut juice and banana palm pith; sometimes it's mixed with chicken or meat (Lombok)

sate *sah-teh* grilled on skewers

–**ayam** *sah-teh ah-yahm* chicken **sate**

–**daging** *sah-teh dah-ging* beef **sate**

–**kambing** *sah-teh kahm-bing* goat **sate**

–**kelinci** *sah-teh klihn-chih* rabbit **sate**

–lilit *sah-teh lih-lit* **sate** of minced, spiced meat pressed onto skewers (Bali)

–Madura *sah-teh mah-duh-rah* **sate** served with rice and a sweet and spicy soy sauce (Madura)

–Padang *sah-teh pah-dang* **sate** served with pressed rice and a smooth peanut sauce (West Sumatra)

–pusut *sah-teh puh-suht* skewered sausage-shaped mixture of grated coconut, meat and brown sugar (Lombok and Bali)

saus *saus* sauce

–ikan *saus ih-kahn* fish sauce

–kacang *saus kah-chahng* peanut sauce (*see* the recipe)

–tiram *saus tih-rrahm* oyster sauce

–tomat *saus toh-maht* tomato sauce/ketchup

sawah *sah-wah* individual rice field

sawi *sah-wih* Chinese cabbage

sawo manila *sah-woh mah-nih-lah* sapodilla

sawokecik *sah-woh-cheh-chik* small, plum-shaped fruit with white grainy flesh and up to five seeds

sayatan *sah-yah-tahn* cutlets

sayur *sah-yuhrr* vegetable; often used to describe vegetable dishes

–asam *sah-yuhrr ah-sahm* sour vegetables in clear broth

–asam rembang *sah-yuhrr ah-sahm rembahng* **rembang** soup (Kalimantan)

–kapau *sah-yuhrr kah-pau* cabbage, jackfruit and shallot shoots in coconut milk (West Sumatra)

–hutan *sah-yuhrr-ahn huh-tahn* wild greens

–sayuran *sah-yuhrr* vegetables

se'i *seh'ih* smoked beef (Timor)

sedikit *seh-dih-kit* a little; not much

segar *seh-garr* fresh

selada *seh-lah-dah* lettuce/salad

–air *seh-lah-dah airr* watercress

selai *seh-lai* jam

selai jeruk *seh-lai jerr-uhk* marmalade

selamatan *slah-mah-tahn* meal that encompasses an abundance of food for many people

selasih *seh-lah-sih* type of basil that has an aniseed-like flavour. Used in sweet dishes and drinks.

selederi *seh-leh-deh-rrih* celery

semangka *seh-mahng-kah* melon/water-melon

sembako *sem-bah-koh* the nation's nine essential foodstuffs

sendok *sen-dohk* spoon

–garpu *sen-dohk garr-puh* 'fork spoon', cutlery

sepat *seh-pat* tart-tasting dish of shred-ded fish in a sour sauce of coconut and young mango (Sumbawa)

serabi *srrah-bih* pancakes made with rice flour, coconut milk and **daun pandan** and topped with chocolate, banana or jackfruit (Solo)

serai *seh-rrai* lemongrass

serbet *serr-bet* napkin

serebuk *srreh-buhk* vegetables mixed with grated coconut (Lombok)

sereh *seh-rreh* lemongrass

serombotan *srrom-boh-tahn* salad of chilli, watercress, beansprouts, yard-long beans and coconut (Bali)

serunding *srruhn-deng* garnish of roast coconut and soybeans, shallots, tamarind and chilli (Central Java)

setengah matang *se-teng-ah mah-tahng* medium (cooked)

setengah mentah *se-teng-ah men-tah* rare (cooked)

silahkan makan *sih-lah-kahn mah-kahn* please eat

singkong *sing-kong* cassava/manioc (a root vegetable with edible leaves)

siobak *syo-bahk* minced pig's head, stomach, tongue and skin cooked with spices (Bali)

sirih *sih-rrih* betel nut

sirop *sih-rrop* cordial

sirsak *sirr-sahk* soursop

soba *soh-bah* buckwheat

DICTIONARY

sohun *soh-huhn* bean-flour vermicelli

sop soup; clear, light broth *(see also **soto**)*

–buntut *sop bu hn-tuht* ox-tail soup

–kental *sop ken-tahl* chowder

–konro *sop kon-rroh* beef-rib soup with **kluwek** (South Sulawesi)

sosis *soh-siss* sausage

soto *soh-toh* soup, usually a well-seasoned broth *(see also **sop**)*

–ayam *soh-toh ah-yahm* chicken soup, usually flavoured with garlic, shallots and turmeric *(see the recipe)*

–Bandung *soh-toh bahn-duhng* beef and vegetable soup with lemongrass (Bandung, West Java)

–Banjar *soh-toh bahn-jahrr* chicken broth made creamy by mashing and mixing boiled eggs into the stock (Banjarmasin, Kalimantan)

–Betawi *soh-toh beh-tah-wih* soup with every part of the cow, including the marrow – made creamy with the addition of coconut milk (Jakarta)

–buntut *soh-toh buhn-tuht* ox-tail soup

–Kudus *soh-toh kuh-duhs* chicken and egg soup (Kudus, Central Java)

–Lamongan *soh-toh lah-mong-gahn* chicken soup with noodles, rice, soybean leaf, turmeric and lemongrass (Lamongan, East Java)

–Madura *soh-toh mah-duh-rrah* soup of beef (any part thereof), lime, pepper, peanuts, chilli and ginger (Madura)

–Pekalongan *soh-toh peh-kah-long-ahn* tripe and soy soup (Pekalongan, Central Java)

–Tegal *soh-toh teh-gahl* beef and noodle soup (Tegal, Central Java)

srikaya *srrih-kah-yah* custard apples; green custard of sticky rice, sugar, coconut milk and egg (South Sumatra)

–nangka *srrih-kah-yah nahng-kah* sweet made with jackfruit (Kalimantan)

stroop *strroop* cordial

subak *suh-bahk* rice growers co-operative which every farmer is a member of in Bali. The subak's most important role is to ensure equable distribution of water resources.

sudip *suh-dip* spatula

sukun *suh-kuhn* breadfruit

sumpit *suhm-pit* chopsticks

sumsum *suhm-suhm* marrow

sunek *suh-nek* water chestnut

susu *suh-suh* milk

–bubuk *suh-suh buh-buhk* powdered milk

–kedelai *suh-suh keh-deh-lai* soy milk

–kental *suh-suh ken-tahl* condensed milk

–masam kental *suh-suh mah-sahm ken-tahl* yoghurt

–panas *suh-suh pah-nahs* hot milk

T

tahu *tah-hu* tofu/beancurd

–gejrot *tah-hu gej-rrot* fried, chopped tofu swimming in spiced soy sauce (West Java)

–goreng *tah-hu gorr-eng* fried tofu

–isi *tah-hu ih-sih* tofu stuffed with beansprouts and other vegetables, covered in batter and deep-fried

–Sumedang *tah-hu suh-meh-dahng* plain, deep-fried tofu (Sumedang, West Java)

talas *tah-lahs see **taro***

tambul *tahm-buhl* Javanese term for food that goes well with drinks

tang *tahng* tongs

tanpa *tahm-pah* without

tanur *tah-nurr* oven

tape *tah-peh* strange-tasting speciality made by peeling, boiling and fermenting cassava in yeast. Tape can be made with rice.

taplak *taph-lahk* tablecloth

taro *tah-rroh* taro, cooked like a potato: boiled or fried to make chips

tauge *tau-geh* beansprouts

tebal *teh-bahl* wide

teh *teh* tea

–gula *teh guh-lah* tea with sugar

–hijau *teh hih-jau* green tea

–jahe *teh* ginger tea

–limon *teh* lemon tea

–manis *teh mah-niss* sweet tea

–mawar *teh mah-warr* rose tea

–pahit *teh pah-yiht* tea without sugar

–poci *teh poh-chih* jasmine tea with rock sugar brewed in a clay pot (Tegal, Central Java)

–susu *teh suh-suh* tea with milk

tekwan *tek-wahn* small pempek dumplings and seaweed in a mildly sweet stock (South Sumatra)

telur *teh-luhrr* egg

–ceplok *teh-luhrr ceh-plok* poached egg

–dadar *teh-luhrr dah-darr* omelette

–goreng *teh-luhrr gorr-eng* fried egg

–ikan *teh-luhrr ih-kahn* fish roe

–penyu *teh-luhrr pehn-yuh* turtle eggs

–rebus *teh-luhrr rreh-buhs* boiled egg

–setengah matang *teh-luhrr steng-ah mah-tahng* half-cooked egg

tempe *tem-peh* fermented soybean cake

–goreng *tem-peh gorr-eng* fried tempe

–kering *tem-peh krring* sweet and crispy fried tempe (see the recipe)

–Mendoang *tem-peh men-doang* thin, fried tempe; speciality (Mendoang, Central Java)

–penyet *tem-peh peh-nyet* deep-fried tempe

tempoyak *tem-poy-ahk* accompaniment of shrimp paste, lime juice, chilli and fermented durian (South Sumatra)

temusu *tem-suh-suh* cow-skin sausage with spiced egg filling (West Sumatra)

tenggiri *teng-gih-rrih* mackerel

tengkleng *teng-kleng* goat curry with coconut milk and all parts of the goat (Central Java)

tepung *teh-puhng* flour

–beras *teh-puhng brrahs* rice flour

–jagung *teh-puhng jah-guhng* maize/cornmeal/polenta

–terigu *teh-puhng trrih-guh* wheat flour

terasi *trrah-sih* shrimp paste; dark and very pungent paste that is used to flavour dishes; also called **belacan**

terigu *trrih-guh* wheat

terong *trrohng* eggplant/aubergine

–belado *trrohng blah-doh* eggplant with chilli sauce (see the recipe)

–hijau *trrohng hih-jau* zucchini

terwelu *terr-weh-luh* hare

timbangan *tim-bahng-ahn* scales

timbul *tim-bihl* breadnut

timbungan bi siap *tim-buhng-ahn sih-ahp* sharp-tasting chicken soup with minced chicken, tamarind, sugar and starfruit leaves for a bitter touch (Bali)

timun *tih-muhn* cucumber

–urap *tih-muhn uh-rrahp* sliced cucumber with grated coconut, onion and garlic (Lombok)

tiram *tih-rrahm* oyster

toko *toh-koh* store

–roti *toh-koh rroh-tih* bakery

–umum *toh-koh* general store

tom *tom* duck or chicken cooked with spices in a banana leaf (Bali)

tomat *toh-maht* tomato

tongkol *ton-kohl* tuna/tunny

tongseng *tong-seng* meat or chicken in coconut milk and spices

tua *tuh-wah* old

tuak *tuh-wahk* palm sap wine; also **balok**

tukang *tuh-kahng* seller

tulang *tuh-lahng* bone

–iga *tuh-lahng ih-gah* spare rib

–kering *tuh-lahng krring* shank

–rusuk *tuh-lahng rruh-suhk* ribs

tumpang *tuhm-pahng* boiled tempe crushed and mixed with coconut milk (Central Java)

tumpeng *tuhm-peng* pyramid-like mound of yellow rice, centrepiece of a celebratory meal

tusuk *tuh-suhk* skewer

–gigi *tuh-suhk gih-gih* toothpick

tutup *tuh-tuhp* closed/lid

U

uang *uh-wahng* money

–persen *uh-wahng perr-sen* tip

ubi *uh-bih* sweet potato

–goreng *uh-bih goh-rreng* deep-fried sweet potato

–kayu *uh-bih kai-yuh* cassava root

–rendang *uh-bih rren-dahng* diced sweet potato cooked in coconut milk and spices then deep-fried (West Sumatra)

udang *uh-dahng* prawns/shrimp

–galah *uh-dahng gah-lah* giant prawns

–karang *uh-dahng kah-rrahng* crayfish/lobster

ular *uh-lahrr* snake

ulek-ulek *uh-lek-uh-lek* pestle *(see* **cobek & ulek-ulek***)*

ulen *uh-len* roasted brick of sticky rice with peanut sauce (West Java)

undangan *uhn-dahng-ahn* invitation

unggas *uhng-gahs* poultry

urab *uh-rrahp* salad of boiled and diced yard-long beans, coconut milk and flesh, chilli, shrimp paste, shallots, salt and garlic (Bali)

V

vetsin *vet-sin* monosodium glutamate

W

wajan *wah-jahn* wok; also called **kuali**

walua *wah-luh-ah* pumpkin

wangi *wahng-ih* aroma

warteg *warr-teg* short for warung Tegal –simple restaurants that sell a wide range of dishes at cheap prices

warung *wah-ruhng* food stall that offers seating and shelter, but is disassembled after closure; street stall

–kopi *wah-ruhng koh-pih* cafe stall serving simple food and hot drinks

wedang *weh-dahng* Javanese for drink

–dongo *weh-dahng dong-oh* coconut drink with black rice-flour drops (Central Java)

–kacang *weh-dahng kah-chahng* coconut drink with nuts (Central Java)

wiski *wiss-kih* whisky

wortel *wohrr-tell* carrot

Z

zaitun *zai-tuhn* olive

Recommended Reading

Cribb, R *Historical Atlas of Indonesia* (Curzon Press 2000)

Gadikas, B, & G Shapiro *Tanjung Puting National Park* (PT Gramedia & Orangutan Foundation International 1994)

Hutton, W, & H Holzen *The Food of Indonesia* (Periplus Editions 1997)

Miller, G *To the Spice Islands & Beyond* (Oxford University Press 1996)

Milton, Giles *Nathaniel's Nutmeg: How One Man's Courage Changed the Course of History* (Hodder & Stoughton 1999)

Peterson, J & D *Eat Smart in Indonesia* (Gingko Press 1997)

Ritchie, C *Food in Civilization* (Methuen 1981)

Mowe, R *South-East Asian Specialties* (Könemann 1999)

Tantri, K *Revolt in Paradise* (Nicolls & Co 1963)

Photo Credits

All photographs taken by Jerry Alexander except page 152 and 166 top right which were taken by the author, Patrick Witton.

A

Ababi 33
Aceh 141-2
agricultural practices 31, 63, 67
air kelapa muda 94-5
air minum 91, 211
alcohol 97-8, 193-4
    arak 97
    balok 157
    beer 98
    brem 29, 97
    palm sap wine 97
    saguer 158
    tuak 97
    wine 97
Ambon 159
anggur 97
animal sacrifice 119, 149, 156-7
apokat 61, 94, 204
arak 97
asam 71
avocado 61, 94, 204
ayam, *see* chicken

B

babi, *see* pork
bacem 53, 167-9
bakso 55, 176-7
bakul 176
Bali 45-6, 48-51, 66, 87, 97, 112-16, 135-9
Bali belly 23
Balikpapan 151
banana 67, 165
    leaves 105-6
bandrek 91
Bandung 48, 88, 127
Banjar, the 152-3
Banjarmasin 41, 151-3, 163-6
Banjarnegara 70

banquets 195-206
Batak, the 45, 142
Batu Sangkar 147
beans 58
    beansprouts 58
    green beans 58
    mung beans 58
    pete 58
    yard-long beans 58
beansprouts 58
bebek, *see* duck
beef 46-8
    coconut curry 47
    rendang 47
beer 98
Bekonang 164
belacan 73
beras, *see* rice
Betawi, the 125, 137
bill, the 189
bir 98
birthdays 114-15
biscuits 81
boogymen 154-5
Brastagi 57, 142
bread & pastries 82, 141, 170-72
    bakeries 170
    bika ambon 141-2
    ikan panada 158
    roti bakar 82
    roti jala 141-2
breakfast 22
brem 29, 97
bubur 22, 29, 58, 146
Buddhism 13-14
buffalo 46-7, 143-5, 155-7
    coconut curry 23, 47, 111, 43-5, 181
    in black sauce 157
    rendang 23, 47, 111, 143-5, 181
    yoghurt with palm sugar 146

Bukittinggi 57, 86, 111, 145-6, 164
bumbu 71
bungkus 171

C
Cafe Batavia 186
cakar ayam 44, 55
cassava 59, 149, 159
celebrations 109-20
    birthdays 114-15
    circumcision 116
    funerals 118, 155-7
    harvest festival 117
    Idul Adha 112
    Idul Fitri 112
    Kedaso 113
    Lebaran 112
    Mitoni 116
    odalan 113
    Ramadan 111-2
    weddings 118
Central Java 129-32
Central Sulawesi 155-7
check, the 189
chicken 44
    claw 44, 55
    fried 131, 139, 184
    in pepper & coconut curry 205
    opor ayam 205
    pepes ayam 135
    porridge 22
    soup 55, 107-8
    spiced cooked in banana leaf 135
children 114-15, 191
chilli 74-7, 150, 208-9
    bird's eye 74
Cianjur 31
Cirebon 128
citrus fruit 63
Ciumbuleuit 127

cloves 71
cobek & ulek-ulek 101
coconut 63, 94-5
    drinks 63, 94-5
coffee 86-90, 157
    arabica 86-90
    Kopiko 87
    plantations 147
    production 147
    robusta 86-90
    serving styles 87
    spiced with coconut milk 127
    with raw egg & sugar 142
coffee growing regions
    Bali 87
    Java 87
    Sulawesi 90
    Sumatra 90
cooking 99-108
    terminology 23
    regional 122
    techniques 23
corn 57, 149
cover charges 193
crackers 79, 146, 164
    emping 79
    kerupuk 79, 146, 164
    prawn 79
    rempeyek 197
    rice 79, 103-4
culture, culinary 9-26
customs 22-6, 171, 197-9

D
Dago 127
Dani, the 160
Dayak, the 152
Denpasar 135
desserts 81, 87, 172, *see also* snacks,
    sweet
Dewi Sri 32

Dieng Plateau 74
dining out 23
dinner 22-3
dog 45, 132, 142, 158
drinks 83-98, 198-202
    alcoholic, *see* alcohol
    non-alcohol 85-95, 132, 183-94
    avocado juice 94, 192
    coconut 94-5
    coconut water 63
    coffee 86-90
    cordial 94, 142
    es campur 61, 93, 183
    es cendol 93
    es cincau 93
    es dawet 93
    ginger tea 91
    iced cucumber 59, 93
    iced orange 93
    juice 94, 192
    milk 95
    stroop 94, 142
    tea 85
    water 91
duck 45
    bebek betutu 45, 135
    coconut curry 45
    gulai itik 45
    stuffed and pit-roasted 45, 135
durian 62
Dutch East India Company 20

E
East Java 133
eating habits 22-6, 171, 197-9
eggplant 59
    terong belado 59
eggs 54
    with coffee and sugar 87
emping 79

etiquette 25-6, 171, 183, 189
    smoking 26

F
fast food 187
festivals, *see* celebrations
fish & seafood 39-43, 133, 138-9,
    147-8, 153, 155, 159, 178
    catfish with pecel 41, 76, 133
    char-grilled 41
    coconut curry 201
    cooked in banana leaves 153
    dried 41, 164
    fish & sago dumplings 148
    fried 41
    ikan panada 158
    pecel lele 41, 76, 133
    pepes ikan 41, 153, 202
    prawns in oyster sauce 41
    shrimp paste 73
    sour shredded, with young
    mango 149
    spiced and cooked in banana
    leaves 41, 202
    with spicy durian sauce 148
fishing 39-41, 153
five-dish feast 113
Flores 149-150
food courts 187, 189
fritters
    corn 57
    potato 59
fruit 61-70, 111-18, 148
    avocado 61, 94
    banana 67, 165
    citrus 63
    coconut 63
    durian 62, 159
    guava 62
    hygiene 209

in coconut milk 111
jackfruit 68-9
mango 66
mangosteen 66
palm fruit tree 61
papaya 67
passionfruit 61, 94
rambutan 66
rujak 62, 66, 81, 101
salak (snakeskin fruit) 70
starfruit 61
water apple 62
funerals 118, 155-7

G
gado-gado 55, 125, 206
galangal 72
garlic 57
general stores 170
geography 11
ginger tea 91
bandrek 127
goat 52
coconut curry 52
sate 52
guava 62
gudeg 46, 54, 69, 129
gula 72, 129
gulai 13, 45, 141

H
health 207-14
Bali belly 23
diarrhoea 213
fluids 211
herbal medicine 212
hygiene 25, 181, 183, 209
nutrition 213
traditional medicine 214
Hinduism 13-14, 46, 97

history 12-16
home cooking 99-108
honey 149

I
Ibu Oka 139
ice drinks 93
Idul Fitri 112
ikan, *see* fish & seafood
influences
Americas 60, 67, 74
Arab 13, 141
Chinese 13, 37-8, 49, 152, 185
Dutch 15-16, 82, 86-8, 98, 133, 155, 186
English 15
Indian 13, 59, 80, 141
Persian 13, 15, 141
Portuguese 158
Spanish 15
US 21, 152-3, 187
western 185-6
intip 29, 79
Irian Jaya 60, 160
Islam 13-14, 49, 97, 111-12, 116, 141
itik, *see* duck

J
jackfruit 46, 68-9, 129
jagung 57, 149
jajanan, *see* snacks
jaje 113
Jakarta 48, 125, 163
jambu 62
jamu 172, 212
Java 87, 123-33
Central 129-32
East 133
West 126-8

Jember 86, 133
jeruk 63
Jimbaran 138-9
juice 94, 192, *see also* drinks, non-alcoholic

K

kacang 58, 72, 76, 206
kaki-lima 23, 177
Kalibaru 86, 133
Kalimantan 151-3
kambing, *see* goat
kangkung 58
Kapau 145-6, 164-5
karedok 60, 126, 137, 204-6
kecap 37, 76
kedelai, *see* soybeans
Kedewatan 139
kelapa, *see* coconut
kerbau, *see* buffalo
kerupuk 79, 146, 164
ketoprak 125
ketupat 29, 112
Komodo 149-50
kopi, *see* coffee
Kopiko 87
Kudus 132
Kuta 137-9

L

Lake Maninjau 147
Lake Toba 142
lalapan 126
Lamongan 133
lawar 113, 135
Lebaran 112
Lembang 48, 52, 57, 127
lemper 31
lesehan 98, 129, 179

leunca 126
Lombok 117, 149-50
lontong 29
lunch 22-3

M

Madiun 133
Madura 46, 48, 133
makan malam 22-3
makan siang 22-3
makanan laut, *see* fish & seafood
Makassar, the 14, 154-5
Malang 133
malls 187
Maluku 159
Mandailing, the 90
mango 66
mangosteen 66
mangga 66
manggis 66
Maribaya 127
markets 42, 163-7
    Beringharjo 129
    Bukittinggi 145-6, 164
    fish 42
    floating 166
    night 38, 80, 175
    Pasar Demangan 167
    Pasar Senen 163
    traditional opening days 164
martabak 13, 54, 80
menus 189
mie, *see* noodles
migration, domestic 21, 133, 149, 160, 190
Minahasan, the 158
Minangkabau, the 143-5
Mt Bromo National Park 133
Mt Merapi 129
Munduk 86, 87, 135-6

N

nangka 46, 68-9, 129
nasi, *see* rice
ngamen 179
night clubs 193
noodles 38, 185
    bean-flour vermicelli 38
    cellophane 38
    flat rice 38
    fried 38
    mie goreng 38
    soup 38
    wonton 38, 55
North Sulawesi 158-60
North Sumatra 141-2
Nusa Tenggara 149-50
nutmeg 73
nuts 58, 206
    candlenuts 72
    peanuts 58, 76, 206
    pecel 132, 133

O

offal 52
oil 73
onion 57
opor ayam 205
oseng-oseng jamur 45

P

papaya 67
passionfruit 61, 94
pa'piong 157
packed meals 171
Padang 143-6
    cuisine 69, 143-6, 181-2, 190
Palembang 41, 148
palm sugar 72, 129
palm sap wine 97
pangsit 38, 55
papaya 67

passionfruit 61, 94
pecel 76, 176
    lele 41, 76, 133
pembantu 100
pempek 148
pepes ayam 135
pepes ikan 41, 153, 202
perkedel, *see* fritters
pete 58
picnics 171
pisang 67, 165
places to eat & drink 173-94, *see
    also* restaurants
    food courts 187, 189
    floating warung 166
    kaki-lima 23, 177
    lesehan 129
    kiosks 98, 170
    lesehan 98, 129, 179
    night clubs 193
    pubs 193
    roving vendors 23, 177
    stick sellers 176
    streetside traders 176
    travelling sellers 190
    warung 23, 178
    warung kopi 98, 179
    warteg 183
plantations 133, 136, 147
    clove 71
    coffee 86-87
    tea 85
Pontianak 151
pork 49, 50-1, 142
    boiled in vinegar & pig's
        blood 142
    spiced minced pig's head and
        offal 135-6
    spit-roast pig 49-51, 111, 115,
        135, 139
    stuffed in bamboo tubes 157

porridge 22, 29, 58, 146
Prambanan 131
pubs 193
Puncak Pass 85

R

rabbit 52
    sate 48
Ramadan 22, 111
rambutan 66
Rantepao 86, 90, 155
regions 121-60
religion 97-8, 111
    Buddhism 13-14
    Christianity 142, 149
    Hinduism 13-14, 46, 97
    Islam 13-14, 49, 97, 111-12,
    141, 149
religious offerings 32, 97, 113-16,
    135, 137
religious prohibitions 194
    alcohol 194
    beef 46
    pork 49
rempah-rempah 201
rempeyek 197
rendang 23, 46-47, 111, 143-5, 181
restaurants 181-3
    Chinese 185
    menus 189
    Padang 181-2, 190
    upmarket & tourist 185
    vegetarian 183, 190
    warteg 183
rica-rica 158
rice 29-38, 149, 171-2
    brem 97
    etiquette 25
    fried 29, 37, 41, 54, 57
    history 30
    ketupat 29

legends 31
nasi campur 181
nasi goreng 29, 37, 41, 54, 57
nasi Kapau 145-6, 164-5
packed meals 171
plain 29
rice cookers 105
steamed in banana leaves 29, 48
steamed in coconut fronds 29,
    112
sticky rice filled with shredded
    meat 31
terminology 36
varieties 30-1, 36
wine 29
rice porridge 22, 29, 58
rijstaffel 15
Rinca 149-50
Roti 149-50
rujak 62, 66, 81, 101
rumah makan, see restaurants
rumah makan Padang, see Padang
    cuisine

S

Sabu 149-50
sago 59, 149, 159-60
salad 60, 204-6
    gado-gado 55, 125, 206
    karedok 60, 126, 137, 204-6
    ketoprak 125
    lalapan 126
    lawar 113, 135
    urab 114
salak 70
sambal 74-6, 101
    badjak 75
sapi, see beef
sarapan 22
satay, see sate

sate 48, 133, 177
  lilit 48, 114, 135
  Madura-style 48
  Padang-style 48, 146
  rabbit 48
sauces 71
  peanut 76, 206
  pecel 132-3
  pelecing 150
  soy sauce 37, 76
sausage 51, 135, 145
sayuran, *see* vegetables
seafood, *see* fish & seafood
selamatan 111
sembako, 28
shops 107, 161-72, *see also* markets
  bakeries 170
  door-to-door grocery seller 107
  general stores 170
  malls 187
  supermarkets 170
  toko roti 170
  toko umum 170
shrimp paste 73
Singaraja 135-6
singkong 59, 149, 159
smoking 26
snacks 23, 79-81
snacks, savoury 58, 79
  emping
  fried peanuts & anchovies 58
  rempeyek 58
  roti bakar 82
  tambul 197
snacks, sweet 29-41, 128, 132, 153
  alam 136
  ampar tatak 153
  black rice porridge 29
  buffalo yoghurt 146
  fried banana 80
  gempol pleret 131

geplak 131
grilled banana 165
kelepon 80, 131
lak lak 136
mung-bean porridge with banana & custard 146
nata de coco 63
roti bakar 82
serabi 80, 131
srikaya 148
Soekarno 22
Solo 103-4, 131
Solor & Alor Archipelagos 149-50
sop, *see* soup
soto, *see* soup
soup 38, 55, 133, 148
  bakso 55, 176-7
  Bandung-style 55
  Banjar-style 153
  chicken 55, 106-8
  Chinese-style 38
  Madura-style 55
  meatball 55, 176, 177
  noodle soup 38
  sour vegetable broth 55
  soto ayam 55, 106-8
  wonton 38, 55
South Sulawesi 154-5
South Sumatra 148
soy sauce 37, 76
soybeans 53
  soy milk 53
  soy sauce 37, 76
  tempe 53, 79, 103
  tofu 53, 79, 104, 127, 167
spice trade 13, 17-20, 71-3, 159
spices 13, 17-20, 50, 71-3, 159
  chilli 74-7, 150, 208-9
  jungle pepper 142
  nutmeg 17
  rica-rica 158
  spice paste 71

staples 27-82
stoves 101
street food 34, 128-9, 155, 175-9,
    see also places to eat & drink
    floating warung 166
    kiosks 98, 170
    lesehan 98, 179
    roving vendors 23, 177
    stick sellers 176
    streetside traders 176
    travelling sellers 190
    warung 23, 178
    warung kopi 98, 179
sugar 72, 129
Sulawesi 90, 154-58
    Central 155-7
    North 158-60
    South 154-5
Sultan Hamengkubuwono IX 129
Sumatra 90, 141-48
    Aceh 141-2
    North 141-2
    South 148
    West 143-7
Sumba 119, 149-50
Sumbawa 149-50
Sumedang 127
supermarkets 170
Surabaya 133
sweets 81, 87, 172, *see also* snacks,
    sweet
sweet potato 60, 79, 145, 160
    dark-fried in coconut milk 145

T
tahu, *see* tofu
take-away 171
tamarind 71
Tana Toraja 155-7
taro 59, 149, 159

Tawangmangu 48, 52
tea 85
    ginger 91
    jasmine tea with rock sugar 132
Tegal 183
teh, *see* tea
telur, *see* eggs
tempe 53, 79, 103
    sweet & crispy fried 53, 205
terong 59
    belado 59
Timor, West 149-50
tofu 53-4, 58, 79, 104, 127, 167-9
    cooked in stock 53, 167-9
    fried 53-4, 127
    jackfruit curry 54
    stuffed & deep fried 53, 58
    tahu goreng 53-4,127
    tahu isi 53, 58
toko roti 170
toko umum 170
Toraja, the 87, 155-7
traditions 99-108
tuak 97

U
ubi 60, 79, 160
Ubud 50-1, 139
Ujung Pandang 155
urab 114
utensils 25, 100-1, 105, 172, 202

V
vegetables 57-60
    acar 126
    beansprouts 58
    cassava 59, 149, 159
    corn 57, 149
    eggplant 59

garlic 57
green beans 58
jackfruit 190
hygiene 209
Kapau-style 145-6
leunca 126
mung beans 58
onion 57
pete 58
sago 59, 149, 159-60
sweet potato 60, 79, 145, 160
taro 59, 149, 159
water spinach 58
yard-long beans 58
vegetarian 183, 190

W
warung 23
water spinach 58
water, drinking 91, 211
wedang 132
weddings 118
West Java 126-8
West Sumatra 143-7
West Timor 149-50
wine 97

Y
yoghurt 146
Yogyakarta 46, 69, 77, 129-32, 179

Boxed Text
Balinese Birthday 114-15
Blood & Guts 52
Colonial Remnants 186
Death of the Party – A Funeral in Sumba 119
Delicious 25
Dining Under the Influence 98
Divine Coconut 94
Dog Food 45
Don't Miss
    Bali 137
    Java 132
    Kalimantan 152
    Nusa Tenggara 149
    Sulawesi & Maluku 159
    Sumatra 141
Featherweight Feast 184
Food on the Run 213
Healthy Land 214
Hot Love 77
Ibu Oka 50
Indonesian Proverbs – Food for Thought 21
Jamu (Herbal Medicine) 212

Kinky Coffee Kitten – Hello Kitty! 87
Living Traditions 117
MSG (Monosodium Glutamate) 208
Nangka (Jackfruit) 68-9
Ngamen 179
Rice 30-6
Rice Legends 31
Rice Tourism – Bali 35
Rice Words 36
Rijstaffel 15
Padang Selection 182
Pampered Cocks 44
Pasar Demangan, Yogyakarta 167
Pepes Ikan 202
Sate Tour 48
Solo Cycle Tour 103
Spice Race 17
Sunday Soup 107
Tips for the Vegan Traveller 190
Titin in Pangandaran 42-43
Toko Aroma 88
Ways Of Cooking 23

Recipes

Bacem (Tofu, Tempe and/or Chicken Cooked in Stock) 169
Bandrek (Ginger Tea) 91
Jus Apokat (Avocado Juice) 204
Karedok (Sudanese Salad) 204
Nasi Goreng 37
Opor Ayam (Chicken in Pepper & Coconut Curry) 205
Pepes Ikan 203
Rempah-Rempah (Spicy Fish in Coconut Curry) 201
Rempeyek (Peanuts Cooked in Rice-flour Crackers) 197

Rendang (Beef or Buffalo Coconut Curry) 47
Sambal Badjak (Dark Chilli Sauce) 75
Saus Kacang (Peanut Sauce) 206
Soto Ayam (Chicken Soup) Asti Mulyana's Recipe 106
Tempe Kering (Sweet & Crispy Fried Tempe) 205
Terong Belado (Eggplant with Chilli Sauce) 60

Maps

Bali 136
Bandung 126
Banjarmasin 151
Bukittinggi 146
Indonesia 6

Jakarta 124
regions 122
Ubud 138
Yogyakarta 130